② Mum and me made an agreement
(a cold! buissness type one). Mum said
I pay £50 and she pays £70. The cost
of the trip is £91 plus a recommended
ammount of spending money £30. The whole
cost is £121. Mum's paid £70 and I've paid
£20 so the trip is paid for but I've still
got to earn my other £30 for spending
money, which they turne to francs.
   My Trip takes me to Lourdes mainly
but we will be stopping of at Paris on
the way for a day or two. The trip is
8 days and my friends are going. I not
only hope to gain pleasure from this trip
but education to. And that means
no chasing french bar maids!
But from what you have told me I
am looking forward to visiting the grotto.
   I didn't to too well in my
exams but I am full of what I want
to do for my O-levels.

Easily Distracted

STEVE
COOGAN
Easily Distracted

CENTURY

1 3 5 7 9 10 8 6 4 2

Century
20 Vauxhall Bridge Road
London SW1V 2SA

Century is part of the Penguin Random House
group of companies whose addresses can be found
at global.penguinrandomhouse.com.

Penguin
Random House
UK

Copyright © Steve Coogan 2015

Steve Coogan has asserted his right to be identified
as the author of this Work in accordance with
the Copyright, Designs and Patents Act 1988.

The author and publishers would like to thank
the family, Martin Glyn Murray, Philomena Lee Ltd,
Pathé Productions Ltd, Pozzitive, Ken Loveday, Getty Images, and PA Images
for the use of images within the book.

First published in Great Britain by Century in 2015
www.randomhouse.co.uk

A CIP catalogue record for this book is available from the British Library.

ISBN 9781780891712 (Hardback)
ISBN 9781780892399 (Trade Paperback)
ISBN 9781448183517 (Ebook)

Typeset in ITC Stone Serif by
Palimpsest Book Production Ltd, Falkirk, Stirlingshire

Printed and bound in Great Britain by Clays Ltd, St Ives plc

Penguin Random House is committed to a sustainable future
for our business, our readers and our planet. This book is
made from Forest Stewardship Council® certified paper.

MIX
Paper from
responsible sources
FSC
www.fsc.org   FSC® C018179

Thank you to Amy Raphael for co-writing the book with me, for guiding me, helping organise my thoughts, making me sound more eloquent and tolerating my endlessly straying off the point with nothing more than a sigh. Without her it simply wouldn't have been written. Thanks to my editor Ben Dunn for telling me when I was boring and self-indulgent. To Paul Stevens at Independent Talent for being a very good agent. To Duncan Heath for his sage-like wisdom. To Anna Stockton for managing my life. I'd like to thank Loretta for making me laugh with her gentle mockery, and for her love. To the two Clares: my daughter, for teaching me more than I've taught her and my big sister for helping with the book, helping me grow up and always being there for me.

To Mum and Dad

INTRODUCTION

Most of my life has been spent wanting to be someone else. If I pretended to be other people, then I didn't have to be me.

Mike Yarwood, a stalwart of seventies television who had as many viewers as *Morecambe & Wise* but who is strangely forgotten now, used to say 'And this is me' after launching into his act. Coming as it did after his impeccable impressions of Harold Wilson and Edward Heath, it was always an anticlimax. We weren't really interested in seeing Yarwood as himself.

When I first did stand-up, I did impressions. When I did my act, I would do a rather distant, pompous version of myself. I continued to do versions of myself in *Coffee and Cigarettes*, *A Cock and Bull Story* and *The Trip*.

All of which was a way of saying, 'This is not me.'

Well, all right, it's a little bit of me.

Until now I have shared only versions of 'Steve Coogan'.

The real me is slightly less desperate for fame than Alan Partridge, slightly less irascible than the Steve who eats his way around the Lake District and Italy in *The Trip*, and slightly less libidinous than the version of me in *A Cock and Bull Story*.

It took me a long time to find out who I was. I certainly didn't know when I was growing up. My views weren't properly informed; I used to parrot opinions that I thought sounded good. I was in some ways tribal. Cloistered by my Catholic upbringing in suburban Manchester. Naive. Unsophisticated.

I used to value the fact that I didn't alienate anyone. I didn't want to say anything that might cause friction. In pursuit of an easy life, I would consciously keep quiet about anything contentious.

When I hear, third or fourth hand, what people think about me and it's ridiculously wide of the mark, I perversely take some comfort from it.

'Oh good, they don't know who I am.'

There are countless examples of those who conform to a role thrust upon them by the media. An unwritten pact to serve each other. I don't like being defined by others, so for those who are interested I will try to do it myself.

It would be ridiculous for me to pretend that I've been a paragon of virtue. Nor have I always been honourable. But it is my work that I have offered up for judgement, not my personal life. I'm proud of my work, and if people don't like it, then I've failed. Judge me on the work, not on the cocaine and the strippers.

You won't find any grief porn in this book. It isn't *Angela's Ashes*. I didn't learn my comedy on the playing fields of Eton, nor am I a horny-handed son of toil. Andrew Collins wrote a book called *Where Did It All Go Right?: Growing Up Normal in the 70s*, a title as apposite for my book as his.

I come from the kind of strong, secure and loving lower-middle-class background that is not celebrated enough. Contrary to what some might think, not everyone from the lower middle class is a xenophobic Little Englander like Alan Partridge.

My parents instilled decency, kindness and a generosity of spirit in me. They may have been baffled for a long time by my career, but I owe them everything. This book is as much about them as it is about me.

PART ONE

CHAPTER 1

I f 1998 was the year that everything came together, it was also the year that everything began, slowly, to fall apart.

The central London hotel room was perfect. When my parents opened the curtains, they could see the Lyceum Theatre. And there in front of them was my name in lights: *Steve Coogan: The Man Who Thinks He's It*.

I was about to turn thirty-three, but I hadn't stopped seeking validation from my dad. My sister, Clare, says I still do it, but perhaps I am less obvious these days.

I should have been luxuriating in my success in 1998 rather than trying to impress my parents. I had the best comedy on television and a sell-out national tour. *I'm Alan Partridge* was incredibly popular *and* liked by clever people. Alan had matured to perfection. The reviews were staggering; it was probably peak Partridge. I had yet to be overwhelmed by drugs and drink, but I can see now that the adulation sent me a bit crazy. I earned well over a million pounds from *The Man Who Thinks He's It*, the kind of money I didn't earn again for a very long time.

The tour culminated in a sold-out ten-week run at the Lyceum Theatre in Covent Garden. Most days, as I was on my way to the stage door in my anorak, ticket touts would try to sell me tickets for my own show at £300 a pop. Six nights a week I dressed up as Alan Partridge, Paul and Pauline Calf, Tony Ferrino and Duncan Thickett in front of 2,000 people. I only stepped down for *The Lion King* to take up residence.

I was determined to create an intimate show on a large scale, with musicians, dancers and a supporting cast. Simon Pegg and Julia Davis provided the best reinforcement available, and the Steve Brown Band, who wrote the title music to *Knowing Me*

Knowing You with Alan Partridge, provided live backing. I knew that having a live band would eat into my profits, but I didn't want the audience to feel cheated when they were faced with yet another comedian muttering into a mic.

Comedy in the late nineties was still embracing jeans and T-shirts, and there remained a residual anti-establishment mindset. I, meanwhile, was trying to reclaim and reinvent the big music-hall-style show that had been denigrated because of its association with politically incorrect comedy.

I wanted to take the format that had once been embraced by the establishment and reinvent it as a proper show with well-observed characters. And it worked. Consequently, both old-timers and young people who came to the show loved it. Simon Pegg gave me a congratulations card. 'Well done,' he had written, 'one day you will throw these BAFTAs through the windows of a large empty house.' It was very funny at the time, but has haunted me ever since . . .

Meanwhile, as if all this wasn't enough, in the midst of the sell-out Lyceum show I was rewarded three times at the British Comedy Awards: Best Actor and Best TV Sitcom for *I'm Alan Partridge*, and Best BBC2 Personality. *I'm Alan Partridge* also won a BAFTA for Best Comedy, and I won one for Best Comedy Performance.

We went to the Comedy Awards after one of the Lyceum shows. During the interval, I watched the Awards live on television with Simon and Julia. After the Lyceum show, motor-bike taxis raced the three of us across Waterloo Bridge so that I could sit in the audience, hear my name and pick up the gong that I was inevitably going to win for playing Partridge on television.

It was everything I had dreamed of since watching *Fawlty Towers* as a child and thinking, 'What an amazing thing it would be to create a character as loved as Basil Fawlty.'

I couldn't imagine anything more satisfying. And I'd done it.

And then my parents came down from Manchester to watch the show and my assistant booked them into a hotel room directly overlooking the front of the Lyceum.

I had unwittingly cast my dad as Doubting Thomas, the Apostle who refused to believe that Jesus was raised from the dead until he felt his fresh wounds for himself. I'm not casting myself as Jesus, but I needed Dad to see my success for himself.

I took Mum and Dad for dinner after the Lyceum show. We didn't really discuss the performance. There is no moment of catharsis when you come from a lower-middle-class background. Nothing is really talked about. So perhaps I got a 'that was very good, son'. But certainly no effusive eulogies.

But then firm handshakes with my dad have only recently progressed to hugs. A tenderness seems to be creeping in with old age. There is acknowledgement of my success, but it's measured. Great shows of anything, from wealth to emotion, have never been encouraged.

In a way, my seeking of approval has turned out to be no bad thing. The verbal diarrhoea you might encounter somewhere like California is the enemy of creativity. It's what *isn't* said that is the lifeblood of any writing. Paradoxically, the way I was raised has empowered me: praise has never been lavished on me and therefore I've never become complacent. I've always had something to prove, to my dad, to my mum, to myself.

I should probably even thank Dad for being dismissive of my playfulness when I was growing up. My parents had six kids, and I was the one they worried about. I was daft. I daydreamed. To cut through the noise, I was always shouting, 'Look at me!'

Drawing attention to yourself wasn't the done thing in our respectable house in suburban Manchester. My parents wanted me to fit in. They expected me to get the kind of respectable job, preferably in the public sector, that would allow me to give back to society. Why would you want to 'act the goat' or have people think you were a halfwit?

For a long time I know they felt both a curiosity and anxiety about my work. It had all happened so fast.

Less than a decade earlier, at the age of twenty-three, I had been a light entertainer in a shiny suit who had appeared on *Sunday Night at the Palladium*. I had shaken Jimmy Tarbuck's hand. And here I was in 1998, an edgy, urbane comedian celebrated for Alan Partridge and performing in front of 2,000 people a night.

★   ★   ★

But all wasn't well: we had to cancel five dates in the middle of the run because I was partying too hard; the official line was that I had acute laryngitis. I was going out every night, getting on it, recovering and doing the next show. The audience didn't know what I was up to because I was looser onstage as a result of my hellraising. I was like a jazz musician who had lost all inhibition. What the show lacked in laser-like precision, it gained in swinging braggadocio. I'd enjoy it even though I was half-cut.

I loved having Simon Pegg and Julia Davis as the support actors. The whole thing was a blast. I was in a fog most of the time, which in itself was amusing. I'd find myself in Soho House, a private members' club, every night. In the end Phil McIntrye, who was promoting my tour, had to send someone to babysit me; their job was to ensure I got into a car to Brighton at the end of the evening. I had to go home: I'd stay up far too late if I was booked into a hotel.

Despite constant partying, I was still driven and rigorous about the show. I still cared about the quality of my work. I knew I cared about the important things; I just happened to be doing all this hedonistic stuff too. I thought I could get away with it.

I had an affair when my girlfriend was pregnant with our daughter, and the story was splashed all over the papers. And then I had another affair. I know it was entirely my fault and I know I behaved selfishly. I became of interest to the tabloids, my behaviour was made public and it was even more traumatic for the people I love.

By the time we recorded the second series of *I'm Alan Partridge* in 2002, I was sometimes falling asleep in the middle of a take because I'd been up all night. I couldn't stay away from cocaine. I couldn't be faithful. I tried to be good, but failed.

Stop. Start. Stop. Start.

CHAPTER 2

I didn't set out to be a comedian. I always wanted to act. Comedy was a way of getting my Equity card after studying drama at Manchester Poly, but I got caught up in a predicament entirely of my own making.

I would do a gig, it would go really badly, and I'd think, 'I can't leave on that note. I have to do one more show. I have to walk away on a high.'

Then I would do a show that went incredibly well. And of course I'd think, 'That was incredible. I have to do it again.'

I loved having 2,000 people in the palm of my hand, all laughing at the same time. I'm not the first comedian to acknowledge how addictive it is to feel empowered on that scale; it's the biggest high you could possibly have, better than any drug. Especially when you do a joke that shines a light on the human condition and everyone, regardless of personal taste or politics, laughs in unison.

This went on for years, until people who recognised me in the street no longer nodded a hello, but shouted out, 'A-ha!'

I soon became used to the instant rewards comedy brings. There's no delayed gratification. You tell a joke and you get a wave of love – bang! You learn fast what does and doesn't work. There's no filter and it's beautifully unambiguous. The audience either make that noise or they don't. You've succeeded or you've failed.

The silence of failure is, of course, deafening.

Comedy is all about precision. Cutting it back until it's razor-sharp. You become conversant with its rules, you become fluent in its idiosyncratic language – so much so that you start to recognise patterns and formulae. Comedy is about having a box of tricks up your sleeve, and that's good up to a point; you can be incredibly proficient at comedy and yet never reach the realm of emotional truth. Sometimes things are funny and you don't know why. Often, when comedy is sublime, there is no apparent explanation for it. Vic and Bob can be like that: hilarious yet impossible to explain.

★ ★ ★

I managed to convince myself for a long time that comedy was important as an end in itself. And of course it is, in certain ways.

People would write me letters saying I'd made them laugh and in doing so had helped them through some personal crisis. This was humbling and helped me appreciate the importance of laughter's medicine. But comedy can also be reductive and limiting.

At least my comedy has a high level of quality control. I've been to Edinburgh in recent years and seen comics who are professional but who don't actually care about anything they're saying. Equally, I've seen young, hungry comics happy to present unpolished material and it's refreshing. Authenticity goes a long way.

Early on in my comedy career, I used to think, 'I can unite everyone in one moment, I can make everyone laugh, ergo everyone likes me. I'm not going to risk that unity by upsetting anyone.'

I thought pleasing all the people all the time was the way forward. It's not. This realisation was only gifted to me following a series of rude awakenings, which certainly took their toll on me at the time, and although I am now able to look at Edinburgh stand-ups with a more discerning eye, my relationship with the festival wasn't always so black and white.

★ ★ ★

Edinburgh Festival in the summer of 1990 was a real eye-opener
for me. Sandy Gort, my first proper agent, asked Frank Skinner
to support me at the Pleasance Theatre. It was ridiculous, because
he was obviously going to upstage me.

Frank had put in the hours. I hadn't.

He was clearly the better act, so the audience responded to
him much more than they did to me. I didn't deliver, because
I was still coasting. Frank would do the first twenty-five minutes,
get the audience on his side, introduce me, I'd do thirty minutes
of old material to a lukewarm reception, Frank would come back
onstage, and we'd sing a song we'd written called 'It's Over Now'.

Frank was always a gentleman, but it was a bit awkward.

Sharing a flat with Frank didn't make it any easier. The phone
was always ringing. I'd always answer it and it was always for
Frank. It would be a TV producer whom I knew and who knew
me. And who always wanted Frank.

The phone never rang for me.

Coming home in the blue morning light of an Edinburgh
dawn, I bought a copy of the *List* from a newsagent's in the
streets at the back of the castle. The review was effusive about
Frank. It said that I came on in the first half as Duncan Thickett
and did a reasonable impersonation of a bad stand-up comedian.
Then, in the second half, I came on as myself and the reviewer
realised I *was* a bad stand-up comedian.

I was gutted.

I got back to the flat and asked Frank if he'd seen the *List*.
He and his girlfriend both looked at me and told me they'd
hidden it under a sofa cushion to spare my embarrassment.

Later on, when we rejigged the show, I decided to get rid of
Duncan Thickett.

I said to Frank, 'Who's going to tell him?'

Frank said, 'I think you should.'

I walked into the bathroom, mumbled quietly behind the
door, then shouted out in Duncan's voice, 'No! Please! Please,
I'm begging you! It's my life.'

Frank was curled up laughing when I emerged, shaken, from the bathroom and said it hadn't gone well.

There were good times to be had in Edinburgh that summer, but I had a horrible feeling in the pit of my stomach. It was as though my success was already slipping away.

One day I had lunch with Patrick Marber, who was performing at the Gilded Balloon with Jo Brand and James Macabre. We'd met in passing before, when we both did an ill-fated, short-lived TV comedy called *Paramount City*, but I'd never sat down with him and talked. Although he is only a year older than me, I came away impressed by how very clever, thoughtful and grown up he was.

I, in turn, was down and probably not great company. I still hadn't found a way to be something other than an impressionist. I talked to Patrick about how I'd had to stretch my material when I'd been a resident comic on *Paramount City*, and how I felt as though I was having to run before I could walk.

Nothing seemed to be going my way and I felt insecure and anxious.

Things in my private life were also just making me feel worse. I was having a fling with an older comedian and Paul Merton was hanging around her Edinburgh flat. Compared to heavyweights like him, I felt slightly naff.

Patrick listened. He told me that Frank wasn't upstaging me as much as I thought; he still insists now that I was really good in Edinburgh that year.

Patrick, in turn, was frustrated with stand-up and wanted to be a 'proper' writer. We bonded over our mutual discontent.

He also responded to my vulnerability; I later found out that, until we'd sat down for lunch, I had struck him as incredibly confident, successful and rich.

I was still earning good money from voiceovers, but I was aware of being regarded as a bit Mickey Mouse. It bothered me for a long time. It's that typical creative angst: you feel like you're going to be found out after your initial flush of success.

I spent far too long thinking, 'I'm a fraud. Everyone is going to realise I'm stupid.'

I've got beyond that now, thank goodness.

The show with Frank was a turning point for me. It was akin to a wake-up call, coming as it did so soon after my first London agent, Jan Murphy, had told me to pull a rabbit out of a hat.

As was Sean Hughes winning the Perrier with *A One Night Stand* that year. It was his first time at Edinburgh, and he became the youngest-ever winner. He looked like a pop star and women adored him. In the summer of 1990 I spent far too much time imagining what it might be like to be Sean Hughes.

And I probably got the crumbs off his table in terms of women. Edinburgh was as much about sleeping around as being funny. It was part of the lifestyle: you did your show, went out, got drunk, had sex, woke up, had a late breakfast, went to see someone else's show if you could be bothered. On and on it went.

It was exhausting, but exceptionally good fun.

★   ★   ★

I nearly had the show ready to take up to Edinburgh in 1991. Jan had secured me a venue and I was very tempted to take it. But the show wasn't quite ready.

I thought, 'I'm going to skip this year, get the show really tight. I'll take it to Edinburgh in '92 when it's dead right.'

Which is exactly what I did.

In the interim, I had to navigate 1991, which turned out to be an odd year. For example, when I decided I no longer wanted to do impressions on *Granada Up Front* with Tony Wilson and Lucy Meacock, Granada threatened me with legal action. If I didn't show up of my own accord, they would issue court proceedings forcing me to show up.

I argued that I hadn't agreed to anything; they said my representative had verbally agreed that I would turn up and do all these shows. My agent was in a panic: she couldn't afford to be sued.

Reluctantly, I went into Granada and did the shows. As I was sitting there writing the topical comedy that I was legally enforced to do, the executive producer of *Granada Up Front* came up to me and said, 'I'm sorry about all that legal business.'

I wouldn't describe his manner as disingenuous, more like fleet-footed. It was as if he'd had nothing to do with it.

My focus was on my prospective Edinburgh show. I decided to take the work-in-progress around arts centres in the north and hone it until it was perfect. I vowed to keep away from London and all those niggly, back-biting bastards. I didn't want the show strangled at birth by some acerbic wanker from *Time Out*.

John Davy and Maria Kempinska, who founded Jongleurs in 1983 in a room above a pub in Battersea, were always in my corner. In the summer of 1991, John suggested I take a trip to Rhodes to do a residency in a resort. It was just something he was into at that time. You'd get your flights paid for, a few days in the sun and a few hundred quid.

And so I found myself, three years after I'd first been on television, standing by a swimming pool, trying to make largely disinterested holidaymakers laugh.

As I was doing impersonations, blokes in trunks kept interrupting: 'Do you mind not swearing? There are kids around this pool.'

I said nothing, but I kept thinking, 'How the fucking hell have I ended up here?'

It was just awful.

My single box room was like a cell. Every time I went back there and looked straight out on to the air-conditioning unit, I would literally put my head in my hands and think to myself, 'This is desperate.'

I remember standing in the gift shop, looking at the over-priced Greek phalluses and thinking, 'What am I doing here?'

The only glimmer of hope on the horizon was my plan of returning to Edinburgh the following year with a brilliant show.

One afternoon I had nothing else to do other than sit alone on my narrow bed and read a copy of the international *Guardian*. The first thing I saw was a story about Frank Skinner winning the Perrier Award. The previous year he had supported me and now he'd won.

Meanwhile, I was in a room with no view in Rhodes.

I felt sick to the pit of my stomach. And so alone. Frank had worked hard and deserved to win. I was full of self-pity. I was a known quantity and I wasn't much quantity. I was a funny voice man from the north.

I thought, 'I've got to do this myself. No one else is going to do it for me. I'm just going to have to put the hours in.'

★   ★   ★

Gradually my attitude started to change and I began to think, 'You know what? I don't care any more about people who don't like me. I'm just going to say what I think, because I feel fraudulent doing otherwise.'

I don't think I had a specific epiphany, rather a slow dawning. I went to see Stewart Lee a few years ago and was really impressed with his refusal to compromise for the sake of a cheap laugh. He was released by his brutal honesty. I was envious.

Deciding not to care what anyone thought about me was incredibly liberating. After years of not speaking up, I stopped giving a damn about how others defined me.

I made a simple but conscious decision to be true to myself, to follow my instincts, to stop trying to second-guess everything or worry about how I'm coming across. The truth, as the Bible says, will set you free. It will also, of course, piss some people off. That's the worst feeling: being authentic and honest and being misinterpreted.

If you are sincere and others judge you as being disingenuous, there's very little you can do about it. You don't have a choice; you just have to carry on. And maybe, if you're lucky, the truth will set you free.

It's not, however, like I'm now a 'grown-up' and therefore constantly in this fantastic place, or that I'm behaving with integrity all the time, because I'm not. It's just that the feeling of acting entirely in my own self-interest was making me feel bad. Making every decision thinking, 'What can I get out of this?' isn't good for the soul after a while.

Compared to my almost overnight decision to stick my head above the parapet, my drift away from comedy has been slow.

By way of example, I like *Saxondale* more than Alan Partridge. I realise I'm out of step with most people. Those who like *Saxondale* absolutely love it and totally get it. And yet the majority would hold it up next to Partridge and insist it's not as funny. It isn't *literally* as funny as Partridge. But there's more depth to it and therefore it's more satisfying to do.

Saxondale marked the start of a shift away from comedy and towards truthful, painful and funny drama. It's more exciting to touch people than to make them laugh. And I don't mean physically. If you manage to make laughter and emotion work side by side, it can be transcendent.

After *Saxondale*, I started to accept straight acting roles in dramas such as *Sunshine*, a three-part BBC series written and directed by Craig Cash in 2008. In doing so, it became clear I was inviting some journalists to mock me.

Caitlin Moran wrote in *The Times* that I was 'faffing around with this wholly forgettable straight role' and that watching me in something as 'outrightly mawkish' as *Sunshine* was 'like watching electricity curdling on a tray'.

I tend to think success is the best form of revenge, but in this instance I decided I could prove whole cliques of naysayers wrong by finding something really positive to say about humanity. I was used to uniting an audience with humour; this time, I wanted to unite an audience with humanity.

And if I failed in doing so, at least I would have failed on my own terms and I wouldn't have anyone else to blame.

CHAPTER 3

I had definitely lost my way before *Philomena*. My advisors spent years trying to position me in the States.

'You need to do a buddy movie with Vince Vaughn! Then you'll finally be successful in America!'

It wasn't what I wanted to do, but at the same time I didn't know what else to do.

In September 2009, I was in New York with my then girlfriend, China Chow, making a film called *The Other Guys* with Will Ferrell and Mark Wahlberg. I played part number three. Will Ferrell is incredibly funny. I just phoned in my performance. I was in a treading-water period, always wondering what the hell I was doing.

One morning, while I was still in New York, I read Martin Sixsmith's story about Philomena Lee on the *Guardian* website. The accompanying photo showed Sixsmith, a former foreign journalist and advisor to the Labour Party, sitting on a bench next to an older woman. The warmth between Martin and Philomena was evident. Sixsmith's piece told the story of an unmarried teenage mother whose young son was sold by Irish nuns to an American couple without her permission. He had agreed to help Philomena find the son she hadn't set eyes on for fifty years.

Philomena's story had an instant and profound effect on me. I immediately wanted to find a way to tell it. On a simple level, it was about two people, Philomena and Martin; one from the Old World, the other from the New World. Intellect versus intuition; open-heartedness versus cynicism; upper-middle-class socially liberal versus working-class socially conservative.

Beyond the obvious dramatic tension, it had a very personal resonance for me. I had been brought up in a Catholic family and spent summer holidays with extended family in Ireland. No one in my family talked about religion. If there was a story on the news about a Catholic sexual abuse case, we wouldn't say, 'It's a real problem for the Church, isn't it?' We'd just go quiet and then we'd start talking about something else. I understood why Philomena had kept her secret for fifty years.

China suggested I have a go at writing the screenplay myself. I'd only written one film before, *The Parole Officer*. It could have been an edgier film; it could have had more substance. My performance is demonstrative and unsophisticated. The script, which I co-wrote with Henry Normal in 2001, is silly because I didn't know what I wanted to say about things then. I thought it might be a fun and interesting little caper about a parole officer framed for murder, but the execution was too broad. It became a paint-by-numbers film.

After the premiere, Patrick Marber, who had helped in the creation of Partridge a decade earlier, came up to me and diplomatically said, 'Congratulations, you've made a film.'

That really was the best thing he could say about it. It really irritated me at the time, but frankly he was very, very generous.

With *Philomena*, I decided to see if I could finally make the kind of film that I wanted to see. No one advised me to do it, which is rare in itself. As co-founder of Baby Cow Productions, a company I'd set up with Henry in 1999, I was at least in a position to take a risk.

But I'd never written a serious drama. I had always thought to myself, 'Other people do serious work.'

At the start of my career, when I'd worked with Armando Iannucci, Chris Morris and Patrick on Radio 4's *On The Hour*, I'd come into contact with an endless stream of people who were uber-confident and educated at Britain's finest universities. I, meanwhile, was a grammar school kid from a Manchester suburb who had failed English O level not once, but twice. I resat it for the first time in the lower sixth and, like a dunce, failed it again.

This might be a class thing, but I never felt like I was the person running the shop. I was never in charge. I wasn't officer material. We, the lower middle class, are destined to be corporals, or sergeants at best. But then, very slowly, I started to realise that my opinions were valid. I had, as all people do, a unique perspective. I realised that in the case of *Philomena*, my background might actually help me.

Also, liberal-leaning intellectuals might worry about castigating the simple world view of an old Irish lady. It wasn't a concern for me. I grew up knowing lots of old Irish ladies and I can say with some authority that they do say lots of daft things. I knew I could mine comedy from playing with Philomena's character and then dignifying the grace and serenity of that same woman.

You can mock the things you love.

Similarly, with Martin Sixsmith I saw an opportunity to exorcise my own cynicism. I identify much more closely with his character's disillusion with religious institutions. I am an atheist but not a nihilist.

Critics tended to lazily define me by my performance as Alan Partridge and seemed to think I was incapable of doing good, serious work. Perhaps it was time to see if I could prove both them and myself wrong.

Of course, I didn't realise all this at the time. I wasn't sitting around feeling insecure and irritated with critics. Nor was I being precious or snobby about comedy. I had just been looking for some kind of artistic nourishment and I found it in the form of *Philomena*.

I didn't tell many people that I had bought the film rights to Martin Sixsmith's book, *The Lost Child of Philomena Lee*. Rather than be accused of failing before I'd even started work on the project, I decided to keep my head down.

Initially, I didn't think I could write *Philomena*; I thought I'd get an experienced writer on board. But the more I thought about Philomena's voice, the more clearly I could hear it.

China introduced me to Gaby Tanner, a great film producer who had worked on *The Duchess* and *Coriolanus*. Gaby and I then went to see Christine Langan, the head of BBC Films. I talked about my ideas for the film and said I needed a good writer.

Christine immediately said, 'You should write it. You just need a good co-writer.'

She suggested that I write the screenplay with Jeff Pope, head of factual drama at ITV. He had co-written *Pierrepoint: The Last Hangman*, which I absolutely loved, and had produced several dramas with Paul Greengrass, including *The Murder of Stephen Lawrence*. He had also produced, among others on a long, impressive list, *Mo* and *Appropriate Adult* for ITV.

I always wanted Judi Dench to play Philomena, and Christine thought Stephen Frears, with whom she'd worked on *The Queen*, would be the perfect director.

Stephen played hard to get. He made me chase him. It was definitely worth it. I found my voice with him. We would have robust conversations in which he would challenge me. He involved me the whole way, asking what a particular line meant in the script and pushing me to think about every nuance. The film is certainly better than the script; Stephen lifted it.

He was a great ally on set too. When the make-up artist made the nuns look too wicked, he understood that we needed to be more subtle. We talked about ensuring that the nuns didn't announce the fact that they are bad; clearly what they've done is bad, but they shouldn't be caricatures of 'bad nuns'.

Jeff was an equally brilliant call on the part of BBC Films. He's the Essex equivalent of me: lower middle class and suburban. Both our fathers are very practical: his worked for Technicolor, helping to develop colour film, and mine worked for IBM. He feels like a brother.

I like Jeff's matter-of-fact, direct and clear approach; it counters the fact that I talk round and round in circles. We are not

natural, lifelong intellectuals, but we share a hunger for knowledge, for learning.

I wasn't intimidated by Jeff. I could say what I thought
without holding back and wondering if I was being articulate
enough. He gave me the space to grow in confidence as a writer;
I could tell him that something he'd written didn't feel right
and he wouldn't get upset.

He is a populist, he has compassion and a sense of the poetic,
and he is also straightforward, a grafter and great company. When
we meet we spend half the time together exchanging anecdotes
and gossiping. I always look forward to working with him.

I was very clear about what I wanted the script to be. I wanted
humour to help tell the story; I knew it would stop *Philomena*
from being portentous. I also wanted it to be a warm film as a
direct response to the irony and cynicism that seem to flavour
everything, and that I ultimately find debilitating and depressing.

It's good to trample on received wisdom. You might think
that you can't poke fun at old Irish ladies because it's bullying
behaviour. Of course you can, so long as there's warmth. You
can have a good raucous laugh at someone and ultimately dignify
them at the same time. That ambiguity is real, it's human; it's
no different from mocking your parents while loving them. You
also need the conviction to say something and not bookend it
with some sort of apology or qualification. You don't have to
parachute humour in as an insurance. If it feels difficult or you
feel self-conscious when you do it, it's probably a good sign.

All these thoughts were racing around my head. I felt
compelled to tell both sides of the story and not to have to
come to a concrete, judgemental conclusion; I've learned late
in life to understand the beauty of thoughts and reflections.
I've taught myself to formulate sophisticated thoughts, and it's
taken a long time. I'm trying to find truths that are under-
represented on screen, to embrace nuance and ambiguity.

★ ★ ★

When I saw the photo in the *Guardian* of Martin and Philomena sitting side by side on the bench, my first thoughts were: 'OK, they took flights together. I wonder if they got coffee from Starbucks. Did he go to WHSmith at the airport? Did they go together? If he got a newspaper, did he ask her what she wanted? Did he buy it for her? Did he react when she asked for the *Daily Mail*?'

I knew I had to talk to both Martin and Philomena in as much detail as possible about their trip to America. I needed all the detail he'd omitted from the book because he didn't think it was dramatic enough. I needed background: how did Martin feel when his parents died? How did Philomena feel when, as an adult, she had a second child? Discovering how excited I was about storytelling was a revelation.

The first time I met Philomena and her daughter, Jane Libberton, was at Martin's house. Philomena was anxious and nervous. Jane was understandably suspicious and defensive; what did this British comedian want from her mother? I knew I would have to work hard to win their trust. I had to convince them that I was honourable.

When I mentioned to Philomena that we were talking to Judi Dench about playing her in the film, she clasped her hands to her chest and gasped, 'Dame Judi Dench playing little old me?'

Philomena soon got used to the idea of her story being turned into a film. I used to joke at Q&As in America that Philomena had kept a secret for fifty years and now you couldn't shut her up.

I was also very keen to play Martin. I related to some of his world-weary journalist persona because I was no longer excited by comedy in the same way. I knew that I could use the fiction-alised version of Martin to get stuff off my chest, to say things that I know are conceited, that are me at my most bilious.

Whenever Martin and I met, we discussed 'Martin' in the third person as if it wasn't quite him. We talked about the film version of Martin as being slightly different from him.

Not long after Jeff came on board as a co-writer, he came with me to talk to both Philomena and Martin. As a journalist, Martin was able to give us notes on the script, to tell us personal details about himself and to help us with the factual background to the story.

During one of our visits to see Philomena, Martin and I played her footage of her son, Anthony, running around the flower garden in Ross Abbey when he was five years old. She had never seen it before, and she started crying. She grabbed my hand as I was watching the footage and said, 'I did love him you know.'

I used that line in the film, when Martin and Philomena are at the salad bar and she grabs his hand. What is strange about life imitating art is that it didn't happen to Martin, it happened to me. And then to me when I was playing Martin.

When I asked Philomena if she could forgive the nuns for what they did to her, she thought about it and said, 'Yes I do.'

Her daughter Jane said, 'I don't.'

Both are valid responses and I wanted them both reflected in the film. I gave the 'I don't forgive' line to Martin and let Philomena have her moment of forgiveness, which allowed us to go from the anger and vengeance of the Old Testament to forgiveness, supposedly one of the central tenets of Christianity.

Almost all narratives are about sating the desire for revenge, because forgiveness isn't sexy. Philomena's clemency, being a rarity on screen, excited me. We can, after all, learn from those we castigate. No one has a monopoly on wisdom.

Jeff and I also retraced some of Martin's steps, including a visit to the nuns at Sean Ross Abbey in Roscrea. I had a difficult conversation with a senior sister of the Sacred Hearts of Jesus and Mary that I felt was reflective of the Church's generally dismissive response to women like Philomena. Historically it has a siege mentality of manning the barricades and refusing to engage in discussion.

I saw 'Sister X', as I will refer to her here, in a car outside the abbey, and approached her.

Me: 'Hello. Are you Sister X?'

Sister X: 'I am.'

Me: 'My name is Steve Coogan. You may know that I'm working on a film about Philomena Lee. I wondered if I could ask you—'

Sister X (interrupting): 'I must say I find it incredibly discourteous of you to come looking around here without first knocking on the door to introduce yourselves.'

Me: 'I thought people were allowed to wander about.'

Sister X: 'No. This is private property.'

Me: 'Why are you presuming that I have negative intentions? If you have nothing to hide, why not be open?'

Sister X: 'I have nothing to hide, but you should have introduced yourself and spoken to me.'

Me: 'Martin Sixsmith called you.'

Sister X: 'No. I was called yesterday by someone else.'

Me: 'Yes, that was my PA. She reported back that you wanted nothing to do with the film.'

Sister X: 'That's right.'

Me: 'So you are refusing to cooperate?'

Sister X: 'What is your question?'

Me: 'I wondered why there are no names of the babies who died, on the wall in the Garden of Remembrance.'

Sister X: 'There is a sculpture to commemorate them; we do not list individual names because there would be an issue of whose names were left off and whose were left on. If the parents wish to place an individual plaque then they can.'

Me: 'There were a number of plaques with names of the dead about five years ago that aren't there any more.'

Sister X: 'There were not. I've been here for nine years and there were never any names there.'

Me: 'OK. This film isn't going to be an attack on the Catholic Church. My parents are Roman Catholic. Judi Dench is going to play Philomena in a film about healing, about acknowledging the mistakes of the past and moving on.'

Sister X: 'Hmmm . . .'

Me: 'Thank you for talking to me. I appreciate it.'

Sister X: 'OK.'

Me: 'Goodbye.'

Sister X: 'Goodbye.'

I walked back to the car and drove away.

Some of the research was tough, but it was a revelation for me to be expressive about things I wanted to communicate through the prism of what had happened to someone else.

And yet perhaps the even greater experience was seeing something through from beginning to end, from reading a newspaper article to seeing it on the screen.

CHAPTER 4

I have never written alone. I like to collaborate and I've never had an ego about the credit being divided. The smartest decision I ever made was to always find the most talented people to work with.

When I was writing Alan Partridge with Patrick, Armando Iannucci or, more recently, Neil and Rob Gibbons, we would record improvised scenes, transcribe them and shape a script. With *Philomena*, I would do all the parts and try to imagine the conversations. The characters in Woody Allen's films all seem to talk with a similar level of articulacy, but I tried to imagine the rhythm of each individual's conversation; I wanted Philomena to talk in that working-class way, with an eloquent brevity.

I've got a good ear for working-class dialogue and I grew up around Philomena's generation of women. I will always remember my grandma saying, when I was full of maudlin self-pity following some self-inflicted personal crisis, 'It's like a cloud, it'll pass.'

There was a rich subtext and a universal truth to her words; she certainly didn't sit around using words like 'duplicity'. My sister, Clare, used to talk about the people we met in Ireland in the summer holidays as having 'a simple faith' and leading 'simple lives, well lived'.

I remember arriving at the moment towards the end of the script in which Philomena tells the nun that she forgives her for what she did to her. I had to think about how she could say it with conviction and honesty. The danger is apologising for it being powerful; you have to *let* it be powerful. Don't be spineless and do a joke. Have the guts to see it through. It's like discovering that the most powerful weapon in writing is love.

It may sound bizarre, but I like the fact that if you get something like that wrong, you look like an idiot. The challenge is attractive to me. But then I'm not a stereotypical writer. When I write with Jeff, I don't look at the script on the page. I'm even superstitious about looking over his shoulder as he's sitting in front of the laptop. I'll stand on the other side of the room, imagine a scene in my head and ask him to repeat it back to me.

'What's the line before that? And the line after?'

Jeff will say, 'Just come and have a look.'

I worry it will break the spell, but I will go over and look. I'm a visual thinker and so the transition between what's in my head and what goes on the page is more evident to me than it might be for others.

We were very aware of keeping the story as simple as possible. I rail against wordy, intellectual writers whose characters talk incessantly, often for the sake of it. It always reminds me of Ken Branagh's fantastic story about the time he met Liam Gallagher.

Liam: 'You're that actor, aren't you?'

Ken nods.

Liam: 'Yeah, I've seen you on the telly. You're that actor in that series.'

Then he makes both his hands talk to each other, like glove puppets. 'Talky talky, talky, talky.'

★   ★   ★

I didn't want Philomena's character to be over-articulate in order to communicate my ideas in the film.

Harvey Weinstein, who distributed *Philomena* in the States, tried to persuade me to add a line at the end of the film. He wanted Philomena to say to the nun, 'I'll forgive, but I won't forget.'

It's a terrible line. I refused.

No one would have a conversation with Harvey, so I had to speak to him on the phone.

He said, 'Listen. I've got so many Academy Awards, I know what I'm talking about. You need to put that line in.'

We argued. At one point I said, 'Harvey, it's New Testament, not Old Testament.'

We compromised in the end by adding the line where Philomena says to Martin, 'I do want you to write your book. People should know what happened here.' It was a note of empowerment; she refused to live like a victim and didn't seek to judge others as the nuns judged her. Forgiveness is proactive, not passive.

One of the agents at Independent Talent had a note for me about Philomena's son, Michael Hess, who worked as chief counsel for the Republican National Committee when Reagan was in power.

'You can't have the son dying halfway through the film,' she said. 'It robs all the momentum of the film. He has to die at the end. Otherwise the script doesn't work. You want to see his life in the White House. You've got to cast a really big Hollywood star as the missing son and make him a central part of the film.'

She said it with such conviction that I had to listen. I had a crisis of confidence.

'That's a different film,' I told her eventually. 'It's not the film we've written. Our film is about two people on a journey. He thinks he's saving her, but she saves him.'

Listening to her point of view and reacting so strongly against it was actually a good thing. It reinforced what Jeff and I had written and I felt more confident about the structure of the film.

I liked the fact that Philomena and Martin would never ordinarily have spent time together. He is, at points, exasperated with her naivety, and is irritated by her enthusiasm for the American hotel breakfast; but then reality kicks in for them both when he discovers her son is dead.

When Jeff and I were writing, I kept saying, 'What would she or he *really* say?' As well as talking for the sake of it, too often what people say in films doesn't remotely resemble what they would say in real life. There's a scene in *Festen*, the Thomas Vinterberg film, where the eldest son accuses the father of sexual abuse. The reaction doesn't feel written; because it's improvised, it feels very real. Some people snigger in the scene because they don't know what to do; others look around the room, gauging reactions. It's far more real than everyone saying, en masse, 'Oh my God, he raped his children!'

You feel, watching that scene in *Festen*, that you've learned something about humanity. Vinterberg is brave enough to ask questions without pretending to have the answers. As Lord Byron said, ''Tis strange – but true; for truth is always strange; stranger than fiction.'

CHAPTER 5

*P*hilomena had its world premiere at the Venice Film Festival in September 2013. I sat next to Judi Dench in a 2,000-capacity cinema. I felt incredibly nervous, partly because it was the first time the film had been seen, but also because we were premiering it in a Catholic country. As producer and co-writer, I'd obviously seen the film before, but it was the first time Judi had seen it.

The audience made plenty of noise, almost as though they were watching a silent movie. Their responses were theatrical: I could hear sharp intakes of breath followed by loud applause in the scene where I say, 'Fucking Catholics.' There was, in fact, spontaneous applause throughout the film and, as soon as the credits were rolling, the audience was on its feet, applauding.

A light picked out Judi, Stephen and me in our seats on the balcony. The audience turned and directed their applause at us. We stood up, feeling happy but a little overwhelmed and almost embarrassed. The applause must have lasted for ten minutes; it felt like it might never end.

I looked at Judi, who simply smiled. I had nothing to compare it to. I didn't know how to gauge it.

Someone leaned over and said, 'This is very good. If they don't like a film they boo.'

So, finally, I allowed myself to enjoy the moment.

The reaction in Venice was surreal. I had hoped for a positive response to the film, but I hadn't been prepared for a standing ovation. And then journalists were voluntarily effusive, and I know from experience that journalists keep their counsel if they don't like something. Some even came up to me on the verge of tears and said, 'Thank you for making this film.'

It was a very strange experience. I felt like someone else. Disassociated. Much like I do when I perform live. Coming from a large Catholic family I have always been on the lookout for approbation, but I don't really know how to deal with it when I get it, so I end up feeling disconnected.

We had a sense that we'd written something good, but we didn't know how people would be affected by the film. The response from women in particular has been incredible. Sometimes three generations of women went to see *Philomena*, and if I met them after a Q&A they would say, 'What a wonderful warm film. We loved it so much.'

It reinforced my earlier point about cynicism. There are films that deal with love and sentiment, but they are nearly always cynical. It's almost as though the film studios have a cynical box that they ask writers and directors to tick. In my opinion, the only sincerity they admire is the big, broad studio type: sincerity that 'tests well'.

I was, on occasion, overwhelmed by the response. After one Q&A in America a large group of middle-aged women hung around to talk to me. My American assistant, Jessica, took a photo of me looking slightly messianic: I'm crouching down, talking to these women from the stage as they look up at me. She said I look like a cross between Jeremy Kyle and Jesus Christ.

I think people responded to the humanity in the film. It's not arrogant, it doesn't claim to have all the answers. There's an imperfection about it simply because there isn't a definitive resolution; nor is there total redemption. It allows both Philomena and Martin to say, 'You don't have to win the argument. Life can move on. It's OK that both of us have flaws.'

Martin is very bullish at the start of the film. He thinks his world view is the right one, but he's wrong. Philomena teaches him a lesson in the end: there is no right and wrong, just different ways of living our lives. That's me admonishing myself for my own cynicism, because I still have to think quite consciously about *not* being cynical.

People also responded to the humour in *Philomena*. I met Tom Hooper, who directed *The King's Speech*, at a party after *Philomena* came out. He said that just as he was convinced he was about to be manipulated he found himself laughing and then, when he wasn't prepared for it, he was karate-chopped with emotion. I was pleased because it was exactly the response I'd hoped for. And it was no accident. I was throwing ideas out during the entire writing process because I'd seen them before and they felt too familiar.

And so the momentum kept on building around the film.

I was wary of dragging Philomena, who was about to turn eighty-one, around the circuit and I didn't want to exploit her for the sake of the film. But she was brilliant. She did Q&As, she talked to the audience and she was very honest about her story.

Sometimes you'd get a curveball in a Q&A.

Audience member: 'Were you really OK with your son being gay, Philomena?'

I'd jump in first: 'I'm glad you asked. Because some people assume that I was being politically correct by making Philomena accept her son in the film.'

Then Philomena would say in a matter-of-fact way, 'I was a nurse for thirty years. I worked with plenty of gay male nurses and they were often the best nurses. They did all the heavy lifting.'

I might add, 'There you go. I didn't make it up. And I didn't make up the scene where Philomena sees her son for the last time in the back window of the car as he's being driven away by his adoptive parents.'

★   ★   ★

I went to so many award ceremonies for *Philomena* that I can no longer differentiate them in my mind. I know that I wasn't allowed to wear the same tuxedo twice. Each one cost $5,000 and had to be measured so that it was a perfect fit around my buttocks. I wore a Dolce & Gabbana suit to introduce Katy Perry and Juicy J to the stage at the Emmys and they sent a letter saying I looked like a proper gentleman.

More importantly, I managed to get in a slight dig at misogynistic black rap music and I made a joke about the Jonas Brothers and The Beatles that got a laugh. But those events are mostly mind-numbing and I only do them because I'm told to. I didn't feel as though I had to sell *Philomena*, because it was doing a pretty good job of selling itself.

On 16 January 2014, the Oscar nominations were announced. I was half-asleep in my Los Angeles hotel room when the phone rang just before 6 a.m. I'd been trying to sleep all night and I was in this semi-dreamlike state in which I was convinced it was midday and I'd overslept. The phone rang and I jolted awake as if I'd had an electric shock.

My American assistant, Jessica, was on the other end. She was screaming. 'You've got three Oscar nominations! Best Picture, Best Actress, Best Adapted Screenplay!'

I didn't watch the Oscar nominations because it would have been excruciating to watch and not get anything. A single nomination would have been amazing. We weren't in any of the American newspapers' Oscar predictions, which made it even more delicious.

It was a very emotional day, not least because Mum left a message in which she was barely able to talk because she was crying.

And then three nominations became four when Alexandre Desplat was nominated for his original score. I absolutely love his score. It's the antithesis of the kind of prescriptive score that tells you what you're watching is either quirky or significant. It doesn't spoon-feed you some kind of emotion in the vein of John Williams, whom I have always found too literal.

It was a whirlwind of an experience. People used to tell me

that I'd be going on a journey, and I was baffled. But that's exactly what happened.

The Oscars are like a political campaign. Winning an Oscar is partly to do with how good your film is and partly to do with how tenacious you are during awards season.

In the US I am sometimes recognised by middle-aged women for *Philomena*, and in Whole Foods by bearded hipsters for *24 Hour Party People* and *The Trip*. No one, however, ever stops me in Wal-Mart. And no one has ever shouted out, 'Aha!'

Not being well known in America really helped. In Britain, when people were coming up to me in 2014 and saying 'I loved your film', they nearly always meant *Alpha Papa*. In the States, however, it was always *Philomena*. They would come up to me there without knowing anything about Alan Partridge, which was quite liberating.

As Oscar night approached, I kept thinking of stories I'd heard in the past.

Stuart Cornfeld, who is now Ben Stiller's producing partner, told me this, my favourite Oscar story. In 1981, *The Elephant Man*, which Cornfeld executively produced, was nominated for a Best Picture Oscar, and Martin Scorsese was nominated for Best Director for *Raging Bull*.

Ordinary People, directed by Robert Redford, won Best Picture and Best Director.

Later in the evening, Martin Scorsese walked up to Stuart and said, 'In twenty years' time, *The Elephant Man* and *Raging Bull* will be considered classics and *Ordinary People* will be the answer to a trivia question.'

Which is exactly what happened.

And I comforted myself by remembering what Denis Healey said about not being prime minister: 'I'd rather people wondered why I wasn't prime minister than why I was.'

It was incredible to be nominated with Jeff for the script. I read books slowly. I like to watch *Air Crash Investigation*. The closest I get to spirituality is watching *Wheeler Dealers*, in which cars are done up and sold for £5,000. Watching a programme that has no real consequence or looking at used cars online is, to me, a form of meditation. It's like doing yoga.

My parents, my daughter and my then girlfriend, Loretta, came to the Oscars.

Of course I was disappointed to lose Best Picture and Best Adapted Screenplay to *12 Years a Slave* (or *Roots* as it used to be called) but it's the taking part that counts.

Steve McQueen said at every opportunity that *12 Years a Slave* wasn't about race, it was about America. And no one is going to vote against America. I said we should take a leaf out of his book, so when I won a low-profile award from the Italian film society in LA, I had a bet with Jeff that I could tenuously and circuitously arrive at a point where *Philomena* was about America.

I went up onstage and said, *Philomena* isn't just a film about a woman looking for a son she never saw grow up. It's about something else. It's about refugees leaving the Old World and coming to the New World. In a way this film is about America.'

Not that it did us any good. Still, I won the bet.

CHAPTER 6

Dad has a great love of poetry. At my mum's eightieth he quoted Shakespeare from memory. I occasionally read poetry to him and he reads it to me, both to find a connection with him and because it makes a change from his favourite subject, engineering. I read him some A. E. Housman and Byron and then he reads me some Rudyard Kipling.

I wanted 'The Garden of Love', a Blake poem, to appear on the screen before the credits at the end of *Philomena*:

> I went to the Garden of Love,
> And saw what I never had seen:
> A Chapel was built in the midst,
> Where I used to play on the green.
>
> And the gates of this Chapel were shut,
> And Thou shalt not. writ over the door;
> So I turn'd to the Garden of Love,
> That so many sweet flowers bore.
>
> And I saw it was filled with graves,
> And tomb-stones where flowers should be:
> And Priests in black gowns, were walking their rounds,
> And binding with briars, my joys & desires.

Stephen said no, but I still think it might have worked, because it's about sexuality and denial. Why would God give us desire and then want us to resist it? And yet I grew up thinking that sex was taboo. It was about procreation, not enjoyment.

Of course I took into consideration the fact that my parents were Catholics when I made *Philomena*, but I could only be true to myself. When I told my parents that I was co-writing it, I think they were anxious, but I didn't want to do anything that would denigrate their faith.

I do think that Catholics like Philomena represent my parents: they live their lives without preaching or piety. It's about being kind and decent, in an unassuming and unremarkable way. My parents aren't talkers, they are doers. Well, they do talk, but not about what they do. They quietly bear witness to their values.

When the film came out, it was a great moment to share with my extended Irish family.

My father's brother was in tears. He had only one criticism, and that was about a scene that was set in the Republic of Ireland but shot in a bar in Northern Ireland: 'On the shelf at the back there was a bottle of Bell's whisky rather than Paddy whiskey,' He looked at me and winked. 'It's just unthinkable . . .'

He also said that when the film was shown in Ireland, there was a great wave of appreciation for the opportunity to reignite the topic of the Catholic Church and its adoption practices.

As far as I am aware, more Catholics embraced *Philomena* than rejected it – apart from the religious right in America, who hated it and dismissed it as anti-Catholic. What enraged the fundamentalists most was that Philomena was willing to forgive the nuns who sold her child. She refused to judge them; they had behaved badly, but she believed they were capable of good.

American fundamentalists don't get ambiguity, self-doubt or humility; they see such traits as weakness. They see forgiveness as unforgivable.

I've travelled a lot around America, but I've never seen a bumper sticker that says, 'I love nuance.'

At the end of the film, Philomena is someone who lives her faith. She doesn't shout it from the rooftops; she isn't one of those people who tell everyone else how they should behave.

She just lives by her own values. Like my parents, she walks the walk while other Catholics talk the talk.

Philomena is not an angry polemic like *The Magdalene Sisters*, Peter Mullan's very powerful film about three teenage Irish girls who are sent to the Magdalene laundries to carry out unpaid labour under the supervision of nuns. There's no olive branch in Mullan's film; there is in *Philomena*. The irony is that the person who had these things perpetrated upon her is herself the best hope for her faith. She is able to show the most dignified serenity to the same religious institution that repressed her. That paradox is in the film.

The things you're not supposed to talk about in films are the same things you're not supposed to talk about at dinner parties: religion, politics and sex. *Philomena* has all three. We revisited, at my insistence, the occasion when the Republicans withdrew funding for AIDS research in the 1980s. It's nice to have unambiguous moments of clarity: Republicans guilty; Democrats not guilty.

All of which made the Catholic League's heads explode. They didn't want an olive branch, they wanted the film to be a polemical attack because then they could attack back. Attrition, black and white. Microwaveable, instant, ready-made religion takes away the pain of thinking for yourself.

Then Philomena and I went to see the Pope, and it basically shut them all up.

When Stephen first mooted the idea at the Venice Film Festival, it seemed utterly bonkers. Stephen said, 'I think the Pope should see this film. It's important. He seems like a good bloke.'

Everyone laughed. It seemed like a preposterous idea; how on earth do you get an audience with the Pope?

But Stephen persisted. 'Seriously, I think he should see it.'

I don't think Stephen would have suggested a visit to Pope Francis's predecessor, but Pope Francis is a bona fide liberal by comparison. I love the fact that he has humility as well as an awareness of the complexities of life. When he first arrived at the Vatican, you could tell that the more right-wing, fundamentalist, intolerant Catholics didn't know how to react to this outspoken liberal guy who had just been made the head of their Church.

He argues for greater tolerance of homosexuality in the Church, has discussed his love of the gay baroque painter Caravaggio and is passionate about Italian neorealist cinema. His favourite films are Fellini's *La Strada* and Rossellini's *Roma Città Aperta*, one about a young woman sold by her mother to an itinerant circus strongman, the other about the Nazi occupation of the Italian capital.

American fundamentalists just scratch their heads at Pope Francis's understanding of nuance and ambiguity. They don't get it at all. The extremists are not, of course, to be taken seriously. Most Catholics understand that life is not black and white.

Some of the often unnoticed victims of the Church's abuse of its position in one form or another are those who have quietly and diligently gone about their own lives. Those people are unfairly judged because of the actions of others.

That an unaccountable institution has wielded so much power over the governance of its people is scandalous. The reason so much abuse went undetected in the Church is because it was shielded from scrutiny.

Ireland is, thank goodness, a new country now, reclaimed by a younger generation.

CHAPTER 7

Our eventual papal visit was the result of a perfect storm. I had seen the Pope before, but only at a great distance.

The first time was in September 1979, when I was about to turn fourteen. My family and I were on holiday in Ireland, and Pope John Paul II came to Phoenix Park in Dublin. No unofficial vehicles were allowed within a ten-mile radius of the city, so we had to walk two miles along a country road and then get a bus to the park.

A nun passed me a camera to take a snap of her as the Popemobile went past, but far more memorable was the crowd: 1.25 million people were there, a third of Ireland's population, and no doubt the biggest crowd I'll ever be in.

Three years later, the Pope came to Heaton Park in Manchester, and we stayed up all night waiting for him. I wandered through the crowd, aware there wasn't the same en masse devotion here as at Phoenix Park. This being England, there were too many latent Catholics.

I knew Bernie Jones, my girlfriend at the time, was there, and miraculously I found her. Just as the light was coming up, we leaned against a fence and snogged.

A policeman walked past with full stripes, leather gloves and a cane. He said, 'If you're going to do that, go and do it over there in the bushes. The Pope has consecrated this path.'

What a wanker.

Anyway, Harvey Weinstein wanted to maximise publicity for *Philomena*, and Philomena wanted to be exonerated by the Pope. Susan Lohan, a founder of the campaigning Irish charity Adoption Rights Alliance, had teamed up with Philomena to set up the Philomena Project, and together they were lobbying for open access to adoption records.

I only found out that Philomena and I might meet the Pope a few days before flying to Rome. There was a cast and crew screening of *The Trip to Italy* on Monday night in London and by Tuesday afternoon I was in Rome with Philomena, her daughter Jane, Harvey, two of his Argentinean friends and Susan Lohan. The Philomena Project precipitated a trip to the Vatican, which was then accelerated by Harvey.

On Tuesday evening, we had drinks with Bishop Sanchez, who is in the Pope's inner circle. He made it clear that *Philomena* was entirely in keeping with the new Pope's tone. There was an overwhelming sense of anticipation: not only would we meet the Pope the next morning at a papal audience, but the film would be screened inside the Vatican.

Papal audiences are held in St Peter's Square on Wednesdays at 10.30 a.m. when the Pope is in town. He gives the assembled crowd short readings and teachings in Italian, English, French, German, Spanish, Polish and Portuguese before saying 'Our Father' in Latin. He then talks to and blesses those who are in the front row of the audience, most of whom are devout Catholics who spent the early morning queuing up.

On Wednesday morning, we drove through a damp, grey Rome in a convoy of black Mercedes and were waved through by the Vatican City State Gendarmerie. Vatican City might be the world's smallest sovereign state, but it is surprisingly big. There's a railway, a petrol station, a supermarket and a post office. I took a photo of the petrol station on my iPad as we drove past.

I kept thinking, 'These cars are full of people who have a vested interest in how *Philomena* is received. There's a lot at stake here. All this has happened because I read an article in a newspaper.'

We waited in the Vatican to be taken into St Peter's Square with the faithful. Everyone was quietly respectful in the Vatican, but once they were out in St Peter's Square, facing the Pope's heated marquee, little groups started shouting for Pope Francis while others sang 'Ar-gen-tina' over and over again. It had the fervour of a boy band concert.

I was guided to the front row, where I sat next to Philomena and Jane. We huddled together under an umbrella while the rain pounded down.

As the Pope came to meet and greet, the sun came out.

In my head I kept going over the short speech I'd scribbled down at breakfast. And then suddenly he was in front of us, a big grin on his face.

'This is Philomena Lee,' I said. 'Our message is your message.'

He nodded. He shook my hand, Philomena's hand and Jane's hand, blessing us as he did so.

Philomena said thank you. The Pope said thank you in return and nodded, grinning more than ever.

He said he was familiar with the film and knew of Philomena's story. But of course he wasn't going to pass comment on it or get into any kind of discussion.

Philomena felt a huge weight had been lifted from her; in blessing her as he shook her hand, the Pope had forgiven her. However much she loved and missed her son, and however wrong she knew the sisters had been, she also disapproved of her own 'disobedience'.

Anyone brought up as a Catholic learns very early on about obedience and disobedience. When I went to my first confession at the age of nine, I had no idea what to say and so was given some ideas.

'Bless me, Father, these are my sins. I was rude to my mum and dad. I answered back. I was disobedient.'

I did absently cross myself during the papal audience, but I did it out of habit and out of respect. Equally, I don't have to be as rigid as Richard Dawkins, even though I'm more sympathetic to his views. I don't believe in religious dogma, but I do still have a slight romantic and cultural attachment to Catholicism. It's part of me, it's what formed me.

I don't think you have to try to embrace Catholicism or kick it to death. And I feel I have a right to take an interest. I don't believe in God. I know one can never be certain, but I've always felt agnosticism is for cowards.

I thought it ironic, too, that the Church of my childhood, the Church I've left behind, briefly figured so prominently in my life. Taking Philomena to meet the Pope felt perfect. I can't pretend it happened organically. Harvey Weinstein was there at every turn, using his unorthodox methods to help the film on its journey to the Oscars. But the film was about so much more than an awards campaign; it was about something real.

When I heard that the people behind the film *Noah* had also sought an audience, I thought it was fatuous. What did they expect the Pope to say? 'Oh yes, that was a brilliantly accurate, literal interpretation of something which never actually happened.'

I mean, the Catholic Church has its faults, but a blindly literal creationist interpretation of the Old Testament isn't one of them.

★ ★ ★

That afternoon we all went back to the Vatican to host a screening of *Philomena*. The papal chair was there, in the middle of this large, wood-panelled room. Bishop Sanchez and Monsignor Guillermo Karcher, one of the Pope's ceremonialists, sat behind the empty chair.

At a certain point it became clear that the Pope wasn't going to turn up, so I had to introduce the film to the assembled throng of church dignitaries, friends of the Vatican, and Cynthia McFadden, a reporter from ABC News.

I felt immense pressure.

My uncomfortable conversation with the senior sister at the Sacred Hearts of Jesus and Mary epitomised the attitude of the

Church, so I had to steel myself and couch the introduction in conciliatory terms, framing it as an olive branch, an opportunity for a mea culpa.

It was more than a little surreal to watch Sanchez and Karcher as they sat very still when Judi Dench, as Philomena, said, 'I didn't even know I had a clitoris, Martin.' They even appeared to laugh when I later said, as Martin, 'Fucking Catholics.'

After the screening, we talked to the Bishop and the Monsignor about the ongoing adoption issues in Ireland and the Irish Church's refusal to be transparent. Philomena, Jane and Susan Lohan were brilliant; their collective passion for the subject would stop anyone in their tracks.

The Bishop listened attentively to Susan's requests regarding the Irish Church and the Irish government and said he would contact his counterpart in Ireland. He added that Pope Francis wanted to acknowledge mistakes made by the Church and to be open to criticism. It seems the 'little monsters', as Pope Francis called poorly trained priests, have yet to adapt to the enlightened attitude of their own leader.

When I said to Sanchez that there were people who were critical of the film in America who called themselves Catholics, he said, 'You don't need to worry about those people. We are not those people.'

I kept glancing at Philomena's face. She is a very composed woman, but I could see she was thrilled to be there. Unburdened of the guilty secret she had kept for fifty years, here she was in the belly of the beast. And the only sin being discussed was the Church's.

I learned something about myself during this time too. I learned that it's OK to acknowledge your weaknesses. It's fine. Not only is it fine, but it makes you stronger, rather paradoxically.

It is generally thought that fallibility is wrong. A large number of people think that you can't openly say you're not very good at something, or that you shouldn't admit to making a mistake. In actual fact, the opposite is true. Admitting to weakness is empowering. It liberates you to take risks in the knowledge that potential failure is OK.

It has taken me decades to fully understand this, and now I'm almost addicted to the risk of failure. I love the idea of doing something that might not be very good and the adrenalin that comes from creative fear.

★   ★   ★

While it's clear that the Church can no longer hide behind the cloak of impunity, a film like *Philomena* can only pull at the thread.

Still, as it turned out, *Philomena* and the Philomena Project effected a change in Irish government policy in terms of access to information. After refusing to tackle historical adoption issues for so long, the government has now publicly said that it is the Church's duty to provide information to help children find their parents and vice versa. The film reignited the adoption debate in Ireland, a debate that some elements of the Church clearly wished would remain unheard.

Although I didn't yet know that Irish policy would change, when we left the Vatican in our convoy of chauffeur-driven black Mercedes I did momentarily feel like a mini-Bono. (Funnily enough, we bumped into Bono and the rest of U2 a number of times on our travels. Bono ended up dancing with Philomena at one point, despite the fact that she insisted on calling The Edge 'The Egg'.)

The visit to the Vatican was a surreal experience. It was almost as if I was in a film, in the sense that I felt I was on the outside, watching it all unfold.

A decade or so previously, I would never have had the confidence to stand in the heart of the Vatican to introduce the film and frame the issues brought up in it in a diplomatic way. Although I felt nervous, I also felt I was capable of doing it.

Sometimes you end up thinking, 'Oh, I suppose I'm a grown-up now.'

CHAPTER 8

In the years before I started work on *Philomena*, I was cut adrift. The people I'd written Partridge with – Armando Iannucci, Peter Baynham – had gone off to do their own thing. If I tried to talk to either of them about doing an Alan Partridge film, they would both drag their feet. It had been talked about for too long.

Understandably, they were both fed up with the character. Half an hour with Alan can be quite entertaining, but imagine spending eight hours a day with him for months.

To use a Bob Monkhouse line, I had a bed with four bedsides to it. I think Armando and Peter were also a bit fed up with me. My abrasive northernness was compounded by my self-induced post-narcotic headache.

I knew some people were already sharpening their knives in anticipation of the Partridge film being awful. But I was driven by my determination not to allow anyone the pleasure of being able to say 'I told you so' or 'I knew it wouldn't be any good.'

Journalists were always asking me one of two questions about Alan. First: when was I going to make a film? I almost wanted to make a bloody film just to stop them asking about it. And second: was I ever going to kill Partridge off because he had become an albatross?

I wanted to have my cake and eat it. I wanted to make a brilliant Partridge film and yet not be defined by Alan. This caused mild outrage: how could I do both? I didn't care. The antipathy simply spurred me on. As did an article in a national paper about why a Partridge film should never be made.

It was a red rag to a bull.

What annoys me the most, however, is people saying, 'You're a bit like Alan, aren't you?' And then laughing hysterically.

To which I reply, 'Well, yes. Of course I am.'

They can't quite believe this admission. 'But he's an idiot! Are you saying he's part of you?'

As patiently as possible, I'll say, 'Yes, because part of me is an idiot.'

I have no problem showing all those imperfections. What liberates me and makes me stronger is utilising all that dysfunction. I really don't care. Especially as I get older. I just think to myself, 'Put in all those negative things. Put in all the stuff that is unattractive, that clearly comes from somewhere, that must be part of me.'

I wouldn't still be doing Alan if he didn't make me laugh. When we're writing, I laugh a lot. Obviously I don't laugh when I'm being Alan, but I do laugh when we're writing and when I watch it back. Which is, I suppose, a bit like laughing at the ridiculous part of myself.

★   ★   ★

Once we had decided to go ahead with the film, Pete Baynham and I went to Los Angeles to secure financial backing. The first producer had white hair and a deep tan; he looked like one of those guys who are born middle-aged and in tennis whites. A healthy, rich, liberal Hollywood producer.

I pitched the film idea to him.

At that point, the plot involved members of Al-Qaeda taking over the BBC. A washed-up Alan, who has turned up at the BBC trying to pitch ideas, ends up electing himself as the key negotiator. When the terrorists want to shoot a hostage, Alan has to decide which one. There is a divorced chap who is clearly depressed and who has even considered suicide. If Alan chooses him, he is simply bringing the inevitable forward by a month or two.

Meanwhile, one of the terrorists is curious about a poster on the wall: it's for an old BBC panto of *Aladdin* in which Alan is blacked up to play Ali Baba. The terrorist sends Alan off to find the tape in the BBC archive. Alan is terrified that the terrorists will be offended by the panto, but in fact they love it.

Pete started to sweat. He realised our pitch wasn't landing. The tanned guy didn't laugh once. He just kept nodding his head, his fingers making a cathedral shape that he held sagely at his lips.

When I'd finished, the tanned guy very slowly said, 'That sounds hilarious, guys. But I'm part of an inter-faith dialogue initiative. I wouldn't be so happy being involved in a script that caricatures Muslims.'

I can't remember if he was drinking Yerba Mate tea or if there was a yoga mat in the room, but there should have been.

Humourless, enlightened liberals bring out the fascist in me. Pete and I just wanted to leave, but we had to listen to the tanned guy's idea. He had Alan working in a chip shop in Norfolk. Alan has to travel the world to find true love and eventually realises his true love was working alongside him in the chip shop all along.

We left, and he presumably went back to making asinine shit and hundreds and millions of dollars.

It didn't knock our confidence; we realised as soon as we walked into the offices and saw the framed film posters decorating the walls that it wasn't the right place for us. I hated pretty much every film they'd done.

We went to Fox Searchlight with the same pitch. They listened. They laughed. They seemed to get it.

It's worth saying that not everyone in the movie business can do comedy; certainly not everyone understands it. I realised this in 1997, when I did a television film with Paul Greengrass called *The Fix*. I put some comedy into my role and Paul was unexpectedly deferential; he held his hands up and said, 'I don't do this.' He couldn't believe how easy it was for me.

Anyway, Pete and I went to see the head of another large film company.

'Sit down,' she said, ushering us into her office. 'How do you find driving on the other side of the road? Isn't it confusing?'

It was an odd opening gambit. I said, 'No, you get used to it pretty quickly.'

I changed the subject by asking the kind of question that usually helps focus the conversation: 'Is there any of my work you specifically like?'

She immediately got to her feet and said, 'Can you excuse me one second?'

She returned with a few sheets of A4 stapled together. 'Well, Alan Partridge is the thing we absolutely love . . .'

Sunlight caught the paper. It was a printout of my IMDb pages.

★   ★   ★

We had to change the Partridge plot after the London bombings on 7 July 2005. Patrick Marber wasn't involved in the script, but I talked to him about it and he rightly felt that this idea was now impossible to do.

Pete, Armando and I talked about the new ideas. Maybe Alan could go to America as a film producer that no one wants to talk to. He has to stand at the gates, trying to get into Universal Studios. But *Borat* was a variation on that.

So we decided to be myopic. As well as now being offensive, the terrorist attack seemed too fanciful. What could we do that was cinematic, but not so grand you lose Alan's very DNA?

I spoke to Ben Stiller and he offered to direct it. Years later, when the film was eventually released, he sent another email: 'I guess I'm not directing it then.'

But he gave me some good advice when we were at prep stage: 'Don't lose the small world that Alan lives in.'

It made me realise we had to shoot the film in East Anglia.

We just had to make sure Alan's parochialism worked on the big screen. We could also use the original hostage idea in a different way: Pat Farrell, one of Alan's fellow DJs at North Norfolk Digital radio, is fired and retaliates by taking the current staff and the new management hostage. He asks Alan, whom he trusts, to negotiate with the police on his behalf. Alan sees it as a chance not to help Pat, but to promote himself.

My two touchstones for the film were both directed by Sidney Lumet: *Network* and *Dog Day Afternoon*. The former is about a fictional television network in the States struggling with poor ratings; news presenter Howard Beale memorably has a meltdown on air.

In the latter, Al Pacino holds the staff of a New York bank hostage. The scene in *Alpha Papa* in which Alan comes out of the building talking on a headset is stolen directly from *Dog Day Afternoon*. The film also has an amateur look to it that I love.

I wanted to call the Partridge film *Hectic Danger Day* or *Colossal Velocity*. I don't know why no one listened to me.

CHAPTER 9

As soon as I'd finished *Philomena*, I had to turn my attention to *Alpha Papa*. I was in this strange position where I knew *Philomena* was a decent film at the very least and as such would establish me as someone capable of good, serious work. I wasn't going to let *Alpha Papa* derail or have any kind of negative impact on *Philomena*.

If I could have done, I would have stopped *Alpha Papa* going into production. But it was too late.

I had already delayed it and no one could really understand why we were postponing it for this other film I was making about an old lady trying to find her son.

Given that I had no choice, I decided to be positive and to look forward to *Alpha Papa*. I'd got my passion project out of my system and I was at least on familiar ground with Partridge. But as soon as I arrived on set, I discovered that *everything* was in a state of disarray. We didn't even get Declan Lowney on board as director until the final stages, which meant he had to deal with the chaos too.

The first week of the *Alpha Papa* shoot was unbelievably hard.

The film very nearly went off the rails: there were issues with funding; the script wasn't ready. Brendan Gleeson had agreed to play Pat Farrell if I attended to the script and improved it. I had been so bogged down in *Philomena* that I never got the chance.

At the eleventh hour I was walking into a cast and crew screening of *The Look of Love* when I got a call from Brendan.

'Steve, I'm out. You said you'd improve the script. You've let me down; it's just not on the page.'

I couldn't even argue with him. He was absolutely right.

I would have pulled out too if I was him. He's a great actor, one of Ireland's finest exports; he didn't have time to wait for me. After *Philomena* and *Alpha Papa* came out, he came up to me and was effusive and generous about both films. Sometimes it just doesn't work out.

Fortunately, into the breach, like a slightly cantankerous white knight, stepped Colm Meaney. He was refreshingly blunt and to the point on the phone. 'I've worked with Judd Apatow. I know a bit about improv. I don't suppose there's much point in asking to see the script?'

'No,' I said. 'There really is no point. Thanks for being so understanding.'

I still felt like I was piloting the *Titanic* straight towards the icebergs. Everyone had thousand-yard stares on their faces. I'd pass Declan on the stairs and he'd say, 'Steve, the crew are here, the actors are here. We have to shoot something. Anything.'

I wouldn't let Declan start shooting until the script was sharper. I knew we had to get two days ahead of ourselves, which meant we weren't just rewriting tomorrow's scenes, but also the day after tomorrow's scenes.

The pressure was immense. I wasn't about to make a substandard film to cash in on Alan's name. I had just made a film about integrity, and I knew that *Alpha Papa* had to be about the number of laughs per page. I also knew that if we didn't hit the audience hard with humour, real, laugh-out-loud humour, we'd be crucified.

I don't enjoy working with my back against the wall. I'd rather have time to refine, refine, refine. When you're up against it, there's so much tension in the writing room and on set. There are also amazing highs: a fantastic piece of dialogue, a great idea, a shot that really works. You have to hang on to those moments and learn to push the anxiety away.

Rob and Neil Gibbons were driven so hard they nearly walked out on me. Every night I'd go into the writing room with them and write till 11 p.m. I'd sit in the car on the way home and think, 'When I get back I can have a break for twenty minutes with a cup of tea and the papers online and then I've got to get to bed.' I couldn't risk having even one drink; I gave up alcohol for the entire period I was working on *Philomena* and *Alpha Papa*.

Once home, I would lie in bed saying to myself, 'Go to sleep, go to sleep.' And then I'd get up six hours later, sleep in the car, wake up as soon as we arrived on set and get to work.

It's the hardest I've ever worked and the loneliest I've ever felt.

★   ★   ★

If I felt alone, it's because I *was* alone. Armando was physically absent throughout the shoot because he was in the States, doing *Veep*. I'd turn round and say, 'What should I do now?' and no one was there. At the start of the first week, I sent Armando an email saying that I needed some stewardship.

I hadn't paid attention to any of his notes and the script had gone in a different direction. It wasn't, he said, his sense of humour.

I've always had more affection for Alan whereas Armando basically regards him as an idiot. There is more we agree than disagree on, but there is undoubtedly a difference of emphasis.

I owe Armando a huge debt: the focus, exactitude and rigour he brought to the development of Alan Partridge helped counter my vagueness and inherent lack of discipline.

But he wished me luck.

A few days into the shoot, I sat down with Neil and Rob. I said the good news was that we'd got clarity. We were definitely on our own. It was gallows humour. In a way it was useful: we could get on with the film in our own way.

I don't think I can go through this book without making special mention of the Gibbonses, who, after a long hiatus, breathed new life into Partridge. They gave him a more rounded personality. The purest, most mature and funniest incarnation of Partridge is, to me, in *Mid Morning Matters*. I think it's as good as the first TV series of *Knowing Me Knowing You with Alan Partridge*. It might even be better. And it's all down to the tenacity of the Gibbonses.

Had it not been for Rob and Neil, Alan would not have had a renaissance. That Tim Key is also part of that renaissance gives me great pleasure; I learned a long time ago how important it is to always be on the lookout for new talent.

One of the problems we had with Partridge is that during his hiatus it became very difficult to find clothes for him that looked suitably awful. Postmodernism meant that everything we had once seen as square or distasteful was now being worn by hipsters, who appeared to enjoy dressing identically to old fogeys. I blame those Hoxton hipsters for confusing things.

The waters of what was uncool became so muddied that it was difficult to find anything that looked bad and not just ironic.

It even made me question if Alan was still relevant.

In fact Alan became relevant again because of Rob and Neil; the writing became more nuanced and complex.

The twenty-first-century Alan is a nicer man. He is more empathetic and less about mocking the fool. More Malvolio than Frank Spencer.

★   ★   ★

I knew by the end of the first week of filming that we were starting to get funny material. Armando saw the dailies and realised we might just pull it off. When he got back to the UK, he came straight to the edit and was fantastically helpful.

I slowly started to grasp that if everyone did as I said, it might just turn out OK. I kept on thinking about something Ben Stiller had said to me a few years earlier: 'When you're on a film set and you've got to make endless decisions, you have to realise that you can't be worried about people's feelings.'

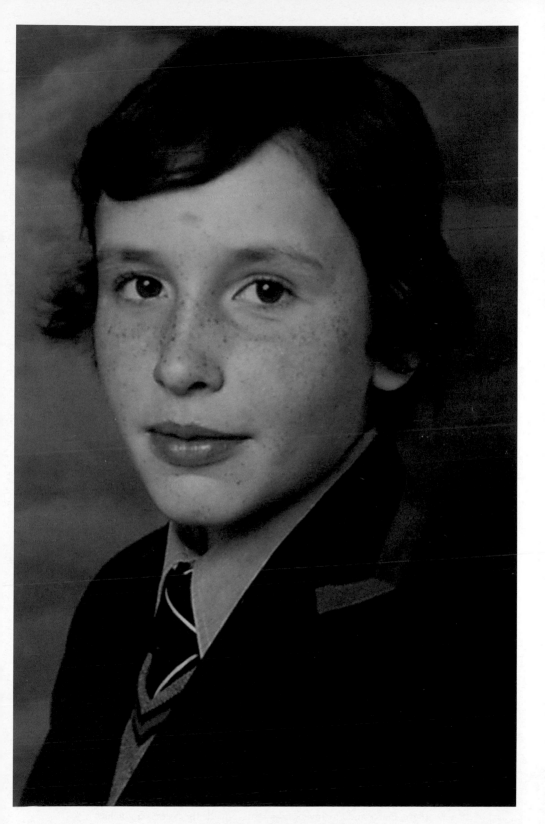

Me, aged twelve, in a Terylene blazer.

Top: Dad carrying Mum over the threshold on 15 February 1950.

Above: Pierce and Flo, my grandparents, outside the Astoria nightclub.

Right: With my great grandmother in the west of Ireland.

Below: David, me in Clare's arms, Martin.

Above : Me aged three in Red Wharf Bay, Wales.

Opposite, top: Martin, me and David
in terrible clothes circa 1971.

Opposite, bottom: My maternal
grandmother Maimi, me, Clare,
David and Martin.

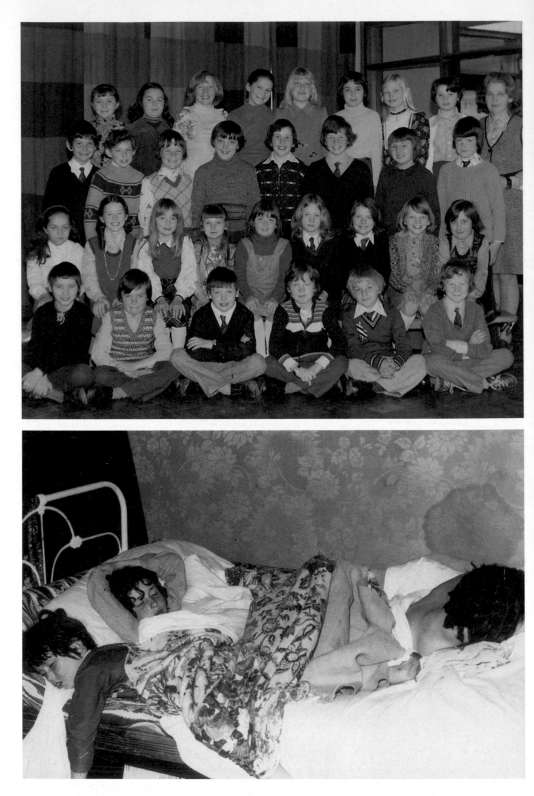

Top: Can you spot me in the school photo? Brendan Tierney's mum, the class teacher, is top right.

Above: Brendan, me and Kevin, top to tail, in Ireland.

Top: The six of us kids in 1977.

Above: Dad in the back garden in Middleton with David, Kevin, me and Martin, 1971.

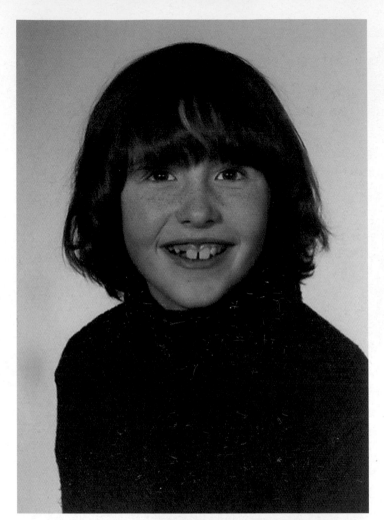

My André Previn
look, aged seven.

In the back garden
in Middleton.

At the time I thought it a selfish approach, but when I was doing Partridge I realised Ben was right. There just wasn't time to be polite.

Julia Davis, who I have worked with for a very long time, was cast as a policewoman. She came up to me after the read-through saying that her character should be a lesbian. I didn't see what difference it would make and anyway the scene wasn't long enough to explore who the hell she was sleeping with. A few days later, Henry Normal told me he'd had an email from Julia.

I got as far as 'Dear Henry, I've been thinking long and hard . . .' That was enough.

I said to Henry, 'Get a replacement right now.'

We were lucky: we got the wonderful Anna Maxwell Martin at very short notice.

The point is, I didn't even have time to read an email detailing Julia's reasons for pulling out. I had to be ruthless, a kind of benevolent dictator. There wasn't time to sugar-coat anything or to make decisions by committee. I didn't have time to talk to someone from the costume department who was asking whether Partridge's shoes should be red or brown.

I certainly didn't have time to make jokey small talk between takes. Humour only mattered if it was on the screen.

In the first week of the thirty-day shoot, Declan had all these tracking shots of Tim Key, who plays Sidekick Simon, as we were DJing at North Norfolk Digital. I would watch the rushes and see that the comedy was being sucked from the scene. It was too fancy.

I said to Declan, 'It's all wrong. Just lock the camera off on a shot of me and Tim in the same frame and that will be the mast for everything.'

I didn't enjoy saying that things were wrong or not working. I felt sick inside, but I had to be brutal. At one point I even had to stop filming and force everyone to take an hour's break so that I could rewrite a scene with Neil and Rob.

Slowly, things stopped falling apart. None of the material we shot on the first day was funny, but by the end of the first week we would be laughing really hard after a take and all the tension would dissolve. I knew it would still be hard, I knew I'd be working till 11 p.m. every night and getting up at 6 a.m., but it would be worth it. You feel very alive constantly being one decision away from disaster.

In a way, having autonomy made me more decisive. At the risk of being mocked by 'Pseuds Corner' in *Private Eye*, I felt a bit like Ernest Shackleton as the ice floe engulfed the *Endurance*. If you all do exactly as I say, I promise we'll get out of here alive.

All right, maybe it wasn't like that. But it certainly felt like it.

★   ★   ★

When we were doing our research for *Alpha Papa*, we went round some of the local radio stations in Norwich that had been taken over by umbrella stations. We saw the same kinds of cards that Alan rips up in the film, the ones that assert inane things such as 'be relevant' or 'local, local, local'. Often there was a timeline of the core audience on the wall to show what they were doing at any given time in their lives: 'Seventies: school. Early eighties: university. Late eighties: career, marriage, kids.' Or: 'Do you remember [insert name of confectionery popular in the seventies]?'

It was really a cynical and horrible way to run a radio station.

Henry sent in a guy called Graham Duff to edit the script when it was all falling apart. Graham helped to keep everyone calm. He told me a really interesting story about a meeting he was called into when he worked at a local radio station in Brighton. The boss started saying that he was perfectly aware of everyone's concern about job security. On and on he went until suddenly the talk ended with, 'Make no mistake, this station *will* get juiced.'

It was an appalling way to suck the life out of a radio station and make it absolutely clear that commerce was the bottom line. I immediately thought, 'That's what I want the Partridge film to be about.' I wanted to use the film to rail against the deification of the businessman. I get angry when I hear about business gurus turning up at schools and colleges. Stay away!

Kids shouldn't grow up thinking that the only thing of any importance is earning money. They should be learning about culture, not business – Albert Camus and John Cooper Clarke, not Grant fucking Shapps.

The Partridge film is essentially about multinational companies taking over local radio stations. It dignifies local radio DJs, who may be cheesy but who are at least serving the local community. Until the cynical Goliaths stride in, desperate to satisfy shareholders while caring nothing for compassion.

I wanted Alan to be heroic, for the audience to sympathise with him while laughing at his world. I also wanted people to think that he dies at the end of *Alpha Papa*. We filmed the final scenes on a desolate, out-of-season Cromer Pier because it has an inherently sad pallor of broken dreams while still looking suitably cinematic.

You have to root for Alan in *Alpha Papa*. You know he's done the wrong thing, but at least he's got some humanity. It's impossible to sustain ninety minutes of good drama without investing in the character.

★ ★ ★

We really did put *Alpha Papa* out against all the odds and all expectation. I'm really proud of it.

My only regret is that we didn't get the chance to film any of the siege scenes in *Alpha Papa* at BBC TV Centre before it was sold off. We did at least manage to film the 'smell my cheese' scene from *I'm Alan Partridge* there; I relished running through the old reception with a large piece of cheese on the end of a fork.

When I recorded *Knowing Me Knowing You with Alan Partridge* for Radio 4 in the Paris Studios, the ghosts of Tony Hancock et al. weren't lost on me; when I ran amok with the cheese at the old BBC I felt the power of *Fawlty Towers*, *Porridge* and *Dad's Army*. I was in the same space they had been in, but with different props. It was truly magical; I had arrived in the place I had loved from afar as a child.

And at least I was there as the sun set on the old world of television.

CHAPTER 10

Michael Winterbottom was one of the few people who always saw beyond Alan Partridge. I have made five films with him now, and working with him on both *24 Hour Party People* and *A Cock and Bull Story* was a revelation.

I'm not in control when I work with Michael, but I'm always very happy to let him tell me what to do. Comedy is about being in control, and Michael taught me that it is OK not to be in control. It's OK to let go, to show naked honesty, which in itself is counter-intuitive to comedy. In drama the responses are much more muted unless laughter is replaced by tears, and even then people don't exactly wail. Both laughter and tears are physical, emotional responses.

Michael pushed me to be uncomfortable with the unknown and to not only do work where every single beat is familiar. It's OK to risk failure as you explore new ideas.

Michael liberated me from the *need* to be funny.

I realised there was a world beyond comedy that I could access. It's not about a total absence of comedy, it's rather about widening out my work in a way that is more interesting and engaging for me.

I have faith in Michael because he has a singular talent. His films always end up being more than the sum of their parts; there is an otherness to what he does that I can't quite understand. I'm just a participant in it really. I'm not the architect, but I'm always happy to come along for the ride.

There's an old adage in Hollywood, 'Ready, fire, aim', and that's Michael all over. Through sheer force of will he manages to make films that probably wouldn't otherwise be made.

Michael likes to run at projects before they are fully formed or financed. There are no scripts to look at per se. The dialogue is largely improvised. There were only around sixty pages of dialogue in the *Cock and Bull* script, but Michael told us not to worry about it. He said we'd figure it out.

Whenever actors turned up on the set of *24 Hour Party People* or *Cock and Bull*, they would invariably ask what was going on. Michael mumbles direction; the set seems to be disorganised. It's not chaotic at all, but it can look that way to an outsider.

I'd say to the actor, 'Just don't try to figure out what's going on.'

Michael has no wardrobe on set, no make-up, no trailers, no script supervisor, no continuity. No indulgences for the actors. He hangs the monitor around his neck and off he goes. I've never been asked to hit a mark in any of Michael's films. Things are shot very quickly; turnaround takes minutes.

In *24 Hour Party People*, the actors playing the Happy Mondays kick over all the furniture at Manchester airport and the security guards throw them out. Those guards were real; Michael told the actors to behave badly until the guards responded. He didn't have permission to film there. He just filmed it secretly. He has a uniquely austere approach to film-making.

There is no safe place to be. There is no such thing as 'off camera', because Michael might turn the camera on you at any point. You have to go and hide in a different room if you don't want to risk being filmed.

I loved living in the world that Michael created in *24 Hour Party People*. It's the only time I haven't wanted filming to stop on a project. There was no catering or lunch breaks; we finished at 5 p.m. and all went out to a pub or restaurant. The next day we filmed again. It all became a blur: we didn't know what was filming and what was hanging out. It was like a dream.

Working with Michael is thrilling. It's the purest kind of work. Every now and again I need a fix of it.

★   ★   ★

In 2009, Rob Brydon and I met Michael for lunch. He asked if we'd be interested in doing a series in which we visit a series of restaurants and review them. He had been inspired by the scene at the start of *Cock and Bull* in which Rob and I are talking in the make-up trailer because the weather is so bad. Playing heightened versions of ourselves, we more or less improvised a scene about Rob's teeth, our appearance and the vanities of growing old. It was a natural, funny scene.

Michael thought we could take the idea of me and Rob as restaurant reviewers and run with it.

Rob and I didn't like the sound of it at all.

We'd already played ourselves in *Cock and Bull*. Playing yourself is not a new thing: *Curb Your Enthusiasm*, *The Larry Sanders Show* and *Extras* had all come before.

The more we thought about it, the more Rob and I thought it sounded awful. Both of us playing ourselves and effectively saying, 'Get a load of us mocking ourselves. Aren't we cool?' Ingratiating ourselves by appearing to be self-deprecating in a way that might have had some cachet a decade ago, but now feels a bit tired and tediously postmodern.

At least *Cock and Bull* had those sixty pages to build on. *The Trip* was just an idea. It was fifteen pages of sample dialogue with the odd vague storyline: 'Steve' sleeps with the receptionist at the hotel; 'Rob' is a family man; 'Steve' is sleeping alone because he's a bit tortured. It pointed out the differences in our personalities.

I thought to myself, 'I know you think it's funny, Michael, but it's going to become boring very quickly.'

It sounded pretentious and tedious; there wasn't enough of an idea to make it work. Rob and I spoke on the phone several times and agreed to say no thanks to Michael. His idea felt like teasing out a quite good but small idea to inevitable failure. Why didn't we make a proper film together instead?

But Michael kept badgering us. And I had always trusted him.

Eventually we met to make a decision one way or the other.

Michael left early and Rob turned to me. 'Should we just do it?'

'Why not? Nothing terrible will happen if it fails,' I replied. 'And you never know, it might be really good.'

The original idea was to film 'up north', but then we decided to focus on the Lake District and Yorkshire because of the proliferation of critically acclaimed restaurants.

Michael gave us homework, mostly poetry by Coleridge and Wordsworth and some books on the area.

I said to Rob, 'Have you read those books Michael told us to read?'

He said, 'No, have you?'

I said, 'Thank God, neither have I.'

I'm genuinely interested in the poets, but I'm always busy. All I had before we started was the kind of smattering of knowledge that any half-educated person might have. I could quote two lines about daffodils and two lines from Wordsworth's 'The French Revolution': 'Bliss was it in that dawn to be alive,/ But to be young was very heaven!'

So I did some poetry cramming the night before and chucked the odd quote into the improvisation.

It annoyed me that Michael wanted to make Rob really enthusiastic about the poets and me a bit ignorant. It wasn't Rob's fault that he was made to be the clever one; I just wanted to share my knowledge, such as it was.

On a day off, Rob and I walked up the Old Man of Coniston. If we saw other walkers approaching, I would shield my eyes, but Rob would greet them with gusto and was happy to have his photo taken. I teased him mercilessly about being an attention seeker.

I then retold the story in a newspaper interview.

Rob was cross. He accused me of affecting a Lou Reed-style disdain of everyone. He said he wouldn't do another series of *The Trip* if I continued sneering at him in real life. It was emblematic of the risky game we were playing in that series, but nonetheless I felt cowed and apologised.

So I confessed: I envied the fact that he found it so easy to be nice to people and to talk to them.

He has since told me he was flabbergasted. He said he always put me on a pedestal, partly because it's such fun to knock me off.

CHAPTER 11

When we turned up at the Inn at Whitewell in the Forest of Bowland, I was still worrying about *The Trip*. As much as I trusted Michael, I still wasn't sure the idea could work. Was it enough to take certain aspects of our personalities and amplify them?

Michael was, as ever, stoic. He kept telling us to do more improvisations and to talk about the north. Michael is from Blackburn and we share a certain northern chippiness. He wanted to show the north in an unclichéd way, to capture its beauty and culinary sophistication. It was funny and slightly abrasive, like two friends fencing.

Suddenly it made sense. I was sitting opposite Rob at the Inn at Whitewell and I said, 'I think this is going to be good. It's definitely going to be different.'

Not only had we started to be competitive with our Michael Caine impressions, but we had also decided to use some of the tabloid stuff that had been written about me. I felt quietly victorious that I'd taken the shit that had been thrown at me, turned it around and made it work for me.

It's all about using everything and spinning it into something creative. Instead of kicking against the pricks, you readjust your trajectory and go with the current. Instead of pushing back against people you feel are attacking you, you use your opponent's momentum to disable them, much as you would in ju-jitsu.

Because we were playing around with the notion of who we are, Rob and I came up with a tacit gentleman's agreement that we wouldn't take anything to heart as it was all for the purpose of making *The Trip* interesting. But it was still tough, at times, to know where the boundaries were.

There's an improvised scene in the Yorke Arms in Ramsgill, where Rob is going on about how great Michael Sheen is, that I really love.

ROB: 'We're not in the same group as Michael Sheen, Anthony Hopkins and Richard Burton.'

ME: 'Straight away let me distinguish. I'm a triple BAFTA Award-winning comic . . . comic actor . . . comic character actor. You're a zero-winning . . . entertainer.'

ROB: 'BAFTA nominated [entertainer]. How many Oscars did Richard Burton win? Do you want me to tell you?

ME: 'Zero.'

ROB: 'Zero. Do you know how many times he was nominated? Seven. Hopkins. Sheen. Brydon. Burton. The Port Talbot four. That's what we're known as.'

ME: 'Really?'

ROB: 'Michael Sheen. We're not the same. We're different animals.'

ME: '*You're* not the same as him. *I'm* more similar to him.'

ROB: 'Well, why don't you do the sort of roles he does?'

ME: 'Because no one will give those roles to me. I've got an albatross round my neck and it's got the face of Michael Sheen.'

ROB: 'Do you try for those roles?'

ME: 'Yes. Michael Sheen gets them all. He's very good—'

ROB: 'He's brilliant.'

ME (getting antsy): 'He's not brilliant. He's good. He's solid.'

ROB: 'He *is* brilliant—'

ME (losing it, shouting): '*I'm* fucking brilliant!'

Somehow the authenticity of that statement transcends the awfulness of it. It shows a vulnerability that people respond to, because everyone wants to be validated. If you think that sounds a bit like Alan Partridge, you're right!

I didn't want to do what I would have done twenty years ago, which would be to try to find the joke, to make people laugh. Instead I frequently chose the darkest, oddest route available because I no longer felt the need to be funny all the time. It was counter-intuitive and sometimes it made me vulnerable, but it was funny in a subtler way. You end up playing for high stakes, with a greater risk of failure, but with a greater prize at the end if it works.

So when I was improvising with Michael I had to forget about trying to be funny and sympathetic and just be honest. In *The Trip* both Rob and I *had* to allow ourselves to be unattractive.

Rob is a brilliant comic actor capable of being much darker as a performer than people possibly realise; he was wonderful in *Human Remains* and *Marion & Geoff*.

I am sometimes a bit jealous that he is more at ease with himself than I am. I know that part of not being at ease with yourself feeds creativity; the American writer Shalom Auslander once told me that his therapist said, 'I could make you feel better, but you wouldn't be able to write any more.'

Rob has made me less intense. I would sometimes become profoundly depressed about other people's cynicism and Rob would say, 'Why are you so het up about this stuff? It doesn't matter.'

Rob might or might not be funnier than me. He is probably more consistently funny. I'm grumpier than he is, but that's OK.

I don't care if people don't think I'm funny as long as the stuff I make matters to enough people and enables me to keep doing it. I'd rather make people think and if they laugh as well, that's a bonus.

CHAPTER 12

The shoot lasted for five weeks and we did two circuits of the Lakes. Michael was very clever: he'd cobble together an edit of stuff we'd done on the first circuit, put it together, see what was working and figure out where the gaps were.

Because *The Trip* is half true and half not, even I get confused when I watch it. Oh, it's not really me, it's not really Rob. Oh, it is. I love that grey area. By the way, it's not my parents in *The Trip*. Or my child. They are very nice people, but they are actors.

When Michael started talking about doing a second series, I asked how it was going to be different. He said it would be the same thing again, only this time in Italy. The food would be better and the locations more impressive.

I'd worked so hard on *Philomena* and *Alpha Papa* that the last thing I felt like doing was going to Italy to have pseudo-arguments with Rob.

But, almost too shattered to argue, I agreed to go.

I got there and stood on a veranda in Genoa in the bright sunshine and had a cold glass of wine with Rob. The first glass of wine I'd had in nine months.

I thought, 'This is rather nice.'

It turned into a five-week holiday, going around the most beautiful places in Italy and eating the most glorious food. It was heaven.

Rob and I would have these slightly cantankerous dinners on camera and then in the evening we'd choose to eat together.

One night we ate in this gorgeous place in Tuscany called Relais La Suvera. Just the two of us, no cameras, no crew, and we talked about our lives. By the end of the meal, we were both crying.

Rob even gave me a hug.

We had, I'd like to point out, both been drinking.

It felt really odd because we were sitting there being quite emotional, knowing full well that in the days to come we'd be picking at each other's scabs on camera.

You can see certain issues – introspection, the melancholy of age, the acceptance of our mortality – running through the series, partly because we were retracing the footsteps of Shelley, Byron and Keats, two of whom had died before reaching their thirtieth birthdays, immortalised in their prime. There was a slight desperation in our trying to reach out and touch them. It was as though being in the places they had been might allow us to find some deeper meaning in an atheistic world.

As André Gide said, 'Trust those who seek the truth but doubt those who say they have found it.'

Again, not much of *The Trip to Italy* was planned; Michael simply wanted Rob to be philandering and me to have found some kind of equilibrium after being lost at the end of the first series.

And, for a second time, we had homework. I watched *Roman Holiday* and *La Dolce Vita*, but Rob didn't. When he was walking around Rome with my assistant, played by Claire Keelan, he had to pretend he knew what was going on.

He says that he was like that at school: he didn't do his homework because he was a hopeless procrastinator and never quite got round to it. So he pretended he'd seen those films. I wasn't much better. Michael was exasperated at times, but we did just fine by winging it.

★   ★   ★

When *The Trip to Italy* was completed, I was caught up by the momentum of the releases of both *Philomena* and *Alpha Papa*. I was disappointed that *The Look of Love,* which came out around the same time, didn't have more impact; it was by far my best performance as an actor. I really went to dark, emotional places to play Paul Raymond, a man so sad he had an empty fridge at home. It was a grotesque rendition of a world I'd moved away from.

Unlike *24 Hour Party People*, I wanted the filming of *The Look of Love* to end. It was an exhausting orgy of hedonism; we did all the sex scenes in three days and it was utterly soulless. I started to crave a lone mountain walk in the Lakes. I didn't even recognise the actresses at the wrap party because they were fully dressed. Be careful what you wish for.

I had almost forgotten about *The Trip to Italy* by the time it came out. The effort involved was so minimal and Michael turned it into something, as he always does, that made it more than the sum of its parts. I would happily do a third one; perhaps we could leave Europe and eat our way around America next time.

Both series of *The Trip* were released in the States as feature films and they had real impact. I was shocked by people's responses to it both in Los Angeles and in New York; I always expected people who approached me in those cities to want to talk about *Philomena*, but it was invariably *The Trip*.

Both *The Trip* and *The Trip to Italy* have a languid quality that is a blessed relief. You are invited to spend time with me and Rob, to immerse yourself in our world as we have unhurried conversations over food and drink. It's a sanctuary for people who've had enough of the digital world; they feel as though they are at the table with us, being irascible yet witty and unapologetically analogue.

It's odd to see how my life changed from one series to the next. When I made *The Trip* in 2010, I was easy to wind up about women, drugs and Hollywood. In an episode in *The Trip to Italy*, Rob talks about how well Sacha Baron Cohen, Ricky Gervais and Simon Pegg are doing in LA. We are sitting in a fantastic restaurant overlooking Capri, and Rob interviews me as Michael Parkinson. I try to get angry with him, but I'm helpless with laughter.

ROB: 'I watched Simon Pegg in the *Star Trek* films.

ME: 'I haven't seen them, but I'm told they're very good. I'm delighted for his success.'

ROB: 'He worked with Tom Cruise on *Mission Impossible*.'

ME: 'I've worked with Tom Cruise. I worked with him on *Tropic Thunder*.'

ROB: 'You died in the first ten minutes, Steve.'

(I'm laughing)

ROB: 'When we think about you, we think about the nineties.'

ME: 'Yeah . . . WHAT?'

ROB: 'We think about the nineties. What a wonderful period that was. We think Oasis, Blur. You're smacked off your tits in a centre-of-London hotel, trying to keep your life together. But you've turned it around now. Tell us about your recovery.'

ME (frowning): 'Well, I'd rather not . . .'

And then we talk about hair loss.

Rob says that it was the type of quasi-aggressive humour that he uses on his audience members; he knows he couldn't usually get away with it with me because I'd come back with something just as good. But he was brilliant that day.

Sometimes I wonder if we will always be playing out those

heightened versions of ourselves. There are worse fates to befall people.

As I've always said, *The Trip* is *Last of the Summer Wine* for *Guardian* readers.

CHAPTER 13

For a while, work provided a distraction from both bad behaviour and press intrusion. I thought that if I kept being funny, the tabloids might eventually go away. Even in my darkest days, when I was messing up my personal life, I still had my career.

I thought, 'I might be a disaster as a human being, but I do good work.'

Creating good art could never justify my behaviour, but it did stop me from going mad. At a time when I didn't feel particularly positive about myself, the work kept me afloat. Eventually, therapy taught me that I should be as exacting about my conduct as my work. But I was a slow learner.

And the tabloids didn't go away.

I never made a Faustian pact with the press. Just as I never bought tabloid newspapers, so I never courted them. I am not famous for being famous. The newspapers did not create my success. I only reluctantly and very rarely spoke to showbiz reporters and gossip columnists. In their absurdly self-deluding terms, I never 'invaded my own privacy'. Just one example: I turned down £30,000 from the *News of the World* for a photo of my girlfriend and me with our newborn daughter.

It was particularly demoralising to be the subject of articles in newspapers that I never looked at. I wanted to be a private person, but by claiming the moral high ground the tabloids kept trying to draw me into a game of self-justification. I wasn't interested; I didn't want to open a dialogue with them in which I had to beg them to think of me as a really nice person. If they were determined to condemn me, I would rather they did so based on a caricature of me. The people in my life know who I am. That's enough for me. It doesn't matter if taxi drivers like me or not.

I have always kicked back against media intrusion. If I misbehaved without affecting wider society, then that was my own business and that of those directly involved only. If I offended people, which I often did, that was also for me to deal with in private. Plenty of people make personal mistakes in their lives; I made mine while living in the full glare of the cameras. My life may be of interest to people, but I still don't think it legitimises press intrusion.

So long as I maintained my 'never justify, never explain' approach, I really believed that the work would articulate itself. We live in a world where everyone mildly despairs of tabloid behaviour but, in the end, simply shrugs their shoulders as though nothing can be done.

I have never believed that celebrities have to allow journalists full access to their lives simply because they are successful at what they do and are in the public eye as a result. It's the intrusive, ugly, immoral and unethical behaviour of certain journalists becoming the norm that I railed against.

One day I woke up and thought, 'Hang on a second, is there a possibility that it doesn't have to be like this?'

You realise that while it may be OK for Piers Morgan to strut around saying, 'You don't get to be the editor of the *Mirror* without being a fairly despicable human being,' it does not have to be that way.

In this case, flippancy doesn't stop it being profoundly true.

Nor is it in any way acceptable for newspapers to practise the so-called 'dark arts' – where editors, executives and foot-soldier journalists or subcontracted private investigators gather information by illegal means.

The first time I was the subject of an intrusive tabloid story was in January 1996, when the *Daily Mirror* published two kiss-and-tell stories about me. 'Kiss-and-tell' is a sugar-coated term which the tabloids invented to disguise the uglier truth – these are actually 'shag-and-sell' stories. Later the same year, a journalist phoned my daughter's maternal great-grandmother and pretended to be doing a survey for the council while asking personal questions about my daughter's mother and me.

In 2008, I agreed to do a profile for the *Sunday Times* in good faith. The paper not only printed photos of my young daughter taken by a paparazzo using a telephoto lens, but also wrote several untruths. These are, of course, obvious breaches of the industry's own 'Editors' Code of Practice'. The paper printed an apology for using photos of my daughter without permission, but instead of being as prominent as the photo-spread, it was just a one-inch item buried on an inside page.

When I lived in Brighton, journalists and photographers regularly camped outside my house. Some went through my bins, some followed my car when I left home, others hung around pubs asking people if they knew me.

As well as being stalked and effectively put under surveillance, I faced blatant falsehoods. Back in the autumn of 2007, the *Daily Mail* printed a number of articles that repeated the lie that I was somehow responsible for or connected with Owen Wilson's alleged suicide attempt.

Although I know Owen, I hadn't at that time seen him for nine months and I hadn't ever taken drugs with him or in his company. My reputation was immediately tarnished: I was forced to make representations to various people in the American film industry explaining that the allegations were completely false. I could have sued, but a legal case would itself have meant more intrusion into the life of my friend.

Those stories are still online and I'm sure the *Daily Mail* is in no rush to take them down.

And then there was entrapment and blackmail. Even earlier, in August 2002, I received a phone call from a reporter called Rav Singh who worked on Andy Coulson's 'Bizarre' column in the *Sun*. He told me that I was about to be the target of a sting from Coulson's office. A girl I'd had an affair with would ring me and try to lure me into revealing details about my private life. Coulson would be listening to the call. When the call came, I gave nothing away. Nothing was printed.

In April 2004, Rav Singh, who now had his own gossip column in the *News of the World*, phoned me. They wanted to print a story that Sunday about a relationship I'd had. If I admitted to part of the story, the paper would hold back on details that might be embarrassing to my family. Because Singh had tipped me off about the earlier sting, I trusted him. I talked to him openly.

And then Coulson, by now editor of the *News of the World*, called my publicist and told him they had recorded the whole conversation. The supposedly confidential conversation would be presented as an interview, as my side of the story. This was by no means the worst thing they did.

The final straw was discovering that my phone had probably been hacked by News International. I decided that I could no longer sit back and do nothing; I had to be proactive and push for press reform, even if the fallout might do me no favours. This was all before 'Dowlergate' – the big hacking revelations of the summer of 2011.

At this point, Andy Coulson had left News International to work as Director of Communications for David Cameron, the leader of the Conservative Party. Coulson was working at the heart of government, and I wanted to show people what he was really like: deceitful and a liar.

Everyone kept advising me not to take action against News International.

I had a frank phone conversation with my publicist, who had connections with Murdoch. He knew Rebekah Brooks, the then chief executive of News International and former editor of the *Sun* and the *News of the World*, as, it seemed of the whole political, media and policing establishment. Scary.

He tried to warn me. 'Do you really want to make enemies

of these people? If you're doing this because you're after Andy Coulson, you'll never get to him. He's at the heart of the government, protected by a ring of steel. This story has gone away, it's not coming back. Maybe you'll get a few quid out of them but . . .' He paused. 'Do you really want to make enemies of these people?' he repeated.

By 'these people', he clearly meant News International.

I asked him to clarify.

'If you're in trouble in the future, I could use this as credit to say that you could have taken action but you chose not to. It will be like money in the bank.'

I put the phone down and considered what he'd said. I had information suggesting that my phone had been hacked, that personal voicemail messages left by friends and family had been intercepted. Could I let that go?

I carefully thought it through. 'Do I really want to open this can of worms? The tabloids aren't writing anything about me at the moment. Maybe it would be better to let it go.'

And then I thought, 'Fuck it.'

I decided it was time to roll my sleeves up. Almost as an experiment, I wanted to see what would happen if I pulled at the thread of News International. I knew it would potentially cost me a considerable sum of money to sue such a powerful company, but I wanted to know exactly what information they had on me. So I applied for a court order to obtain it, and the police provided me with the incriminating documents.

Both the Met and News International were hiding behind the so-called 'rogue reporter' explanation of why, in 2006, a royal correspondent and a private investigator had been arrested for voicemail interception. But I was in the paperwork, and I was as far as you could get from royalty. Only three or four other people were taking legal action at the time, so we were hardly part of a mass movement. More like a fringe sideshow.

Martin Sixsmith once said to me, 'You're a bloody northerner and you like a fight.' But I wasn't looking for trouble. I just didn't want to be one of those people who thinks, 'Anything for a quiet life.'

I knew I was about to lay myself open to a press revenge attack, but at least I would be in control this time. The *Sunday Times*, the *Daily Mirror*, et al. were no doubt hoping that I wouldn't take legal action because I wouldn't want my past raked up again. Ironically, because the tabloids had emptied my closet of skeletons, it made me invulnerable to their bullying tactics.

I had nothing to hide.

CHAPTER 14

After the astonishing revelation in the *Guardian* in July 2011 that the *News of the World* had illegally accessed information from the phone of murdered schoolgirl Milly Dowler in 2002, while she was still missing, the police finally agreed to give information to the lawyer of anyone who suspected their phone had been hacked. I had got a court order and the police were obliged to give me all the information I required, but it still wasn't straightforward: various officers had blanked out parts of phone numbers to try to limit the amount of information they divulged.

I felt as though the police were resisting, but eventually I started to uncover what had been going on.

I discovered a number of distressing things, the most inoffensive of which was that private investigators had been following me to cashpoints and watching how much money I withdrew. I was then presented with pages from Glenn Mulcaire's notebook. Mulcaire was a phone-hacking specialist at the *News of the World* who appeared on their payroll soon after Rebekah Brooks's appointment. He referred to himself as 'Dr Evil'. He had served a short prison sentence back in 2007 for hacking the voicemails of the royal household, when all the time the police had thousands of pages of his notes showing thousands of non-royal targets. Between then and 2011, Rebekah Brooks had time to implement her infamous 'email deletion policy'. Millions of records were destroyed.

Mulcaire's notebook was full of numbers that appeared to be from my phone. I phoned a girl I'd being going out with and she recognised the redacted numbers. I returned to the police with the missing digits; as far as I was concerned, it was proof that Mulcaire had hacked my phone.

I then discovered that Andy Coulson had phoned this girl personally and suggested she dress up in sexy clothes for a *News of the World* photo shoot and in turn the paper would run a story in her favour. Otherwise they would print a not-so-nice story, since they already had the information about her affair with me.

This woman nearly gave in, but at the last minute changed her mind. Her instinct was right: it seems they obtained the information about her relationship with me illegally and couldn't use it without her side of the story. It's what those journalists and editors specialise in: calling your bluff. Getting you to talk so that they don't need to use the original, illegal source of information.

It is shocking when you sit down and really think about it: 'public interest journalism' is another planet for certain parts of the press. Their output is nothing to do with free expression and everything to do with business. It's about selling newspapers. It's just about the only business left that doesn't have any system of accountability.

★   ★   ★

It was strange to be simultaneously seeking legal action and watching the story unfold in the press. But as soon as the Milly Dowler story broke, I was on the right side overnight.

I used to go into the newsagent's and see endless hacking stories on the front pages of all the papers. While Paul Dacre, editor of the *Daily Mail*, was predictably defensive of his paper's journalistic methods, Nick Davies led the way in the *Guardian*. With his rigorous, conscientious reporting, Nick revealed the dark heart of the worst kind of journalism.

Nick may have been the pioneer, but he wasn't alone: the *Financial Times* and the *Independent* also covered the story honourably and properly. *The Times* and the *Sunday Times* were, however, slow to join in. Either they thought the story was irrelevant, or they had decided it was in the interest of Rupert Murdoch, their proprietor, not to cover it. Some say Murdoch's main motivation is that he has a political axe to grind, but I think ultimately he is more concerned about preserving his business interests and maximising his profits at any cost. As a businessman, however, he has to be accountable for his employees acting in an abusive way.

It was all very well suddenly being on the right side. I still stood to lose a considerable amount of money. I quickly decided that I didn't care. I thought, 'I'm going to ask questions. I might not win any damages, but those questions have to be asked.'

At the eleventh hour, News International's lawyer said to me, 'Look, whoever loses or wins, do you want to split the legal costs?'

I said, 'No. If I lose, I pay. If you lose, you pay. I'm not splitting anything.'

The lawyer came back and said, 'OK, News International will give you £250,000 to go away now. If they win the appeal, they'll take all the money off the table and they won't give you a dime. They'll see you in court.'

At that point, I'd spent way more than £250,000 on legal fees and would be considerably out of pocket even if I accepted the News International offer.

I went home and asked myself what the worst-case scenario would be. My life wouldn't be destroyed. I probably wouldn't lose my house, against which I was borrowing, but I might be financially crippled for a few years. I might have to do well-paid work I wasn't interested in. I was lucky that I was able to take that kind of financial risk.

News International was gambling on the fact that I had limited resources and would therefore snap up their offer. The truth is that most people, regardless of their financial status, would accept such an offer. It's very easy to compromise one's ethics when the financial stakes are so high.

But I had a point to prove and I didn't want to give in to

bullies. I wanted to make public the behind-the-scenes behaviour of some journalists who think 'ethics' is where Page 3 girls with lisps come from – either that or they are pressurised into finding stories with no-questions-asked methods to satisfy editors and proprietors. It has everything to do with profit margins and nothing to do with freedom of expression.

So I stood firm and waited anxiously for the judge's decision that afternoon.

The judge decided in my favour. Later, News International had to give me an apology in open court and pay me damages. After I had paid my lawyers I still ended up £30,000 out of pocket.

Until the judge gave his verdict, I had no idea if I was going to win. It was certainly a close call. I don't think I ever proved beyond reasonable doubt that my phone was hacked, but the judge said it was a reasonable assumption that News International had tried to get into my phone.

The money had become largely irrelevant. People would ask what was in it for me and the answer was simple: beyond wanting answers, I wanted to remind News International that power comes with responsibility.

And the fight gave me back my self-esteem. Thanks, Rupert.

★ ★ ★

After I sued the *News of the World*, I agreed to give evidence at the Leveson Inquiry. Set up by David Cameron in July 2011, it was a public, judge-led inquiry, divided into two parts, that explored the relationships between the press and the public, the press and the police, and the press and politicians.

In the same month, July 2011, Rupert Murdoch announced the closure of the *News of the World*. It was still flogging an astonishing 2.8 million copies a week, but the torrent of hacking allegations and accusations of a cover-up forced Murdoch's hand. The tipping point was not the hacking of Milly Dowler's phone coming to light, it was the flight of advertisers. Like I say, for Rupert Murdoch and his ilk, it is all about business. I still think it's unforgivable that, until phone hacking became a matter of public knowledge, the bribing of public officials was not taken seriously by the police.

Standing up to Murdoch had been nerve-racking, but it meant I was ready to give evidence at Leveson. It was bloody hard-going; it made me appreciate writing stupid, funny gags with Neil and Rob. I really missed the levity of Alan Partridge.

I don't regret speaking up, but it was a huge learning curve for me.

This may sound naive, but what shocked me most was the way some journalists behaved as though their job had nothing to do with the truth and everything to do with being tribal. And those who do strive to uncover the truth – such as the Guardian's Nick Davies – are reviled by some of their peers for not being a journalist's journalist, for not displaying loyalty at all costs. Revealing the truth made him a traitor. Somehow, your first loyalty as a journalist shouldn't be to the truth or to the public interest, but to your fellow hacks and your proprietor. Always the company, right or wrong.

By closing ranks, the journalists and editors who oppose effective press regulation are trying to put a stop to any kind of productive or sensible discussion. They would rather fight than talk. Because if you fight, you don't need to get into the detail of the argument. You don't have to defend your appalling behaviour. And the truth will never out.

The dark underbelly of how some journalists and editors behave may have been exposed by the Leveson Inquiry, but people are still arguing that an unaccountable and feral press is the price we have to pay to live in a democracy. It is not, of course. Just look at any other healthy Western democracy and their newspapers. Free and feisty, but not out of control.

There's also an element of what I think of as intellectual, middle-class, liberal guilt applied to working-class journalists.

They're working class, ergo they're allowed to behave badly. It's misguided and it's patronising.

Whenever I talk about press regulation, certain parts of the media caricature what I say. They distort my words and mock me and Hugh Grant as nothing more than poster boys for Hacked Off. We laugh at the fact that tabloid editors (including the once-proud *Times* and *Telegraph*) would rather target us than refute us.

Far from being a well-funded PR machine, we really are a motley crew. According to the papers we are two vain/failed/rich actors, some 'ambulance-chasing' lawyers, a few dandruffy professors from 'provincial' universities, and the odd (very odd) lefty activist. What they do not mention – because they dare not admit it – is that at the heart and soul of Hacked Off lie the real victims of press abuse, including the McCanns, Milly Dowler's sister Gemma, and Bristol landlord Christopher Jefferies.

It's easy to get sucked into a debate about press responsibility that you could, of course, argue matters to no one outside the M25. But I want to see an effective system of independent press self-regulation. An effective system of redress for the disempowered is, of course, entirely consistent with free expression.

I'm certainly not alone. In November 2013, 100 prominent figures signed a declaration urging newspaper and magazine publishers to embrace the Leveson Royal Charter. The signatories included Stephen Fry, John Cleese, Stephen Frears, J. K. Rowling, David Hare, Tom Stoppard, Salman Rushdie, John Pilger and Will Hutton, many of whom know perhaps a little more about free speech than Kelvin MacKenzie or Piers Morgan.

For some reason, those signatories are seen as difficult targets for the papers to attack, whereas I'm slagged off as a 'celebrity', used, in this instance, as a pejorative term to try to undermine the credibility of what I say.

When Andy Coulson was finally sentenced to eighteen months in prison, Hacked Off was asked to respond on television. Executive Director Joan Smith, a writer and journalist, and herself a victim of press abuse, went along with Gemma Dowler. And guess what? The producer was frustrated because Hugh Grant and I weren't there to put 'celebrity' into a news programme. And the press were frustrated too because we are so much easier to attack when they can write about how we are only out to avenge all those nasty little tabloid stories about us.

It's worth remembering that Lord Leveson said he would be watching the *Daily Mail* carefully during the inquiry because their attacks on Hugh Grant and me were likely to prove intimidating to other witnesses.

Since then I've always regarded attacks by the *Daily Mail* as a badge of honour. Paul Dacre is, like all bullies, a coward. Although some people remain intimidated by him, I find that it helps to think of *The Wizard of Oz*.

Far from being this big, booming voice, the *Daily Mail* is just a little man behind a curtain.

★   ★   ★

When I was suing News International and giving evidence at Leveson, my publicist was convinced I was on a suicide mission.

By early 2014, when *Philomena* was Oscar nominated and *Alpha Papa* had proved a huge success, he had changed his mind: 'Look at you now. You just set yourself free.'

Was I playing with fire? Yes. Would people have me buried alive if I fucked up? Yes.

I can see why some people would rather I keep my mouth shut unless I'm shouting 'A-ha' every now and again.

But that's not me.

I am a serious person. I like to do funny things. The fact that the 'me' who has emerged in recent years isn't consistent with the earlier tabloid perception of 'me' as always shagging some bird is not my problem.

I haven't changed. The perception of me has changed.

PART TWO

CHAPTER 15

On 27 January 1979, when was thirteen, I wrote a four-page letter in green ink to my older sister, Clare, who was at university. I began with:

> Sorry I haven't written for ages and I said I would, but I just couldn't be bothered.

What a wag and a wit I was.

I went on to tell her about my morning paper round and how I had recently been given a rise from £2.64 to £3 a week.

> Do not think that as soon as I get my wages I spend them.
> Oh! no! Definitely not, no! No!

I was saving assiduously for a school trip to Lourdes, the cut-price Catholic Mecca. I kept my money in a small but weighty cast-iron piggy bank that my dad, unable to walk past a skip without having a rummage around, had no doubt salvaged.

> Mum and me made an agreement (a cold! business type one). Mum said I pay £50 and she pays £70 . . . My trip takes me to Lourdes mainly, but we will be stopping off at Paris on the way for a day or two. I not only hope to gain pleasure from this trip, but education too. And that means no chasing French bar maids!

The trip was my first one abroad. The coach had no air conditioning, but we were happy to sweat and laugh our way across the Pennines and on to Paris. The French teacher, who wasn't remotely religious, sat at the back of the bus telling dirty jokes. He wore Cuban heels, flared trousers and a shirt that, slashed to the waist, revealed a medallion and a hairy chest. He looked like the fourth Bee Gee. If The Bee Gees had ever had a Pete Best, it would have been him.

Even then we knew he was slightly ridiculous. He loved *Saturday Night Fever* and insisted that disco was where it was at; he dismissed punk and new wave as noise. At the same time as being a good Catholic altar boy, I was also getting into slightly nihilistic music that was, as far as I could tell, mostly about concrete urban decay.

The soundtrack to my life as I entered my teen years included The Jam and Blondie, and The Human League, who were like a northern Kraftwerk.

The lyrics to The Undertones' 'My Perfect Cousin' encapsulate the period for me perfectly, conjuring up that sense of finding a new, exciting sound and using it to define who you are. The line 'Playing along with the art-school boys' always comes back to me when I think of that time.

So I was a snob. And I didn't hold back in my letter to Clare.

> Our French teacher is INSANE. He is in his early 20s and has a moustache and shoulder-length hair. He's just one big corny cliché. He's into Bee Gees, 'Grease' and other commercial rubbish. I'm really into heavy punk, Clash, Sex Pistols, Siouxsie and the Banshees, but I do like Buzzcocks. I hate ELO and I'm going to get a Sex Pistols LP called 'Never Mind the - - - - - - - - Here's the Sex Pistols'. I also like X-Ray Specs [*sic*].

We were, however, happy to hear the French teacher's dirty jokes, which weren't really appropriate for a coachload of Catholic schoolboys.

Not that I was offended: I wasn't religious, beyond thinking Catholics were sort of right and everyone else was sort of wrong. And I was a bit confused about sex; not long after the school trip, sex became the most awkward thing in the world.

We went to Biarritz on a day trip and walked up and down the beach, looking sideways at all the women sunbathing topless. It was incredibly exciting; in the days before Internet porn, the sight of a woman's breasts was something to be savoured and logged in the memory bank (mammary bank?).

Apart from this, the journey proved to be the most exciting part of the trip: the getting there, the being somewhere else.

I wasn't particularly impressed by Lourdes. I knew that Our Lady, as we called the Virgin Mary, was quite a pop star in the Catholic world. She has always got top billing. She's the head-line act. I'd seen the 1943 film *The Song of Bernadette*, in which the teenage peasant girl Bernadette reports countless visions of the Blessed Virgin Mary in a grotto in Lourdes, but I didn't experience any such visions myself.

All I can recall of Lourdes now is a huge basilica, the grotto and endless stalls selling religious paraphernalia. I spotted some giant wooden rosary beads and thought they'd make a fantastic gift for my mum and dad. How could they not appreciate supersized rosary beads?

Now I barely recognise the boy who went to Lourdes. I had a blessed upbringing, but I was an awkward, dreamy kid prone to outbursts of attention seeking. I certainly wasn't naturally cool like some boys.

It's no accident that Alan Partridge exploits those traits of mine that I know might generally be described as failings. A lack of self-consciousness coupled with acute self-consciousness.

Grasping at knowledge; Alan knows a bit about everything, and we all know a little knowledge is a dangerous thing.

Like Alan, I spent much of my childhood on the outside looking in.

CHAPTER 16

I am a product of my Catholic upbringing. Of my Irish roots. Of my lower-middle-class background. Of the north. Of suburbia. Of the grammar school system. Of the television generation.

I'm the fourth of six children, five of whom are boys. Our house was a colourful, noisy environment. Quiet contemplation was saved for church on a Sunday.

When I was a teenager, my parents fostered a series of kids because they took the view that, if you can look after yourself, then you should look after others less fortunate. Mum and Dad came from working-class backgrounds, but were socially mobile, aspirant.

And education was the way to a better future; knowledge was something to be acquired and appreciated. My dad decided to buy the *Encyclopaedia Britannica*, which meant that knowledge could be accessed without a trip to the library. It was a step closer to Google, which itself has supported the Coogan trait of presenting an educated guess as an incontrovertible fact.

My parents' Catholicism is the left-wing, Irish kind. The monarchy and the establishment were held at arm's length; the brutal repression of the Irish by the English informed a scepticism which has served me well.

My parents are both left of centre. They have traditionally supported the Labour Party because it represents working people and they were working people, but they have coupled this with a natural conservatism that is born of hardship.

Mine was a household in which everyone was more obsessed with grammar than literature. The illumination of the human condition through good literature was less important than dotting your 'i's and crossing your 't's. And never, ever pronounce 'h' as 'haitch'.

Dad always thought that grammar was more important than creativity. The whole family went to Tuscany for Mum and Dad's fiftieth wedding anniversary in 2008 and Dad, who is not usually demonstrative, gave an emotional speech in which he qualified his gratitude at our collective good health with a tinge of regret that not all our marriages had gone according to plan.

One of my brothers shouted out, 'At least none of us are gay!'

Another brother immediately countered with, 'At least none of us *is* gay!'

Sexual orientation might be met with a furrowed brow, but grammatical transgression was unforgivable.

The curse of being lower middle class is knowing just enough to be aware of what you don't know. There is no blissful ignorance.

I was born and brought up in Middleton, Greater Manchester. It had been Middleton, Lancashire, until the boundaries were redrawn in 1974 and my father still defiantly insists on saying 'Middleton, Lancashire'. He thinks 'Greater Manchester' has a horrible, municipal, bureaucratic, soulless sound to it and I agree with him.

Manchester was the birthplace of the Industrial Revolution and the cooperative movement and was where Engels wrote his letters to Marx. Middleton was a dormer suburb, a former mill town dotted with abandoned cotton mills, sad monuments to a more glorious past. In the nineties, those that hadn't been demolished had been turned into loft-style living.

However, I grew up convinced that Middleton was the centre of the universe. There was a small element of Little England about Middleton, and the London I saw in television shows such as *The Saint, Department S, The Champions, Randall and Hopkirk (Deceased)* and *The Baron* provided an escape. These shows bore little resemblance to reality: suave men in suits drove Bentleys,

and stunning women wore cocktail dresses to impossibly glamorous parties in Mayfair, where they held arch, mannered conversations. It seemed so very far away from my life.

As you approach middle age, you start to think about where
you come from. You start to realise that there is more life
behind you than in front of you. It's where the midlife crisis
is born. You see your attitude changing; you do the things
that, as a younger person, would have horrified you. What I
perceived as weaknesses – inconsistencies, contradictions,
prejudices, vanity – I now perceive as strengths. I have become
empowered by them.

As I age, my childhood is a place I increasingly visit in my
head. I often think of the opening line of the L. P. Hartley novel
The Go-Between: 'The past is a foreign country: they do things
differently there.' It's been quoted so much that it's become a
cliché, but it remains a germane observation.

My childhood is a wonderful place to visit. Our parents didn't
tell us they loved us – it's since become the norm; I tell my
daughter every day – but we never doubted we were loved.
When you're from a working-class background as my parents
were, you are defined by your actions. Rhetoric was an indulgence. Talking about your feelings was a luxury only afforded
to people with 'too much time on their hands'.

★   ★   ★

Both my parents were keen on elevating themselves, but equally
they felt self-conscious about moving up the social ladder. This
could easily be judged as materialistic; there certainly wasn't
much spirituality about it. Yet they wanted their kids to have
a grammar school education and they were keen on respectability. Not in a *Daily Mail*, curtain-twitching, Hyacinth Bucket
kind of way. It was all about having a sense of Christian philanthropy, in which you helped the less fortunate. All, of course,
without making a fuss.

My parents were of the generation that skipped rock 'n' roll. Their generation moved from childhood to adulthood very quickly; they weren't forever young like my generation. 'Teenager' was an American term that only gained currency in the bountiful fifties, whereas my parents came of age in the immediate post-war years of austerity Britain.

There was no time to 'find yourself' or all those other self-indulgent things we're so familiar with now. Gap years were a madman's dream.

Mum and Dad didn't have the time to navel-gaze. For them, life was about finding a decent job, making enough money to get by and contributing to society. Once they could look after themselves, they could look after others who were less well off. My parents always maintain it was the simple Catholic, working-class ethos of feeling responsible for the people around you.

Both my parents came from poor backgrounds. My mum's family was originally from Ireland. By the 1930s, a significant section of the population had emigrated. Mum, who has a breathtaking archive of letters and school reports, once showed us a heartbreaking letter that my great-aunt Maggie sent her daughter, Mum's aunt, when her daughter left for America.

She wrote: 'I can still remember the last time I saw you, walking up the hill to catch the train . . . I may as well have dug a hole and buried you in the ground.'

In the days before commercial flights, it wasn't as though they could easily come back in the holidays; once they had gone, it was goodbye for ever.

The shockwave of the Irish famine in the 1860s and the subsequent Irish diaspora meant the country was in a very slow decline. The shrinking population only started to expand again in the 1980s, and even now abandoned, broken mills and cottages litter the west of the country. There was no employment in Ireland; unless you had land or property you simply left as soon as you were old enough to work.

My maternal grandparents came to England in the 1930s. My

maternal grandad (Pop) was a labourer who became an expert floor layer for Semtex, and his wife (Nana) did various jobs and in later years looked after the brethren and students at De La Salle teacher training college. After Pop retired, he worked as a cleaner at the Arndale Shopping Centre in Manchester. He would bring home shoes he'd salvaged from the skip. The shoes were ruined one way or another to stop people from wearing them – they had either been slashed down the side with a knife, or the heel had been 'cored' because they'd been on a shop dummy. If it was the latter, my enterprising grandad would make the shoes wearable again by hammering a cork into the hole and shaving it until it was flush with the heel.

My mum was born in Manchester in 1933. She had a tough time when she was sent back to Ireland during the war. She lived with her uncle and her grandparents while her parents stayed in England to work. Each time the history teacher found a reason to say, 'And that's the fault of the bloody English!' all the children would turn and stare at my mum.

★　★　★

My dad's family originally came from Ireland too. My great-grandfather was Irish; 'Coogan' is an Irish name. My mother's maiden name was 'Coonan', so she only had to change one letter when she married my dad. It was slightly confusing for us kids: Nana and Pop *Coogan* and Nana and Pop *Coonan* (I have asked my parents why they simply didn't call one set of grandparents 'grandma and grandad', but they have never given me a straight answer).

My dad was born in Manchester and stayed there during the war. My paternal grandmother worked in the cotton mills and talked just like Les Dawson's old woman character Ada, who theatrically and almost silently mouths most of what she is saying to her friend Cissie, played by Roy Barraclough. The looms in the cotton mills were so loud that the women who worked there had to mouth their words and learn to lip-read. Once home, they would often extend the miming so that the kids wouldn't know what they were saying.

Nana Coogan told me a story once about a night during the war.

A bomb was dropped on the house directly opposite. My dad and his younger brothers, Tommy and Peter, were all in bed together. They were about seven, five and three years old. None of them woke up when the window was blown in, even though the entire bed was covered in tiny shards of glass. Nana spent all night silently picking fragments of glass off them while they slept peacefully.

Both world wars cast a long shadow: Nana's neighbours, Agnes and Betty, lived together because they'd lost their husbands in the first world war. So many women widowed by the war ended up living together rather than alone. Looking back, it's so poignant, but at the time they were just dotted around and we didn't think much of it.

Dad grew up in a strict Catholic household; as a kid his father had truanted and misbehaved until he was 'saved' by the Christian Brothers. Pop Coogan felt he owed them and so became an upstanding member of the community. Rather like my dad some years later, Pop was the only person in his social circle who had a car, so people were always asking for lifts in his Ford V8.

Pop Coogan leased the Astoria Ballroom in Plymouth Grove in Manchester in the early 1950s so that he could put on big-band nights for the local working-class Irish community. The Irish were ostracised, so they had to look after each other. But their embracing of big band rather than Irish music showed their desire to assimilate, as did their propensity for dropping 'O' from their surnames.

The ongoing love of all things Irish is a modern phenomenon. In 1970s mainland Britain, in the shadow of the IRA Guildford pub bombings of 1974, the Irish were viewed with suspicion. Ross McWhirter, the co-founder of Guinness World Records, went as far as to suggest that it should be compulsory for Irish people to carry ID. He paid for this with his life when the IRA murdered him on his doorstep. I remember a tearful Roy Castle trying to explain his death to viewers of *Record Breakers*, a BBC TV children's favourite.

Anyway, my dad played sax in a band while his brothers played the trumpet and drums. We were constantly meeting people in the Irish community in Manchester whose parents met at The Astoria, and as a result everyone knew Pierce Coogan.

Josef Locke and Bernard Manning both sang there before the latter decided to pursue a career as a mildly funny racist bigot.

Dad was appalled by Manning's racism and grotesque sexual explicitness. Dad would say that if only he had had his wire cutters with him, he could have cut Manning's microphone lead and silenced him.

I didn't like Bernard Manning either. There is a simple yet significant difference between Les Dawson, whom I respected, and Bernard Manning: the latter's humour came from a place of contempt and the former's from a place of love. I used to loathe Manning because he brought northern humour into disrepute.

I worked at a petrol station for three years when I was in my teens and sometimes Manning would pull up in his white Lincoln Continental. The largest car in America, it had real presence on the road but looked incongruous in the suburban enclave of Middleton. His number plate was 'I LAF', which I always read as '1 LAF'.

Not bothering to get out of his car, he'd bark, 'Fill her up, sunshine, and watch the paintwork.'

To fill up his car cost about £40, which thirty years ago was a substantial amount of money. Each time I would stop filling it at £36 and pocket the change.

I'm still happy to have fleeced him out of a bit of cash.

★　★　★

Pop Coogan was an exceptional MC. He once sat a drunken Irish ogre down and hit him with a non sequitur.

'Is your mother alive?'

'She might be,' came the surly reply. 'What's it to you?'

Pop looked at him. 'What would she say if she could see you now? Her son, the apple of her eye, a grown man, fighting like an animal.'

This triggered a moment of introspection. The young man then slumped on the chair with his head in his hands and wept tears of remorse for himself and his mother. A more inflammatory situation had been averted – and of course it's always nice to give someone something to think about.

Pop also used to own a minibus, which he used to deliver all the Irish nurses home. He never made any money out of the club; he was doing it for the Irish community.

★   ★   ★

More importantly, for me anyway, my parents met at the Astoria in 1951. My mother noticed my father playing sax and quite liked the look of him. He noticed her for the first time on St Patrick's Day. There was a big crowd with two bands playing. One was an Irish band with squeeze boxes and banjos, the other the more modern band in which Dad played. As Dad was coming off stage, two girls, one of whom was my mum, asked if they could sit with him.

My mum, Kathleen, was eighteen and my dad, Tony, was not quite seventeen.

My dad thought, 'Gosh, she's got legs all the way up to her armpits!'

They both say it was love at first sight. But, this being the 1950s, it wasn't a wild romance. Not at first. They were friends for a while, meeting up at the dance hall, slowly getting to know each other. She used to wait for him at the school gates, feeling like a cradle snatcher.

Dad, who had always tinkered with crystal sets and was more brains than brawn, registered for mandatory national service and was fast-tracked after excelling in his radar exam. He returned home after a year, my parents were married in February 1958, and their first child, Clare, was born in December that year. Dad was playing in the band when the news came through. There was a public telephone at the Astoria. Mum said that someone phoned the hospital for news, and after that the band struck up with 'Thank Heaven for Little Girls'.

Dad did an engineering course and in 1967, by the time I was two, was working for IBM. We used to see huge computers with tapes going *whoosh!* on sci-fi programmes; his job was to fix them for IBM in real life.

I recently heard a song on Classic FM called 'IBM 1401, A User's Manual' by an Icelandic composer called Jóhann Jóhannsson. I was driving at the time so just glanced at the title displayed on the digital radio. I thought it must be wrong; it was so evocative of my childhood that I couldn't believe it was actually the name of a song.

As soon as I got home, I looked Jóhannsson up. His father worked at IBM as a maintenance engineer, but he was also a musician. He programmed the IBM 1401's memory so that electromagnetic waves could be picked up by a radio receiver sitting on top of the computer. In 1971, when the magnetic tape drive computer was rendered obsolete, he said goodbye to the 1401 by playing the strange, maudlin music he'd recorded on a reel-to-reel. It was as though he'd given this huge computer, big enough to climb inside, a personality.

Many years later, Jóhann used his father's recordings as a starting point for a series of songs about technology's inevitable obsolescence. A music critic described the 2006 album, also called *IBM 1401, A User's Manual*, as 'a pang of longing engendered by the aching nostalgia of a future imagined in the recent past'. It's exactly that; I was overwhelmed by the music's nostalgia. I played it for my dad, who was silenced by his memories of a future imagined.

I remember being asked what a computer was at school and I couldn't find an easy way of explaining it. Eventually I said it calculated things and processed information. Still nobody really understood. Everybody was sceptical, as though computers might disappear if we ignored them.

I was more au fait with them than most, but even for me they were part of a future that I couldn't quite imagine. In the late seventies, Dad took us round the IBM headquarters in Sale in south Manchester when there was an open day. You needed a plastic credit card to get from one area to another and the doors slid back electronically. It was as exciting as being in a sci-fi film.

We were shown a printer that could produce pictures of famous people in binary numbers. Most people were printing pictures of Mickey Mouse, but my older brother Martin chose 'Eve'. An image of a topless woman in binary numbers slowly appeared. I thought she looked quite sexy. Mum moved us on with a polite smile.

Mum didn't pursue a career, because she was raising six children and running the house. She wanted to give us a better life. She effectively had a full-time job looking after us and, later, the children she and Dad fostered. She was suspicious of feminism; it made her feel slighted, as though being a housewife and bringing up a house full of kids wasn't a proper job. But she always managed the family budget.

That was the deal: Dad earned the money, she managed it.

We weren't on the breadline, but every last penny had to be accounted for. Everything was stretched a long way. As far as my parents are concerned, there are only two types of food: enough and not enough. When you come from a background where things are in short supply, as my parents did, you appreciate things just by virtue of their quantity.

When my parents were growing up, Britain was still recovering from the war, most people were living hand to mouth and everything was at a premium.

By the time they started to have kids, they made sure that we had enough food and second helpings were encouraged. Mum would always give us more, even if we'd had enough, because in her mind her greatest achievement was having more food than we wanted.

By dint of economic necessity we mostly ate fresh food, which was cheaper in the sixties and seventies than processed. Mum cooked food bought fresh from the Co-op, the butcher's and the greengrocer's, and most of our meals consisted of meat and two veg. It was a real treat to have Smash, Bird's Instant Whip or Angel Delight; I used to covet the Findus Crispy Pancakes enjoyed by my more well-off friends.

The 'save, make do and mend' mentality of the ration years was never completely abandoned. My sister, Clare, remembers that Mum used to cut up Dad's old work shirts and discard the worn bits, to make school shirts for us boys. My brother jokes that we always had fresh bread in the house, but we never ate it; we were always finishing off the slightly stale loaf first, by which time the fresh one was turning.

What makes me feel wealthy as an adult is not having a nice house or car. It's stopping at a service station and being able to pay through the nose for overcooked, tasteless food. As kids we used service stations just for the toilet facilities and the car park, where we'd eat frankfurters cooked on a Calor gas stove as part of a makeshift picnic laid out on a tea towel in the boot of our Morris Oxford Estate.

I might read the latest copy of the *Beano* on those journeys and it would make me salivate. If my memory serves me correctly, there were two outcomes to most stories involving Roger the Dodger and Dennis the Menace. A negative one in which a series of people had been offended and the final frame of the cartoon strip showed a long line of aggrieved people waiting to give Roger/Dennis a beating. And a positive one in which one of the protagonists had inadvertently – normally through sheer luck – won someone's approval and was rewarded with a five-pound note. This would be brandished in the air by Roger/Dennis and accompanied with the triumphant words, 'And now for a feast.'

The final frame was always a long party table laid out with jelly, trifle and sandwiches, as if the best thing a child could hope for in those days was an abundance of food. Now of course it seems strangely quaint, but as you read the comic you'd look on enviously as you chewed slowly on your half-penny Fruit Salad sweet or quarter pound of cherry bonbons.

★   ★   ★

Culinary treats were so rare in our house that my dad even considered Easter eggs a rip-off. He thought you were over-charged for all that cardboard and fancy foil, and it wasn't as though you even got that much chocolate. Instead we were given a big bar of Dairy Milk and I was left to dream of breaking into egg-shaped chocolate. To an engineer, it was never about the aesthetic but always about the measurement.

Sometimes money was tight. Once Dad came home with cream cakes for us all and Mum was furious.

Mum, horrified: 'What's this?'

Dad, sheepish: 'I've bought us all some cream cakes.'

Mum, frowning: 'We haven't got the money for that kind of thing.'

Dad, not quite knowing what to do with the box of cakes: 'I thought it would be a nice treat . . .'

Mum, contemptuous: 'I can't believe you're throwing money around like that when I'm counting every last penny.'

Some periods were financially tougher than others. We would manage to eat out as a family twice a year, mostly at a steak house called Smithills near Bolton. It was a huge outing, with all eight of us crammed into the car, and memorable because it was exceptional.

Most of the time Mum was very careful with money, and Dad would quickly acquiesce on all things financial. She wrapped plastic bands around money-off coupons from Tesco. I was sent off to Asda for some things and Tesco or Macro for other things. Tea was cheaper at Tesco, coffee cheaper at Asda, and so on.

Mum's friend owned a butcher's shop and had access to a warehouse, so she would often shop there because buying in bulk was cheaper. There might, at any given time, be a dozen boxes of cornflakes in our attic. Not Kellogg's: buying brand names was an ostentatious, reckless use of money.

Then, in the middle of all this, when I was thirteen or fourteen, Mum won £1,000 on the St Clare's lottery. We were all given £50 each or a new bike, Mum's friends were given sherry and a joint of meat to feed their own big families, then we all went out for a meal with the whole family, including grandparents. In among her altruism she even found £100 to buy my dad a stainless-steel Seiko watch, which I thought was the apotheosis of urbane sophistication.

It is strange to think that money, and the luxuries it afforded me, became synonymous with memories of my childhood in later years. I bought a Morris Minor Traveller because of the incredible rush of nostalgia that hits me as soon as I sit inside the car. The smell of vinyl seats, petrol and, more subtly, oil. A slight trace of damp that takes me right back to summer holidays in Uncle Johnny's farmhouse in a sleepy Irish village. I can smell wet turf and even burning peat. It's the most powerful smell in the world for me.

Nothing else is so transporting, so evocative. As I sit in the car I experience an overwhelming feeling of warmth, security and extended family. The details of the holidays there flood back. I used a penknife to sharpen sticks and make bows and arrows. I remember walls covered in dark, dank patches. And the absence of hot water. A jug of water was heated up slowly on the fire and we would stand naked in a tub as Mum washed us down with a sponge. The adults would lean over the sink and just do 'pits and face', which I believe is known as a 'Glasgow bath'.

There was no cooker in the house; food was cooked in a big iron pot hanging over an open fire. We would have boiled bacon, cabbage and potatoes enriched with a big knob of butter, served alongside tea with milk straight from the cow. When we were small, we could stand in the fireplace and stare at the flames, warming our damp bodies as best we could.

There was a large kitchen table lit by a single naked bulb. Other local families still had oil lamps, so this was progress, of a sort.

The local pub, just down the road from Uncle Johnny's house, was also a grocer's, petrol station and undertaker's. The publican would give you beer, food and petrol, and eventually he'd bury you. The grown-ups would go off to the pub and come back with Coke and crisps as a treat.

We'd stay up with our books till all hours, reading *The Secret Seven* and *The Famous Five* in a large old bed that we had to share. The mattress had no springs and sank in the middle; by the morning, we were all in a heap in the dip.

The working dogs on the farm weren't friendly. They snapped at us because we were relative strangers. I didn't mind; I liked the fact that it was a working farm. I'd get up at 6 a.m., while everyone else was still in bed, pull on my wellingtons and go out with Uncle Johnny on the tractor to dig turf.

I would stand on the footplate – I was still quite small for an eight- or nine-year-old – hanging on to the side of the tractor and watching the big back wheel move swiftly through the thick, wet mud. It was dangerous, but I didn't care. I was clinging on, just inches from the wheel, trying to make it look as though I was just hovering there. Of course no one was watching, but I felt very manly.

It was another life, a different world. The antithesis to my safe, suburban life in Middleton.

It's a world that has disappeared: old, rural Ireland. It was still James Joyce's Ireland. I realised sometime later that I was seeing a way of life that was trailing behind our own English one. As recently as the 1960s, women bringing condoms from Northern Ireland into Ireland by train were arrested. It's the kind of reactionary behaviour that makes me furious with the Church.

I wasn't aware of such dogma as a child. Nor did I think it odd that when I first started going to Ireland at the age of around five or six, Uncle Johnny's only form of transportation was a donkey and a cart. It took him a good couple of hours to get from his farm into town, which was ten miles away.

I didn't see it as a peasant way of life. Even at a young age, it seemed romantic to me. The world is much bigger when you're younger, and my life in Middleton seemed incredibly far away. It felt even bigger in the seventies because travelling generally took so much longer. It felt like a real journey. We spent two days getting to my uncle's house from Middleton because the 'motorways' were really just single-track roads. It took a further eight hours to get across Ireland; now you can do it in under three. We had to break up the journey by staying in Dublin after crossing the Irish Sea.

A few of my friends still went to Butlins, but package holidays were the new thing and Spain in particular was a very fashionable destination. Friends started coming back from the summer holidays with *tans*. I, in turn, would return to school looking paler than when I left.

★   ★   ★

We didn't go abroad until I was sixteen, in 1981. My sister, Clare, was working at the L'Arche community in France, and I went to visit her with my parents. L'Arche was set up by Jean Vanier, an aristocratic French Canadian who, in the early sixties, invited two adults with learning difficulties to move into his house in France. At the time it was an incredibly radical thing to do because people with learning difficulties were pretty much institutionalised without question. Vanier was making the point that these people, regardless of their disability, should live among us rather than be ostracised.

When Vanier set up L'Arche in 1964, he was offered psychiatric treatment by those close to him because they couldn't believe he had no interest in pursuing a highly remunerative, glittering career. He wanted to devote his life to this not-for-profit organisation in which people with and without disabilities live and work in the same community. There are now L'Arche communities all over the world.

Clare held Vanier up as a hugely inspirational figure. It was essentially Catholic, but non-denominational. L'Arche encouraged people from all over the world to go and work there for short periods. She worked at the original L'Arche for a couple of years and some of the adults with learning difficulties later came to visit our house.

My brother Kevin now runs a branch of L'Arche in Manchester with his wife. He's a much better example of a human being than me: he used to go into school early to do sport, he worked hard, he got good results. He has always been the most intrepid of the six Coogan kids, and went off to Gaza to work with Palestinians with learning disabilities and eventually did the same thing in Calcutta.

He nearly died after catching hepatitis. When I met him and his future wife at the airport, he was emaciated and in a wheelchair. He made a full recovery, but it still upsets me when I think of my little brother like that.

Generally speaking, my family have a philanthropic attitude to the world. I feel guilty sometimes that I have never rolled my sleeves up, but I content myself that while they are doing all the good stuff, I am earning money doing what I like and I help them out when I can. A great example of the public and private sector coming together for the common good.

When we were young, however, I wasn't envious of my

friends' holidays: I loved the adventure of Ireland. The *clang clang* as the car drove slowly on to the ferry. Even now, when I occasionally drive on to a ferry going over to Ireland, I still feel a childish fizz of excitement. The other smell that evokes happy childhood memories for me – rather counter-intuitively in this case – is the combination of sea, salt, beer, fags, puke and urine on a ferry. It reminds me of the one we used to get from Liverpool to Dublin, with the promise of two or three weeks' holiday to come. There might no longer be the stench of fags, but the smell is still pretty foul and it triggers a really strong Proustian response.

We were allowed one fib as kids. It was free to travel on the ferry over to Ireland if you were under seven, so us younger ones had to be prepared to lie. I used to sit in the back of the car feeling slightly sick, because lying was normally forbidden. But it was also exciting to lie, especially with permission.

Once we were on the ferry to Dublin, I used to sit there relishing the fact that I had the holiday stretching ahead of me. Heading back to Liverpool at the end of those weeks, I'd be overwhelmed with sadness. It's odd how bereft I felt given that all we did was run around with the sticks we had sharpened or go to a rain-soaked beach.

Dad would often join us in Ireland later because he was off on some training course to keep himself updated with new technology. Sometimes, when it was raining, I'd fold down the seats in his Volvo estate, pretend it was an exclusive two-seater sports car and go on an imaginary adventure. I'd be sitting in a respectable car in front of a cottage in the middle of *Ryan's Daughter* countryside, pretending to be James Bond.

I might ask Kevin to come and sit in the passenger seat and, without warning, leap out of the car with my toy gun and shoot an imaginary villain. My fantasies were like very bad films: I'd always be escaping from or chasing baddies.

I remember being in the kids' pool at the swimming baths and instead of swimming or splashing around with my brothers,

I would imagine I was wading through a car park after an apocalyptic flood. I'd shout at my brothers in an American accent, 'Follow me! This way!' – as if I was the only one who could save them.

Once, in 1971, a Scottish IBM colleague of my dad's lent us his caravan for a holiday on the bonnie, bonnie banks of Loch Lomond. When we arrived at his house in Glasgow, he kindly offered to tow it to the campsite. There, hooked to the towbar of his Triumph Herald, was the smallest caravan in the world. And there were eight of us.

Fortunately, there was a half-tent that could be attached to the side of the caravan and it was here that the three oldest, Clare, Martin and David, slept. They woke up crying because the ground was soaking wet, and had to move into the caravan with the rest of us. There wasn't an inch of space to be found without a slumbering body.

One afternoon, I sat in a canoe, unable to swim, the black water lapping at my sides, convinced the lake was bottomless. If I fell in I might well die. I needed my imagination to distract me. While my family trudged around the edges of the lake, my brother Brendan in a child carrier on Dad's back, I escaped to my fantasy world. I ran up and down the hills, thinking, 'I'm driving a Jeep!'

I had nothing at all to play with, not even a fake steering wheel, but I didn't care. It was enough to amuse me.

CHAPTER 17

In the summer of 1970, when my mum's younger brother Bernard got married, my three cousins came over from Ireland for the wedding. They were all attractive teenage girls.

I was not yet five, but I sat there slack-jawed. 'Wow! One, two, three, all in a row.'

A few summers later, when I was seven, I was in Ireland and my female cousins were now in their late teens and early twenties. They were all beautiful. They were goddesses. I watched as Marion, who was nineteen, got dressed for a night on the town. She put on these huge flared trousers, which she explained were culottes. I sat there, mesmerised. She was so glamorous that she was almost an alien creature.

I wrote a card, drew a heart on it and gave it to one of the sisters. My brothers found it and mocked me till I cried with humiliation.

We wanted to go to Ireland every summer. Not only because of the girl cousins growing impossibly beautiful, but also because it was a change from Middleton.

Mum used to say, 'Please God, we can afford to go to Ireland. But, if we can't, we'll stay in England and have lots of days out.'

I would hold her to her promise and she would honour it. I recently looked on Google Earth at all the places she used to take us. They look so small now, but they seemed huge then. Rivington Pike. Queen's Park in Heywood, a cheap day out in a local municipal park. Hollingworth Lake, a reservoir on the other side of Rochdale where I learned to swim.

We went to the reservoir with a picnic, often with Mum's

best friend, Mrs Knibb, who lived down the road and had six kids and the same Morris Minor Traveller as us. Mrs Knibb didn't have a phone, so I was forever carrying messages between her and my mum. Like Leo Colston in *The Go-Between*, but without the scandal.

Mike Knibb, who was the same age as Brendan, was very interested in electronics. He would often come round to our house and sit with Dad at the kitchen table, chatting and fiddling with electronic equipment. Dad was part of the Meccano generation who had grown up learning to take things apart and put them back together again; that was just what boys did.

I think Dad hoped that one of his five sons might show an interest in his job, and he was slightly disappointed when we didn't. Martin understands electronics to an extent, but he's not very interested in it. So Mike Knibb became, for a while, the son Dad never had. And Mr Knibb had died, so Dad in turn filled a gap.

When I was in my twenties, I put some shelves up in my London flat. They were straight and attached properly to the wall.

Dad came to visit and said, 'Who put those shelves up?'

I said, 'I did.'

Dad was absolutely delighted. 'Have you seen these shelves, Kath? Stephen put them up.'

I'd been on television for a while at that point, and he was impressed with that, but the shelves overshadowed any comedy achievement. Dad thought there was some of his DNA in me somewhere.

Anyway, on these summer-holiday days out, my younger brother Kevin would sit around reading or run off exploring with his best friend, Timmy Knibb. Kevin's adventurous spirit was evident even then. He was very *Lord of the Flies* while I, nearly always sitting in my long trousers and shoes, drinking tea and listening to my mum and Mrs Knibb gossip, was salad days without the salad.

I didn't want to read or explore. Sometimes I might bring a friend and we'd go for a swim, but I liked sitting there on my own, listening to adult conversation.

★   ★   ★

As much as I liked to observe, I wasn't a lazy kid. I learned from my dad how to make do. He once brought home discarded phones that he'd found in a skip outside a telephone exchange and wired them up so we could use them as home-made walkie talkies. In turn, I learned how to build my own bikes. I would save £3 or £4 for a new wheel, using my paper-round money and maybe some cash from Mum. While I was saving, I'd find an old, buckled wheel and straighten it with a spoke key and a hammer. It wouldn't be perfect, but you could ride it. When I finally bought the new wheel, its symmetrical smoothness was a luxury.

I grew reasonably adept at building and mending bikes, and my friends would bring theirs round for me to tinker with. We'd strip down a racer frame, prime it, paint it in hot-rod colours and finish it off with wide handlebars. The satisfaction when the bike was ready was palpable; you could tear off on this thing made out of a box of bits. It almost felt as though you were flying.

In June 1977, in my last year at primary school, I was knocked off my bike, suffered severe concussion and lost my memory for about six months. I remember waking up in a bed and seeing a high ceiling above me. I looked around the room and realised it was a hospital ward. I brought up my hands, which were cut, and felt my face, which was covered in wounds and scabs.

I lay there thinking, 'What happened to me? Have I been knocked down by a car? That's generally what happens to kids my age when they end up in hospital with cuts and bruises.'

I had to crawl to the toilet because my body was so badly battered.

When my mum came in with the doctors, I asked what had happened to me. No one knew. And I couldn't remember.

I asked Mum if I had passed the 11-plus.

'Yes,' she said. 'Don't you remember, we bought you a camera because you'd passed.'

A camera? I had no idea.

Some eyewitnesses came forward and said that I'd been riding my bike with my arms folded, which I could do very well. A lad had swung his bike out, doubtless thinking I looked too cocky, and caught the handlebars. I had flashbacks of tarmac rushing towards my head very quickly for a while afterwards.

Martin went out looking for the boy, and Mum was worried he would kill him if he ever found him. It was often useful having a big brother. If I was picked on, he would pick on them.

I stayed in Booth Hall Hospital – the same one I'd been in as a very young child with meningitis, now shut down – for a week. I was fascinated that children on the ward were able to watch *Play School* at 6 a.m. When I enquired how this was possible, I was told about something called a video recorder. At the time it cost an exorbitant £1,000, just under a quarter of my dad's annual salary. In those days the NHS had money to spend on a video recorder . . .

It was interesting to watch the comings and goings and I liked the attention. At least I forgot, temporarily, about the terrifying prospect of Cardinal Langley, the secondary school I was due to start at.

My accident didn't put me off cycling. We would still go to the woodland opposite the house and get lost on our bikes, or cycle to each other's houses and listen to music.

We didn't have Choppers. They were for kids whose parents had Ford Cortinas and thought catalogues were aspirational. I remember looking in a catalogue and thinking, 'My life will be complete if I can have these kung fu pyjamas.' They were orange nylon with brown braiding, and a brown belt to tie around the waist. I stared at the catalogue for a long time. 'Wow, the kid in the pyjamas looks so happy. If I had cool pyjamas like that, I know I wouldn't want for anything else.'

In the pre-Internet era, catalogues allowed a glimpse of a possible lifestyle and women in underwear. Some of the bras might be slightly see-through, so there was a good chance of seeing a nipple. The Grattan catalogue was particularly reliable for nipples and it was easy enough to turn to the camping pages if anyone walked in the room.

★   ★   ★

We talk about Detroit as this post-industrialist landscape now, but that's what the north of England was like when I was growing up. Cotton had once been king and Manchester had been at the forefront of the Industrial Revolution, boasting over 100 mills at its mid-1850s peak. By the time I was born, the cotton industry had long since vanished but the landscape was still littered with these ghostly cathedrals. Decades before they were redeveloped, those neglected mills – Times Mill, Warwick Mill – became our playground.

Brendan, Ged and I used to climb up a drainpipe and sneak in through a broken window. The huge spaces inside were dusty and dark and littered with shattered glass. I doubt we even gave a second thought to what the buildings had once been. We didn't think of them as huge red-brick monuments to industry any more than we thought about the danger of breaking in.

We walked across steel cross-beams, our arms stretched out wide, our breath held, not daring to look at the 100-foot drop below. Sometimes our youthful fearlessness would recede and we had to shimmy across the beams on our bums. We were unbelievably stupid, in retrospect.

It was the kind of adventurousness that led to public information films warning children of the perils of unsupervised outdoor activity. A message rendered obsolete now that most children are glued to their iPads. That's progress.

We knew that what we were doing could get us into trouble, so we never told our parents what we were up to and they never found out. On Saturdays and Sundays and during the holidays we were free to go out all day, with very few questions asked. We would stay out on our bikes till it was dark, riding for miles and miles.

If I lost track of the time and came home very late – with no mobile to ring ahead – Mum would be worried out of her mind and Dad would be furious.

'Why have you been out so late? It's ten thirty, it's dark and Mum has been worried sick.'

Dad never drank, so his anger wasn't fuelled by alcohol, but his temper was nonetheless frightening. Sometimes he would threaten to give me a 'thick ear' by clouting me with the flat of his big, leathery hand. When he did, my ear would ring for at least twenty minutes.

But I was never quite sure of the consequences of staying out late because discipline wasn't consistent. Sometimes I'd come home to find Dad working on the car and I could breathe a sigh of relief. If he was distracted then I probably wouldn't get a thick ear.

As I grew older, so my father became more moderate and less tyrannical. As we all grew older and developed our own personalities, the authoritarian side of his nature visibly receded. Martin and I were even able to mock his awful jokes openly, without fear, especially if our mother was laughing at him at the same time.

★　★　★

In my family, discussions about feelings were seen as a bit of an indulgence, a kind of non-essential luxury. As far as they were concerned, getting through life meant putting food on the table and paying the bills. We shared affection with each other by gentle mockery and well-aimed retorts around the dining-room table.

On occasion we have been forced to have a conversation about feelings. Such as the first time I was involved in a 'scandal' – I slept with someone in the wake of winning the Perrier Comedy Award in Edinburgh in 1992 and the tabloids thought it worthy of column inches – and I went home to explain myself.

I have become inured to people discussing my private life over the years, but the first time it happens it's a big shock. You feel naked and vulnerable.

'I'm sorry, Dad,' I said. 'I've embarrassed the family.'

He hugged me. There was a touching moment of awkward-ness because Dad is from the handshake generation and has had to learn the modern act of hugging.

'You don't need to apologise.' He looked at me. 'None of us is perfect.'

It showed his generosity of spirit.

★   ★   ★

If Dad was occasionally like a Victorian father, then Mum was the pragmatist. Mum wasn't touchy-feely or indulgent, nor did she spoil us – I'm not sure it's possible to spoil six kids – but she was fair. We could talk to her about things, but when we misbehaved all she had to say was 'I'll tell your dad' and we'd beg her not to. We'd immediately get in line. Dad was a discip-linarian and none of us wanted to feel his wrath – though one of my earliest memories is of him grabbing hold of me, growling and tickling me with his whiskers.

Mum has always been more progressive than Dad.

After I'd left home, she met James Anderton at some local event. Anderton was the homophobic former chief constable of Greater Manchester who infamously said that everywhere he went he saw 'evidence of people swirling in the cesspool of their own making'. He also claimed to have heard the voice of God.

When he leaned across and asked Mum about her children, she mentioned me. He asked what I did.

She handed him a photo she had in her bag of me dressed as Pauline Calf. 'This is him.'

He gave her a thousand-yard stare.

Mum has a great sense of humour. She enjoyed doing this and relished telling everyone about it afterwards.

She is, unexpectedly for a woman of her generation, passionate about football. I cherish that about her. She loved Roy Keane when he was at Manchester United and she got cross when people criticised him for being violent. She thought he was picked on for being himself; he might occasionally hit someone, but he was the real deal. She doesn't like people who are flash and super-slick. Keane was a bit more earthy.

She loved glamorous stars like Veronica Lake and Elizabeth Taylor and, in the years before television and before we were born, she often went to the cinema with her friends. Dad was less interested because there was nothing technical or factual involved.

Mum and Dad were different in many ways, and yet there was tenderness in their relationship. When I was a child, Dad used to pick her up, give her a squeeze and spin her round the kitchen. They would bicker too, of course. I would hear them arguing when I was upstairs in my bedroom. And, very occasionally, there was a full-blown row.

My dad was – and still is – a charmer. He still cuts quite a dashing figure. When he met Judi Dench, he genuflected and kissed her hand. His is an old-school charm that might be considered inappropriate in these more modern times, but he's not lascivious. He's courteous, definitely flirtatious and prone to flattery.

He cut a very striking figure, especially when he was younger

SCHOOL REPORT.   ST. THOMAS MORE SCHOOL.   DATE: MARCH
                                                                      ~~JULY~~

CHILD'S NAME *COOBAN STEPHEN* .... CLASS ... *2.T.F.* ....

ENGLISH ... *A good result. Stephen does good*

77% *work, but is a very slow worker.*

Grammar work very good.

MATHEMATICS ... *Tables very good. Problems present*

79% *some difficulty. Can do good work.*

....

GRADING IN AGE GROUP ON TEST RESULTS

N.B. | *C+* |

C = Average child comprising approximately 40% of age group

              A   B   C   C-   Very weak

             10%   20%   40%   20%   10%

GENERAL COMMENT *Stephen is a very keen worker.*
He can be easily distracted though
which slows down his work.

CLASS TEACHER   HEAD TEACHER. *G. L. Farrell*
Am Capani.

Above: My primary school
report containing the title of
this book.

Left: In a photo booth aged
seventeen, embracing the
eighties.

Top: Me and Dad bonding in a Morgan three-wheeler.

Above: My YHA card from 1981.

Above: My drama class at Manchester Poly. I'm on the far right, in the row second from the back.

Professional Name
STEPHEN COOGAN
Equity Details
Yes
Height
5' 10"
Eyes
Brown
Extra Details

Professional Experience
Writing and performing on BBC
Radio Manchester's 'The Buzz'
Performing on Phil Sayer's Special
BBC Radio Manchester.
T.V. and radio voice over's
Soldier in 'Oedipus' at Royal Exchange theatre.
Parts Played Include
Nicky – The Vortex
Tusenbach – Three Sisters
Hugh – Joking Apart
The Son – Six Character's in Search of an Author
Skills
Fencing – 1st Foil, 1st Sabre
Piano
Vocal mimicry

Left: My first CV.

Around the time of *First Exposure*, my first TV experience.

Awkwardly wearing my first suit to my sister Clare's wedding in 1983.

Above: Mike Taylor and me in 1985, in an amateur dramatic production of *Song of Norway*.
I played Henrik Ibsen and Mike was a dancer.

Opposite: A black eye from
falling off a sledge in 1991.

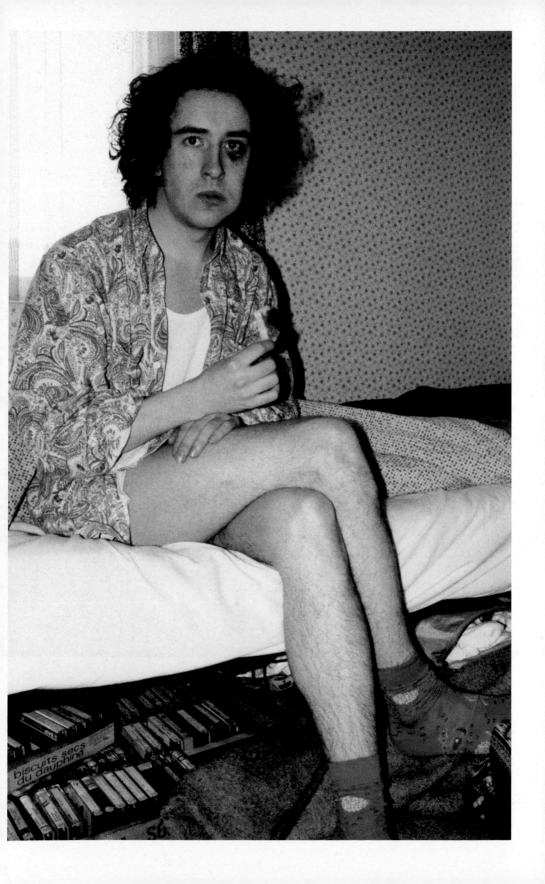

Me, Martin Murray and Alan Francis in 1991.

and his beard and hair were both midnight black. Kids at school used to say he looked like the devil, and he can't have been offended because he went to a couple of fancy dress parties as Beelzebub.

I remember once, on the way back from church, with a car full of kids in the back and my mum beside him in the front, Dad wound down the window of the Morris Minor Traveller, leaned out and wolf-whistled at the primary school teacher, who was walking in the opposite direction.

He said, in a way that Alan Partridge would have approved of, 'Where did you get those pins?'

The teacher laughed and my mum vaguely admonished him by saying, 'Tony, don't!'

In his head he was probably thinking he was the Laughing Cavalier and had momentarily forgotten that his car was crammed with his wife and six kids.

Despite Dad's occasionally provocative behaviour, he and my mother have mostly had a calm, loving relationship. They hardly ever had a drink and Dad never went to the pub. They had fewer parties as more children arrived, but often had friends round. There was lots of laughter. Life was about restrained enjoyment. Sex was essentially about making babies; we shouldn't get too distracted by the fact that it's enjoyable as well. And yet Dad was romantic. He was always buying my mum anniversary cards, chocolate and flowers. On more than one occasion I remember him buying what must have been the most prestigious cards that John Menzies (a now defunct newsagent and stationery outlet) had to offer – usually padded and covered in satin with a watercolour of a slender woman in floaty chiffon.

CHAPTER 18

My parents moved into the large family house in Middleton in December 1963, two weeks after John F. Kennedy was shot.

They still live in the same house. The drinking tap I reach to get a glass of water now is the same tap I had to stand on a chair to reach some forty years ago. The spare bedroom I sleep in when I visit now is the one in which I was born.

Barney the dog, who died on Good Friday in 1978, is still buried in the front garden. I wanted to help Dad bury him, but he insisted on doing it alone. I watched through the bedroom window as he wrapped Barney in canvas and placed him in a deep hole in the garden.

The house is largely unchanged. It still feels like a sanctuary, a reassuring constant in a turbulent, shifting world.

Middleton is an old town, a little isle of suburbia where people mowed their lawns and washed their cars on a Sunday when I was growing up. Kids rode their bikes round the streets from dawn till dusk, and everyone we knew lived half a mile away. Dad had a car and there was a phone in the house, both of which were still relatively unusual in the 1960s.

In the early 1950s, people were always popping into my grandad's house to make calls and eventually he put a bucket under the phone because it was an expensive business. My dad inherited the same generosity coupled with thriftiness; he used to say the phone was only for exchanging information, not for gossiping. He considered extended conversations a waste of money.

Dad would chat to anyone who would even half listen to him. He can talk endlessly about airships, trams, canals, architecture and anything to do with science and engineering. We used to laugh at him when he said that electric cars were the future.

Everyone said Mum and Dad were foolish to move from an ordinary detached house to a bigger – but not grand – house with a reasonable back garden and its own drive. But Dad was quite well paid and he often did overtime. He wasn't interested in being promoted at work and moving to London because he thought it would unsettle the family. Putting the family first meant that he remained a basic engineer.

The house cost £2,500 – just over £44,000 in today's money, which seems ridiculously good value. It was built in 1902 and back then banks wouldn't give mortgages on properties that were more than fifty years old; old houses would inevitably fall down, whereas new houses would last. The slums were cleared away. It was symptomatic of how excited everyone was about the post-war world in which everything was going to be bright, new and modern.

★   ★   ★

I was the first to be born in the house, on 14 October 1965. Mum had an early miscarriage before she had me. If she hadn't miscarried, I might never have been born. I'm the fourth of six: Clare, Martin, David, me, Kevin and Brendan. I was the oldest of the 'three little ones'. As I've said, Kevin was an adventurer who read books; I was a chatterbox who watched telly. He was often barefoot; I didn't like getting dirt on my trousers.

Being one of six seemed normal to me. My friend Brendan Tierney was one of eight, and the Cliffs, another local family, had thirteen kids.

Ours was a very male house. Clare was the oldest and most sensible sibling. She was head girl at her convent grammar school. She's seven years older than me and has always been a kind of surrogate mother to me. She was the touchy-feely one.

If I was in trouble with Mum or Dad and didn't know why, I would go straight to Clare, often in tears.

She would sit me down and say, 'What's wrong, Stephen? Mum and Dad might get annoyed, but they do love you. And I love you.'

Clare was demonstrative, Mum and Dad less so. Clare has told me since that I was like a doll for her. I was definitely malleable and a bit soft.

Mum and Dad were committed Catholics. My dad is a non-elitist Catholic who is now a minister of the Eucharist. My brother Kevin and I went to a local public speaking event when I was about seventeen and I told Dad that the chairman from the Catenians was going to ask him to join. The Catenian Association was founded in Manchester in 1908 and has around 10,000 lay members, most of whom are wealthy businessmen. Rightly or wrongly, it has a reputation for having an air of elitism.

Dad chose to decline the invitation in a polite manner, choosing to avoid any derogatories.

He would conspicuously avoid swearing: 'balderdash' replaced 'bollocks'. Fiddlesticks = bullshit. Upstart = dick. Sling yer hook = fuck off. Bamboozled = fucked over.

I only heard him say 'shit' twice as a child. Once when he was gingerly removing a ceramic tile that he hoped to maintain in one piece. He did so successfully, only to notice a hairline crack just before it broke into two in his hands.

The second time was when he cracked the front indicator lens of his newly acquired Volvo. It would cost £17.50 to replace and he didn't have that kind of money to throw around.

A member of the parish, who lived locally and had a lot of children, was a member of Opus Dei. My mum and dad used to whisper about it. Being a member of an elitist, misogynistic, essentially right-wing Catholic institution didn't sit well with us. It was sinister and weird. And, frankly, a bit nutty. Why would anyone choose to hold Latin-only Masses? We knew that kind of extremism could only give our more liberal Catholicism a bad name and we distanced ourselves from it.

I went to about three open-air ecumenical services that were held outside the local United Reformed church, in the woods across the road. The local Reformed church, Methodist church and Catholic church would come together for Mass. My dad was very keen on ecumenical services as a way of showing that we might be from different churches, but we're all friends together.

My dad is very egalitarian. He made a point of opting out of the private health care that came with his job at IBM. He didn't think that health care should have anything to do with money – and he's right.

In Matthew 6:1, Jesus says: 'Be careful not to do your acts of righteousness before men, to be seen by them. If you do, you will have no reward from your Father in heaven.'

Plenty of people in the Catholic Church pay no attention to the Sermon on the Mount. They talk it, but they don't live it. My parents, like Philomena Lee, mostly live it.

I wanted to dignify my parents' simple faith with *Philomena*. But the Catholic faith is more complicated for me. For a long time I was drawn to the intellectual, left-wing Catholicism favoured by Clare. But when I reached my teens I started to question my faith. I would love to believe in God, but I can't. I'm not being a nihilist. I just believe we are all mortal. There is no afterlife.

One of my favourite passages in the Bible is from Genesis 3:19: 'For you are dust, And to dust you shall return.'

Being an atheist is OK: I can still appreciate churches.

As a child, however, it didn't occur to me to question the existence of God.

All I thought was that it took a bloody long time to say prayers by our beds each night: 'Bless Mummy, Daddy, Clare, Martin, David, Kevin, Brendan, my cousins and all my friends. Bless all the people who are sick and dying, all the people who are at war, especially in Vietnam, Cyprus and Northern Ireland . . .'

Once I prayed for an Aston Martin at church.

'Dear God, when I grow up, I promise I'll be really good to people and I'll try to live a good life, but please, please, in thirty years' time can I afford to buy an Aston Martin?'

My mum cites that as the existence of God, because I have a couple of classics now.

I disagree. God exacts a tsunami on the innocent and gives me two Aston Martins. As divine justice goes, it strikes me as a bit unfair.

★   ★   ★

Years later, in 1990, Tony Wilson asked me if I was still Catholic.

'Yes,' I said. 'In the Latin American Marxist-affiliated sense.'

Tony looked at me and said, 'So am I.'

Although I no longer believe in God, I will always carry elements of my Catholicism with me. I like the idea of people trying to be decent to each other. I must admit that on some level it's intellectual posturing because I can be cantankerous, irritable and juvenile. But on a bigger scale, I want to be decent. To be kind, to show compassion.

★   ★   ★

I sometimes miss going to church on a Sunday morning and hearing my dad read at Mass. He would go up to the altar in his suit and do two readings before the priest read the Gospel. The readings were done by my father and two or three other pillars of the parish. Good family men leading diligent lives.

I certainly miss that feeling of Mass ending, when I felt like I'd done my bit for the day. We would go across the road, buy the papers and go home for Sunday lunch. There was a proper structure to my life, the kind that children need to feel secure. Going to church was a ritual that was not only part of a kind of suburban respectability, but also an indelible part of our family life: we all went to church on a Sunday. I would get up every Sunday and do my best to get to 11 a.m. Mass because going to Mass at 6.30 p.m. had the potential to ruin the entire day. I might not have looked forward to Mass, but equally it didn't occur to me to question my attendance. It was simply the done thing in our parish.

In 1976, when I was ten, nearly eleven, I started training to be an altar boy with my two primary-school friends, Gerard McBreen, known to all as 'Ged', and Brendan Tierney. I was an altar boy until I was sixteen and, for a brief period, I trained young altar boys how to serve. I took my duty pretty seriously, telling them off for wearing trainers instead of regulation black shoes. Everyone knew who I was. I had an identity in the parish as one of the Coogan kids.

John Richmond, the fashion designer, used to attend my church. He turned up every Sunday looking like David Bowie, accompanied by his mum and dad. He was androgynous, with orange hair, a pierced ear, a leather jacket, red winkle-pickers and studiously sucked-in cheeks. My brother Martin was the same: he turned up at church in a bright red leather biker jacket, crimped hair and mascara.

It was as if he was saying, 'I might have to go to church on a Sunday, but I'm an anarchist for the other six days of the week.'

Martin and John used to go to youth Mass together. Although the organ was replaced by an electric guitar and a synthesiser and the hymns were more up-tempo, it probably wasn't nearly rebellious enough for them. And yet they both went.

I was at the end of my time as an altar boy when Jerry Kidd, the singer in an indie band called Red Guitars, got married in the church. They did a John Peel session and had a minor hit with a song called 'Good Technology'. I've still got a photo somewhere of me in my cassock standing next to Jerry.

A few years later, in 1984, Red Guitars supported The Smiths at the Free Trade Hall in Manchester. The Smiths were sublime onstage. So different, in my mind, from what had come before. Very un-American, very dour, bleak and northern but funny at the same time. You can almost hear the overcast Manchester skies in their music.

I was invited backstage and was stupidly excited at the prospect of meeting Morrissey, who said hello and bought me a drink. I remember being very aware that I was present at a special time that would be talked about in the years to come.

★   ★   ★

I had a one-sided view of religion as I was growing up. Protestantism, as far I was concerned, existed because King Henry VIII wanted to bed as many women as he could. I knew nothing about Martin Luther, the German friar and Catholic priest whose writings inspired the Protestant Reformation. I knew nothing about his protests in Germany in the 1500s. He railed against the idea that you could pay your way into heaven, believing salvation to be a free gift of God's grace.

Because I knew so little, I could never work out why anyone would want to be a Protestant. The king who had separated the Church of England from the Catholic Church was a sexually voracious bloke who cut off his lovers' heads and destroyed all the monasteries. He was a horrible, horrible man. Why would you choose to be in his Church?

I was naive enough to be convinced that one day we'd all be Catholic again. Nor did my early education exactly promote Protestants. We learned about the Catholics being persecuted, about priest holes in York where priests would have to hide because otherwise they'd be put to death. As far as I was concerned, it was only Catholics who were persecuted. I knew nothing about how it had flipped the other way at various times in history, at least not until I reached secondary school. I only learned about the Spanish Inquisition from Monty Python.

On my way to St Thomas More RC Primary School in Middleton, I used to walk past the Protestant school and think they were all a little bit evil. They worshipped a fat king with gout, and we deified the man who opposed him. *A Man for All Seasons*, the 1966 British film based on Robert Bolt's play of the same name, was all about Thomas More standing up to Henry VIII. My parents loved it, and in 1995 the Vatican listed it among the greatest religious movies of all time, which tells you all you need to know.

Of course I didn't know about Thomas More's pursuit and burning of those who had committed the heretical act of translating the Bible into English.

I have become, over the years, slightly obsessed with Thomas More. There's a fascinating book by his adopted daughter, Margaret More Roper. Thomas More could not support Henry VIII's divorce, or the king's decision to separate from Rome, and so he was sent to the Tower of London and beheaded. Roper managed to bribe someone to hand over her father's head and she kept it, pickled, till her death. With her brother William she wrote Thomas More's first memoir and in doing so became one of the first women of literature.

When I was ten, I went on a school trip to London to see Thomas More's cell in the Tower of London. I was interested in the history, but it was my first trip to London and that probably made more of an impression. It was as though the world had suddenly, briefly, switched from black and white to Technicolor.

I was catatonic with religious zeal. After all, I'd seen Rolls Royces, Ferraris and Porsches being driven around Trafalgar Square. Previously I'd only seen pictures of them in *The Ladybird Book of Motor Cars*.

★   ★   ★

There was a simplicity to life in the sixties and seventies that I miss. There was a sense of 'We've done it! We've got our home, our garden, our healthy family. We are not living on the bread-line. We survived the war and we're happy. We have a job for life.' I can see why some people are nostalgic for that last hurrah of a uniform equilibrium.

In those days there was a sense of a homogenous nation. Three TV channels aimed at the white middle and lower middle classes but nevertheless part of the fabric of the nation. Everyone, regardless of creed and culture, watched *Morecambe & Wise* at Christmas.

The notion of family values is sometimes hijacked by the Conservatives; but in a more general, apolitical way, those values should be about philanthropy, extended family and community. People move around so much these days that community and extended families have largely disappeared. We are more restless than our parents, we have more expectations. I'd hazard a guess that there was less unhappiness back then.

Our suburban existence was very pleasant. It was a kind of utopia. 'Pleasant Valley Sunday' by The Monkees reminds me of where I grew up, particularly the line about people in the street being able to hear the local rock group rehearsing their new song.

Although, as a small boy, I didn't quite realise that I lived in suburbia. As far as I was concerned, no one lived in the big cities that were full of smoke and traffic. Visualising people living there was beyond me. In fact, no one did live in the city centres: the centre of Manchester in the seventies was unrec-ognisable compared to its present-day hub of students and affluent young folk.

Manchester was just under half an hour away on the bus, but my only forays there were to visit Virgin Records and to buy cool music that wasn't in the charts. If you wanted to order non-chart music, you either bought it directly from Virgin in town or went to the local Boots.

Half of Middleton was an aspiring suburb and the other half council estate overspill. Both sets of grandparents lived in council houses. While we lived in Alkrington, a part of Middleton, my dad's parents were in nearby Blackley Hill and my maternal grandparents lived on a council estate in Langley, adjacent to Middleton. Langley overspill estate was part of the post-war building programme that, by the 1970s, had already soured.

Mum was affectionate about her parents, but she always felt sad, I think, that they had missed part of her childhood. My maternal grandparents' house was different from my parents'. There were tabloids everywhere, they both smoked and there was often a faint smell of beer on my grandad.

Langley council estate had Lake District-inspired names such as 'Windermere Drive' and 'Coniston Way', none of which remotely reflected the densely crowded urban living space.

Mum was forever defending Langley: 'The people are lovely. Salt of the earth.'

I would ask, slightly pushing my luck, why we didn't live there if it was so lovely.

She would say, 'Hmmmm?' as though she hadn't heard the question.

I slowly became very aware of living in a nice part of town. I realised Mum was generous about Langley because she was slightly self-conscious about being materially aspirant. I recently teased my mother by taking her to an upmarket eaterie and saying, 'It's nice here, no riff-raff.'

'WE are riff-raff,' she retorted.

CHAPTER 19

In September 1972, Mum walked into the bedroom with tears in her eyes.

'They've killed them all,' she said.

I asked her who had killed whom. She explained that eleven Israeli athletes had been killed by Arab gunmen at the Munich Olympics.

The same year Watergate was unfolding.

A peaceful civil rights demonstration through the streets of Londonderry ended with British soldiers shooting dead thirteen civilians. It wasn't until 2010 that David Cameron finally called the Bloody Sunday killings 'unjustified and unjustifiable'.

But more importantly, on 14 October that year, I became the first person in my school to invite girls to my birthday party. Until then, boys had invited boys and girls had invited girls. But on my seventh birthday, I decided to shake the system up. I felt risqué breaking ranks, and I didn't care if anyone thought I was a sissy for inviting girls.

I was young, but it felt like an important moment.

The presents started to pile up: a *Look-in* annual with a watercolour painting of Ed 'Stewpot' Stewart on the front; *Beano* and *Dandy* annuals; perhaps a comic about the Second World War, because it was still very much in the received consciousness. We were, for example, still playing war games in the playground. Those who were playing the Germans shouted 'Achtung! Schnell!' Those playing the English would say a little more tentatively, 'Who goes there?' And I'd do a rather too realistic impression of a gun: '*Duh-duh-duh-duh. Rat-a-tat-tat.*'

There was probably a football colouring-in book with the

faces of both Manchester United and City players to colour in. We supported United as a family and therefore City were the enemy; we punished their players by drawing lipstick, eyelashes and earrings on them. I'm not remotely interested in football, but I made Paul Calf a City fan in the early nineties because at that time they were by far the less successful team in Manchester. I wanted him to be cursed by supporting the local team that never won.

I wasn't generally expected to share my presents with my siblings. My brothers, especially David, made Second World War planes with Airfix kits (Dogfight Doubles were a cheap way of getting two planes for the price of one: Spitfire versus Messerschmitt, Mosquito versus Me 262) and dangled them from cotton tacked to the bedroom ceiling. Even today I can spot and name the silhouette of any fighter plane from that era in the sky.

We played pass the parcel, musical statues, musical chairs, and ate white bread sandwiches, Ritz crackers, crisps, jelly and trifle.

I liked being around girls, even at seven. I liked talking to them. I was too young to know how to flirt with them; they were just good company. Two of the girls I invited were super-smart and both ended up going to Oxford. I could tell they were unusually clever, even at primary school; I quite liked the fact that they were much brighter than me.

I also invited Brendan Tierney, who remains a close friend. The Tierneys were conservative, with a small 'c', and I had endless arguments with Brendan about politics and ideology. He was strong like an ox, but never struck me with a blow when we fought. I would hurl my fists at him and he would just grab me in a bear hug and squeeze me so hard that I couldn't move.

Mum and Dad gave us various quaint options on birthdays. We could have a party at the house or we could go to Blackpool and drive up and down the Golden Mile, looking at the Illuminations from the car. Staggering though it may seem now, it was exciting to see trams covered in light bulbs to look like a steam train or a rocket.

We didn't even get out of the car except to buy fish and chips. We were all crammed into the Morris Oxford Estate, no doubt illegally. It was like a slave ship.

Another option was the pictures. I thought sitting in silence in a darkened cinema was the most exciting thing in the world. There was a cinema in Middleton called the Fleapit. For a long time I thought that was its name; I didn't realise it was a generic term for cinemas with flea-infested velvet seats.

When Dad was young he used to go to the local cinema every Saturday morning to watch films like *Flash Gordon*. In the post-war years there were beautiful old cinemas on every street corner, but as I was growing up they were being demolished. Television was taking over.

Still, it was an occasional family treat for us to go to the cinema on a Saturday morning. Dad took me to see two Jacques Tati films – *Mon Oncle* and *Mr Hulot's Holiday* – at an art-house cinema in Hulme called the Aaben. He thought he'd take me to see some 'proper comedy' as I appeared to like it.

He loved science fiction, so he took us to an 11 a.m. screening of *2001: A Space Odyssey* years after it had come out; there was no other way of seeing it in the days before VHS players. I found it an odd, disturbing film. I didn't quite understand it, but Britain seemed smaller afterwards and I felt as though I'd been on a strange journey.

My dad was unusual in that he was religious *and* believed in science. He thought science would answer all our problems; as old-fashioned as he was about many issues, he generally considered progress a good thing.

He particularly liked Isaac Asimov and Arthur C. Clarke because they paid proper lip service to logic. George Lucas, on the other hand, was bollocks.

★   ★   ★

Most of all, though, I was obsessed with Bond films, where the sun shone and everyone looked beautiful. They were uniquely immersive. I'd step out of the cinema after watching gorgeous people on expensive speedboats in the Everglades in Florida into a slightly damp, overcast former cotton-mill town.

In 1974 Mum took me to see a James Bond double bill for my birthday. *On Her Majesty's Secret Service* starred George Lazenby and *Live and Let Die* was Roger Moore's first outing as 007. It was the kind of magical experience that stays with you long into adulthood. I still remember the blue-white light of the Swiss Alps flooding into the cinema during *On Her Majesty's Secret Service*, and John Barry's score filling the theatre.

The atmosphere was electric and yet somehow otherworldly.

I remember looking across at my mum and seeing that she was fast asleep. I was appalled.

I didn't care that Bond films embraced style over content. Everything about them was exotic. It was the first time I realised there was a world out there that was very different from Middleton. A world outside my own. One full of glamorous people with fast cars and stunning women. I didn't know any women of that age. People in their twenties were alien to me: everyone I knew was the same age as me, or one of my siblings, or my parents, who were in their late thirties when I was growing up. And my parents weren't exactly hip and happening.

Dad turned forty in 1975, so I remember him very clearly in his late thirties.

I remember coming back from church one Sunday and discussing Elvis's death.

'How old was he?' my dad asked.

'He was quite old,' I replied. 'He was forty-two.'

'Do you mind?' said Dad. *'I'm* forty-two.'

★   ★   ★

When Mum's youngest brother, Bernard, got married in 1970, the wedding was full of guys with big hair, beards, bell-bottom trousers and unbuttoned shirts with flappy collars, who looked like Mungo Jerry. Bernard, who is my godfather, dressed well. He worked for a shirt company and for a while we all got free ties. Big, fat, satin ties.

Everyone had big hair in 1970. Everyone, that is, except my dad. Even at the age of five, I was aware of my dad always being one step behind. He had a short back and sides when the whole world had long hair.

Only my dad and NASA ground control had short hair.

And a Polish boy at school called Marcus. Heartless as we were, we used to laugh at his short back and sides. We'd say, 'The war is over, Marcus.' He also wore drainpipes; we thought his dad must have been so cruel to make him wear narrow trousers. Didn't he get where it was at?

Of course, although when I started at school it was patch pocket trousers and fat knotted ties, by the time I was leaving everyone was wearing thin ties and drainpipes.

The most risqué thing Dad did was to grow a goatee beard.

He was cornered at a works do by a member of senior management.

'Tony, the beard . . .' someone said from IBM. 'What are you hiding?'

It wasn't, they explained, part of the company image. Perhaps, as an American company, they thought there was something slightly subversive about having a beard.

There was, ironically, always something vaguely cultish about IBM, which is manifest in a quote attributed to its founder: 'There are two kinds of people in the world, IBMers and everyone else.'

With so many hippies around, Dad's beard may have been seen as a threat to the very fabric of society, but he didn't shave it off. He had, thank goodness, a certain polite defiance and a measured individualism. He loved the 'white heat of technology' but didn't want to become a robot. He wanted us to be morally upstanding and respectable without fitting in.

He would always say to us, 'What's wrong with you, don't you want to be different?'

No. We wanted to fit in. We certainly didn't want to be different if it meant driving around in a knackered old Morris Oxford Estate. All my mates' dads had brand-new Ford Cortinas in primary colours, Choppers, colour TVs and central heating.

Towards the end of his time as a computer engineer, Dad carried on wearing a suit even though the younger engineers, the Steve Jobs generation, were turning up to work in more casual clothes. And he always kept his tools in a nice attaché case.

He eventually left IBM and went to work for a rival company that maintained IBM equipment. He knew his role was obsolete when he went to mend a broken printer and someone helped him download a program that diagnosed the problem and fixed it remotely. While the computer was fixing itself, he just sat in a chair and waited, his attaché case unopened.

★   ★   ★

I can admire his style now, but I was constantly embarrassed by my dad when I was growing up. I thought I knew about fashion. Dad and kids like Marcus had *no* idea. It was all about having your hair combed over your ears, bell-bottom trousers, spearpoint collars and penny round collars.

At my first communion in 1973, I wore a white nylon shirt with a penny round collar. I must have been pretty trendy for an eight-year-old. This was the era of elasticated snake or 's' belts, which had an elongated 's' as a buckle, and we never seemed to be out of nylon-rich skinny polo necks.

By the time I was ten, however, I was wearing a dark brown cheesecloth shirt with a white tie and I thought I looked like Al Capone.

Mum kept, rather randomly, a drawer full of old pairs of jeans. In the mid-seventies, my brother Martin would choose a pair, unpick the stitching and add four triangular denim pieces. The drainpipe jeans were transformed into bell bottoms.

Meanwhile, I became increasingly aware of Dad being a good decade out of fashion. He had a fifties suit in the sixties, and a sixties suit in the seventies. The suit he wore until 1974 was from about 1965. He was still wearing a suit that he'd bought *ten* years before. To me, that was a lifetime ago. The suit was prehistoric.

Then one day he went to Marks & Spencer and bought a flared suit. It blew our minds that he had finally bought a suit that looked good. It was pale blue, had flared trousers, white lapels and two vents in the back. My brothers and I were properly impressed. Even better, Dad's hair was now nudging his collar. It was 1974 and he was finally with it.

★　★　★

The media representation of society often skews reality. The 1920s weren't, for 99 per cent of the population, about the Bloomsbury set. In the same way, the 1960s weren't, for most of Britain, about the sexual revolution and the emancipation of women.

The media has long been obsessed with the notion that the world changed in the sixties. The truth is that while London changed, we were simply playing catch-up in suburbia. My parents read about women's libbers, but they didn't actually know any. There might be hushed whispers of, 'She's a women's libber . . .' It was all a bit *Invasion of the Body Snatchers*: some of *them* are among *us*.

There was a local woman, Mrs Walker, who was formidable, a kind of Amazonian Margaret Thatcher. She was very tall, her husband slightly shorter. We heard these stories about how she *made* him iron his own shirts.

'The poor man,' I thought, 'he must have been enslaved by his wife.'

Hippies remained equally foreign to my parents. They didn't dismiss them as terrible people, but I think their general view was 'Peace and love is all very well, but taking your top off and running around in the mud is unacceptable behaviour.'

In lieu of not making a fuss or showing off, my parents felt it best to embrace modesty. As a family we were imbued with the ethos of keeping our heads down while taking care over our appearance and looking smart. Dad showed us how to polish our own shoes when they got scruffy in the hope that they would last as long as possible. The polish is still in the same drawer in the kitchen.

Once or twice a year we'd all go on a trip to Tommy Ball's shoe warehouse in Blackburn, which only closed down in 2008. It was a near-legendary day out for northerners of a certain class. All the shoes were tied together with a piece of string that was fed through a hole drilled in the side, and thrown over a wooden horse.

You could try on as many pairs as you liked, but you couldn't really practise walking in them. At best you could have a bit of a shuffle.

Not only was the promise of a new pair of shoes ridiculously exciting, it was also dressed up as 'a day out in Blackburn'. Wow.

My friends had dads who were not respectable and who wore their shirts open while driving slightly sporty cars. My parents weren't impressed by a local guy, a judo instructor, who wore a medallion *and* drove a very flashy Ford Capri S John Player Special. It was black with gold detailing. He looked like he was driving around in a giant packet of high-tar cigarettes.

Dad always took pride in his appearance, carefully curling his moustache at the ends before going to church. Even now, he styles his moustache and always wears a tie under his sweater.

But style was one thing, fashion something else entirely.

He was still dressed like Don Draper in *Mad Men* when everyone else, wearing brown flares and kipper ties, looked like they were in *The Sweeney*.

He used to spit out the words 'fashion and fad' as though simply saying them might bring an end to the world.

CHAPTER 20

My dad could be very black and white, with very few grey areas. It took me a long time to realise that you don't have to make your mind up definitively. You can float somewhere in the middle and shift from one opinion to another.

I'd watch a film with my dad and he'd make an instant moral judgement about a character: 'What that man did was totally wrong. He should never have killed that man. It was totally unnecessary.'

I used to think, 'Why are you spoiling the film? It's just a bloody film.'

Sometimes he would say that a television character should behave in a more Christian way and I would surreptitiously raise my eyes to heaven. Ultimately, however, I knew that my parents' eagerness for social justice was a positive force: they were determined to do the right thing and treat people properly.

My aunt Molly tells a story about my parents.

When she got pregnant out of wedlock in 1967 and decided to give her child up for adoption, Dad, who was thirty-three and had five children of his own at this point, asked if he should contact the father. Molly declined.

Towards the end of her pregnancy, she chose to go to a place in Wales run by nuns.

I asked her about this when I was making *Philomena*. She told me how cruel the nuns were. They tried to make the young women clean the floor on their hands and knees even while heavily pregnant and insisted all washing was done by hand despite the presence of a working twin-tub washing machine.

Because Aunt Molly was in her twenties, she had the fortitude to refuse. She found a mop to clean the floor and used the twin tubs to do her washing.

The nuns' lack of compassion continued when Molly gave birth. She was scolded for holding on to the bedstead as she pushed the baby out; a nun slapped her hand away and said, 'Pull yourself together.'

It was almost barbaric.

While Molly was still pregnant, Mum and Dad offered to adopt her child. They wanted to keep the baby in the family; he and Mum would be happy to say it was their child. Molly agreed, so, while she was in Wales, Mum and Dad were busy buying baby clothes, a pram, a cot, nappies, and so on.

As soon as the baby was born, Aunt Molly changed her mind. She rang her mother and said, 'She's beautiful. I want to keep her.'

Hilariously my nana said, 'You can't let Tony and Kath down. They've been looking forward to this.' As if a deal was a deal.

In tears my aunt rang my dad. All the preparations my parents had been making for the new arrival had been a charade.

'We knew you'd change your mind,' my dad said. 'We just didn't want anyone else to be let down.'

Molly said that as soon as she arrived home and stepped through the front door, all the things my parents had bought for baby Sarah were waiting there.

★ ★ ★

At some point when I was growing up, I said to Brendan Tierney, 'Someone says my cousin is a bastard.'

With great authority, Brendan said, 'She's only a bastard if your aunt had sex with someone. Did your aunt have sex with anyone before the baby?'

I replied, 'No. Definitely not. She would never have done anything like that.'

'In which case,' he said, 'your cousin is not a bastard.'

★   ★   ★

My mum and dad started fostering kids when my brother Brendan, the youngest, was five and Clare, the oldest, was sixteen and in the sixth form. The Catholic Children's Rescue Society was run by nuns, but the kids they placed in foster homes weren't necessarily religious.

The kids would stay in the guest bedroom for a few months, sometimes more. I was probably a bit resentful when they came and a bit sad when they left. My parents would always cut the adopted kids a lot of slack, but we got on with them and had days out together.

Every now and again a social worker would come round to check on the kids. Sometimes I was interviewed separately from my mum and dad, but I didn't mind; for the most part I enjoyed having new people around the house.

Sarah and Cheryl came in 1975. I fancied Sarah, who was eleven to my nine. I used to play 'murder in the dark' and use it as an excuse to grab hold of her and have a grope. Does that constitute an historic sex crime? I'll expect a knock on the door soon.

They went to a Protestant school around the corner, so I'd walk part of the way with them. They would turn one way and we'd turn another.

Sometimes the kids would be crying when they first arrived because they'd left their mum behind.

Two brothers, Kurt and Rolf, came the same year. Kurt was five and Rolf was just three. I remember sitting on the stairs with them when I came home from junior school at lunchtime. Kurt was crying because their mother had left them in this strange house and Rolf was comforting his older brother. I felt so sorry for them.

I did a half-hearted song-and-dance routine, pulling faces and generally being silly. I felt great satisfaction in giving them some momentary respite from their sadness.

Then came Edward and Michelle. Edward had a wonky foot, so he wore callipers. He was always falling over but would just pick himself up and carry on running.

John Madden came in 1976. He was a very affable chap.

Debbie and Andrew turned up as newborn babies and stayed until they started responding and interacting by smiling and waving. It must have been very hard for my mum. We heard his adoptive parents changed Andrew's name to Lee. What can you do?

Jerry came in 1978 when she was sixteen. She had a troublesome relationship with her father and stayed for a few years.

Tina came the same year, when she was fourteen. She'd been adopted but her new family were too strict; they wouldn't let her watch *Top of the Pops* because they considered it to be morally degenerate.

Both Jerry and Tina stayed in touch with us.

Lam Dien, a Vietnamese boat girl, came and stayed with us for about a year in 1983. She loved Benny Hill and the *Carry On* films, which always left me a bit nonplussed. I would sit there watching such dross because we didn't have a remote control and I couldn't be bothered to get up from the sofa. Meanwhile, Lam Dien would be drowning in tears of laughter.

One evening, when the TV channels had closed down, as they did in those days, and the brain-numbing monotone signal finally dragged me off the sofa, I switched off the TV and chatted to Lam Dien about fleeing Vietnam.

We stayed up for hours while she told me in quite graphic detail about her escape, those she had left behind, those who had been killed. She told me very matter-of-factly how gunmen had opened fire on the boat and how she had lain down as her friends returned fire at the government forces.

I finally understood why she needed to laugh.

Finally, Maria came in the early nineties, when she was eleven. She eventually asked if my parents would adopt her and she took our name; she's still very much part of the extended family.

★   ★   ★

The police once came round and thought our house was a community centre. There were kids everywhere and a pinball machine in the corner of the living room. Mr Eddisford, who lived next door, used to come over and play pinball without even saying hello. He would simply nod at us as he walked past the kitchen table.

Mr Eddisford was a butcher. One Christmas, in the days before organic food, he bought us a 48lb turkey which must have been pumped full of steroids. It was so unwieldy that we had to kick it into the oven and slam the door shut. It probably came out square-shaped.

On the other side of the house was Mrs Howarth, whose first name I never knew. She was very conservative, like a very old Margaret Thatcher. She'd been a magistrate and pretty much lived in the kitchen; despite being very well off, she only wanted to heat that one room. Her house was like Miss Haversham's in the sense that it was frozen in the 1930s.

Mum still sent us round there because Mrs Howarth was a 'lonely old lady' and Catholics always have to see past people's faults.

Tina was mixed race and Mrs Howarth used to say to me, 'Aren't your parents worried about having a brown girl in the house?'

I would reply, 'I love brown girls. In fact, when I grow up I think I'm going to marry a brown girl and have lots of caramel-coloured babies.'

Mrs Howarth would wince and clasp her hands to her chest as though she was almost physically in pain. 'If your mother could hear you now!'

She would discuss her Conservative politician relatives, telling the same stories time and again. 'My uncle ran for the local council . . .'

There was a large park in Blackley called Boggart Hole Clough which had a lake in it. The uncle's campaign was: 'Vote for Bennett and a lake in the Clough.'

My brother Martin would say, 'That's not very good. Loads of people are starving and can't pay their rent and he's basing his campaign around a lake in the Clough.'

Mrs Howarth would say, 'Oh no! Everyone loves the lake.'

Sometimes Brendan Tierney called for me and Mum would tell him I was next door, with Mrs Howarth. So he would knock on her door. He'd been round a dozen times before, but her memory was shot.

She'd peer at him and say, 'Do I know you?'

Brendan would ask if I was there and, when she didn't register, he'd sigh then say, 'Vote for Bennett and a lake in the Clough' as if it were a Cold War password.

She'd warm up immediately. 'Oh, *do* come in!'

★   ★   ★

Mr Stott the tramp would appear once a week for a cup of tea, a sandwich and yesterday's newspaper. He was invited into the hall, where he had a comfortable seat and a small table. We were always very polite to him as children, and he was a regular visitor from the late sixties right up to the early eighties, when he died.

He was never allowed in the living room, but he was relatively respectable and didn't drink. Sometimes he'd ask to borrow a razor and would disappear into the bathroom. He was an old-fashioned, Roald Dahl-style tramp in an overcoat, and sometimes wore a stained tie with his frayed shirt. His glasses rested on the end of his nose as he read the newspaper in the hallway.

He always called me 'lad'.

'Lad, can I have a word with your dad?'

Mr Stott might need money for the bus, but he'd never ask me because I was a child.

Once a drunk bloke came to the door asking for money and Mum said, 'I'll give you food if you're hungry, but I'm not giving you money, because I think you'll spend it on alcohol. I'll make you a sandwich if you like . . .'

My parents were generous and liberal, but they believed that the family was the most important thing. They believed a man should stay married to his wife. Divorce was wrong. As a boy, I was always slightly shocked if someone got divorced. It was almost as if they'd murdered someone. Marriage was a commitment you didn't just wander away from, it was for life.

My parents found themselves in a brave new world where the Pill had given women unprecedented sexual freedom and social mores were being challenged. As children we were, of course, aware of this encroaching modern world. But, like London, it was something of a mirage.

Progress was easier for my siblings and me to accept, but we were nonetheless the last generation to experience the pre-digital age. We grew up in a world that was always looking to the future.

My dad was rather adept at anticipating the development of technology. By the seventies, technology was already getting smaller and smaller and Dad made a series of predictions.

One day, he said, we would all have pocket phones. Cordless phones didn't even exist at this point.

Secondly, we would all listen to music on a small machine that didn't have any moving parts. We were baffled. A record went round and round. As did a tape. We asked where the music would come from and he said, 'Information.'

Information could be stored on a machine that didn't have any moving parts. It would be, as he called it, 'solid state'. But what happened when the machine was switched off? Wouldn't all the information be lost? That was the issue they were struggling with in the seventies. They knew that magnets could help retain information. And that's exactly what happens when the iPod is turned off: tiny magnets retain the information.

He predicted the eventual demise of the internal combustion engine. The electric car, he said, would rise like a phoenix.

Finally, he predicted the return of trams on the basis of their environmentally friendly nature. They had been removed from cities when cars were seen as the future. The car has been, for a long time, king. We all thought we'd be driving hover cars by the turn of the century. But we're not and, sure enough, the trams are back in Manchester and other British cities.

Of all his predictions, freight transport via airships and/or a renewed canal network have yet to materialise.

Still, he didn't do too badly in his predictions of the future.

For a boy growing up in the seventies, the notion of the future was incredibly exciting. When the Pulp song 'Disco 2000' was released in 1995, its lyrics were so evocative they reduced me to tears, in particular the line 'Won't it be strange when we're all fully grown'.

Throughout the seventies and early eighties, my friends and I were obsessed with the year 2000. We wondered what we'd be like and if we'd meet up. I remember thinking that I'd be thirty-four and my life would be over. I wouldn't be attractive to anyone. If I was lucky I might have a year or two left.

★   ★   ★

I have always been fascinated by how we mark the passing of time.

In a general sense, I think about Joni Mitchell being in her heyday in the early 1970s, just over four decades ago. It's quite a long time ago, but nonetheless it's a world that is recognisable. But forty years before *that* was the 1930s – a totally different universe.

More specifically, when I was seven, I stood in the playground on my own and imagined how far away the age of eleven was.

'One day,' I thought to myself, 'you're going to be in junior four and you're going to be eleven. It might seem a long way away now, but it will happen one day. And when you're eleven, you will think back and remember yourself standing here in the playground, aged seven, thinking how far away this moment is.'

When I was eleven and about to go to secondary school, I remembered being seven and thinking about being eleven. I used to do that all the time. I'd be cold and wet and happy in the middle of a field in Ireland in the summer holidays, thinking that in a few weeks I'd be in a warm classroom remembering playing in the fields. I'd feel sad and think I should have enjoyed being on holiday more because I wouldn't return to Ireland for another year. And then I'd remember that I wasn't yet in the classroom and I could enjoy the moment. I had to drag myself from the future and back into the present.

I remember 12.34 p.m. on 5 June 1978 very clearly.

Because it was the moment a self-congratulatory fat boy in the class said, 'Sir, it's 12.34 on the 5th of the 6th, '78.'

The form master said, 'So?'

'Well, sir, that means it's 1, 2, 3, 4, 5, 6, 7, 8.'

Funny what sticks in your mind.

During the 1980s I would think about how people in the 1990s would reflect on the previous decade. I was acutely aware that the present would one day become the past. I clearly had too much time on my hands and nowhere to channel my imagination. When I started to work, that sense of wonderment became part of my job, part of being a creative person.

There's a story we used in *I, Partridge* that is true.

On 31 December 1979, I went and sat alone on a bench under a tree in Alkrington Woods across the road from my parents' house.

I thought, 'This is the last day of the 1970s. No one will

remember this decade, nothing defines it. What a shame I'm not sitting here at the end of the 1960s instead.'

I was fourteen and it was the first decade I could remember vividly. It was a sort of orangey, mustardy-brown decade, but of course when you're still in it you can't define it.

I thought about it some more. 'There are going to be eights at the beginning of the date tomorrow, and I can't remember when there weren't sevens. I wonder what I will be doing in ten years' time.'

On 31 December 1989, I was at my parents' house and once more I went into the woods and sat on the same bench.

I was there on my own, thinking, 'It's ten years since I last sat on the bench and what have I been doing? Wow, I went to drama school and now I do voices for *Spitting Image* and I do comedy onstage and I earn a living.'

I suppose in my suburban universe it made me feel poetic and interesting. I thought I might be 'deep'.

Ten years after that I was in Devon getting drunk with Simon Pegg, celebrating the new millennium. We had a jolly night, but there was a nagging feeling that I should have been under the tree.

I went back to the bench in 2009 with my daughter, Clare, who was thirteen. I told her how I used to sit there on my own and contemplate the end of a decade; I was her age when I first did it.

'Hmmm, that's interesting,' she said, probably while texting someone. She knows how to humour me, in the same way I do with my dad.

Then I told Neil and Rob Gibbons about my bench experiences. 'It's hilarious,' they said. 'We can use it in the Partridge book in a slightly different way.'

I still think about the passing of time.

When I was about to go onstage in front of 2,000 people, I'd often feel strangely detached and disconnected. Slightly numb.

It's a strangely, lonely place to be.

I'd be standing in the wings, dressed as Pauline Calf, listening to the hubbub of the crowd and feeling petrified. You're playing for very high stakes, risking abject public failure.

All these questions would race through my head.

'How did I end up dressed like this?'

'Who are these people? Why have they come to see me?'

'What if it goes wrong?'

The curtain would rise and I'd walk out in my heels and start singing. It would be like a weird, abstract dream. It's almost as if the sound recedes.

My mouth would be moving, but my mind would wander and create a kind of soundtrack in my head.

I'd look into the audience and start wondering. 'Is she married to *him*?'

'She looks a bit grumpy. I wonder what's wrong with her.'

'*He* wanted to come, but *she* didn't. He's dragged her along and she's not impressed. She's trying not to laugh. Fuck her. I'm going to make her laugh.'

I was always more determined to win women over than men, possibly because I was worried about Paul Calf's ironic sexism. To win the approval of a humourless middle-aged woman was probably a sign of the gig having gone well.

'Why did they laugh so loudly at that, it's not very funny . . .'

'Why didn't they laugh more loudly at that, it's very funny . . .'

And then I'd think, 'What if I forget the words?'

And then suddenly I would be flying. The exhilaration you feel onstage when the show is going well is something else.

You feel very alive in those moments.

You know there's a killer line coming up and you relish delivering it. You fine-tune it till it's razor-sharp and the timing is perfect. Sometimes I'd play with the gag and strip it back. Try to get the audience to laugh with the minimum effort.

The Friday night audience was generally a joy as everyone wanted to be there; couples tended to come on Saturdays and that's when you got the stony-faced girlfriends.

Sometimes I would loathe these audiences in equal measure. They would reflect back my own intellectual schizophrenia: I'd be contemptuous of the philistinism of the lager boys for being mystified by some of Alan Partridge's subtleties, and wishing the chin-scratching *Guardian* readers would loosen up a bit with my end-of-the pier humour and just 'have a laugh'.

Whatever else I might have been thinking, one of my main preoccupations would be time and its inevitable passing.

I would always end up with the same thought: 'At some point this gig will be in the past. In a couple of hours' time, I'll be sitting in the bar thinking, "It's over."'

CHAPTER 21

Dad often napped in the car when he came home from work. The driveway was at the bottom of the garden and his car was just out of sight. Mum would send me to tap on the window to wake him up and tell him tea was ready. He always nodded but didn't move or attempt to turn the radio off.

It was a brief hiatus between maintaining IBM System 34s and the maelstrom of a chaotic household.

After we'd watched *Blue Peter* and *The Wombles*, Mum would rap the butt end of a serving spoon against the wall that divided the kitchen from the living room. Like Pavlovian dogs, we would start salivating as we headed for the kitchen table where tea (dinner) would be served.

Mum: 'See if Dad's car is in the drive.'

I would walk down the garden and knock on the car window. His eyes would usually be closed and he'd be listening to Radio 3.

Me: 'Dad, tea is on the table.'

Dad: 'All right. I'll be there in a minute.'

Mum would send me back out five minutes later.

Me: 'Dad, your tea is getting cold.'

Dad: 'Right. I'm coming now.'

Other days he'd come home, have tea, swap his suit for overalls and do heavy-duty DIY. He installed the central heating system on his own. He removed the chimney by renting scaffolding and winching it down. His brother and a friend sometimes helped; no one else could be trusted to do a good enough job and it was cheaper.

On Sundays after church we'd be introduced to all sorts of

interesting people. In the late 1970s I met a woman in her eighties who had survived the *Titanic* as a teenager; she talked about the mayhem on board and the noise of the ship going down.

On another Sunday, Dad pointed someone out as we were leaving church.

'That man told me how a toilet cistern worked when I was a child,' Dad said. 'He explained how simple the mechanics of a ballcock are. He opened my eyes to engineering.'

Dad built everything in the house. He made a stool by fixing a bathroom tile to some reclaimed wood. You can't reach the bath taps while you're in the bath, a safety measure designed and installed by my dad in the sixties to prevent us kids from turning the hot tap on. I thought all bathrooms were like that until I left home.

When he put the central heating in, he lifted the floorboards to lay the pipes. He was so proud of the pipe junction work that he wanted to lay a sheet of Perspex above it so that he could roll back the carpet to show it off to visitors.

Instead he wrote detailed notes explaining how he'd built the central heating system, sealed it in polythene and placed it under the floorboards.

He said, without a glimmer of a smile, 'When the central heating breaks, I won't be alive and I want whoever fixes it to know exactly how I put it together.'

One of the most exciting things about the early seventies was the power cuts that came as a result of the miners' strike and the three-day week. There were candles everywhere and an open fire in the lounge. Until, that is, Dad rather spoilt the effect by rigging up an emergency lighting system wired to disused car batteries.

I have acquired some of Dad's wisdom over the years and, according to my daughter, I put my hands behind my back when I'm studying something technical and I look just like him.

As a precaution, when touching anything live, Dad would fiddle with equipment he was unsure about using only his right hand. He would keep his left hand firmly in his pocket in case an unexpected electrical charge crossed his heart.

He once resolved a tricky technical issue with the microphone pack I used on live tours. A tiny mic was taped to my cheek and the wire ran down to a battery pack on my belt. I would put the battery pack in a condom to keep it dry, but the sweat would still make its way into the battery pack and fuse it. I couldn't figure out how to solve the issue, so I mentioned it to Dad.

'Just turn the battery pack upside down and put a loop in the wire,' he said. 'That way the sweat won't fuse it.'

It's a simple enough solution, but it took an engineer to solve it. I'll never be as scientific as my dad, but I have at least inherited a sense of how the built world works.

When I was a sometime actor in Los Angeles in the 2000s, I drove my hired sports car to the gym one morning. I found myself looking at the structure of the gym car park and wondering why the concrete cross members went into a hole instead of joining up with the wall. I realised the beams were suspended on tiny rollers to protect the car park in the event of an earthquake.

I wasn't even discussing it with anyone, I was standing on my own in this semi-lit car park. I'm not remotely embarrassed by my techie moments: I have great admiration for the beauty of good engineering.

When I was growing up, I didn't see Dad for hours at a time because he was in the cellar working on one thing or another to improve the house. He couldn't stop fixing things; he still says there aren't enough hours in the day.

He once salvaged a couple of discarded phones and rigged them up inside the house for us. Stuff that was a bargain or free was the subject of endless discussion.

When he worked at IBM he would always rather fix a part

on the computer than replace it. He was obsessed with built-in obsolescence and wary of buying new things for the sake of it. He thought there was something slightly distasteful and vulgar about showing off new things.

I was very aware that we couldn't just have anything we wanted. Especially if it could be made from scrap for virtually no cost. Dad was thrifty – the Formica kitchen table was ex-army, cost a tenner and is still in use half a century later; the carpet in the front room was only replaced after seventy years – and he embraced recycling long before it became fashionable and the thrift and recycling of the post-war years finally dovetailed with the environmentalism of the new millennium.

In the early seventies, he constructed a Wendy house out of a huge wooden mainframe computer box. He salvaged it from work, took it apart so that it would fit in the back of his Volvo, and put it back together with brass screws that would resist the rain. The 'diddy house' is still standing in my parents' back garden nearly fifty years later.

As a kid, I much preferred the diddy house to playing soldiers at war. I would play with girls in the diddy house, pretending I was an adult. I liked the drama of it. It was far more enticing than soldiers killing each other, although I'm sure some of my peers considered me a bit of a sissy.

My dad once found an old, battered pedal car, stripped it down to the metal, resprayed it, added electric lights that turned on and off, and made rubber bumpers from old strips of pipe insulation. I watched him doing it up and it was worth the anticipation – much more gratifying than just wandering into a shop and buying a new one. I can still recall the smell of paint on this good-as-new pedal car as I climbed into it for the first time.

We never had new bikes – we had to fix them or make new ones out of the component parts – and Mum had to make do with the 1950s washing machine. She still uses the kitchen knife she bought on holiday in Wales in 1975. It's not even an especially good knife. It doesn't even have a bolstered shank where the blade meets the handle.

And of course my mum had her Morris Minor, which my dad liked because it was so robustly engineered and could be kept on the road for ever.

'They forgot to build in the obsolescence!' my dad would say with great satisfaction.

It was half timbered and blue; someone once described it as 'broad of beam', like a spinster in tweed. The perfect car to eat sandwiches in while parked at the beach on a rainy day. Very British.

Specifically, I loved my mum's Morris Minor, and so I bought myself one that is identical to the one my mother had until it was stolen in the mid-seventies. I went to a Morris Minor garage in Bristol and said, 'I want you to build a Traveller exactly to this specification and it has to be Trafalgar blue with dove-grey vinyl seats.'

Much as I loved the Morris Minor, I was embarrassed by Dad's Morris Oxford. It was a dull, functional post-war car that reeked of austerity. It seemed dusty and grey compared to the sleek, bright cars that were on American TV shows, so unglamorous compared to the yellow, red and orange cars that most people drove in the seventies. I wanted Dad to have a car that looked a bit more American, that was a bit sexy.

Dad's car was the equivalent of a man with a trilby, pipe and slippers, but he didn't want to upgrade to a sexy car. For him, it was all about the engineer versus the designer. The beauty was in the engineering and not the form. He has very little truck with architects who design from an aesthetic point of view and worry about how they are going to construct it later. I said to him once that form follows function, and he did at least agree.

When Dad announced he was buying a Volvo, I said to myself, 'Thank God! Anything that's new will do!' At the age of nine, I scoured the car section of the local newspaper day and night. I found as many Volvos as I could, including an M-registered model for £1,750. We went to see several together. I was heartbroken when we went to look at one that was £2,000 and some bloke turned up with the cash in a suitcase and took the car away. Dad looked so dejected. Accessing that kind of money would have been a lengthy process for him.

I was stupidly happy when Dad finally bought one.

My car-loving friend at school used to persecute me about the Morris Oxford, and was always reminding me that his dad bought a brand-new Datsun every two years.

'It's got tinted windows and air conditioning.'

Then he'd twist the knife. 'Why does your dad drive a crap old Morris Oxford? They're rubbish. They look horrible.'

I knew he was right. I was tormented. But I had an ace up my sleeve.

'Well . . .' I hesitated. 'Your dad has a limp and walks like this.' I hobbled round the playground as he looked on, crestfallen.

I knew I'd gone too far.

The next day at school he said, 'I told my mum what you did. She said you must be a very sick person.'

You can see why I'm not on Twitter.

CHAPTER 22

I nearly died when I was two. My older brother David and I both had meningitis (Mum thought that it was polio and that the doctor wasn't telling the truth) and we were put in an isolation room at the local Victorian hospital. It was a small room with two beds side by side. I would sit in bed and drive a Matchbox car over the sheets and then get up and give the car to David, who was seven, so he could do the same. At some point a nurse looked in on us and I thought she had a nice, kind face. It's a simple memory, probably my first.

My mother later told me that I had had a lumbar puncture, in which a needle is inserted into the lower part of the spine with no anaesthetic. Mum wasn't allowed in the room because they thought she might get hysterical, which in turn might upset me, and it was critical I didn't wriggle. Some men in white coats took me into a room, held me down and drilled a hole in my spine.

When I was returned to the isolation ward, Mum tells me that I gave her a look as if to say, 'You betrayed me.'

In the years following my time in hospital, I had waking nightmares and wet the bed. My brothers, with whom I shared a room, would go downstairs and get Dad, who would try to pacify me. It must have been distressing for him because I was screaming wildly and telling him to get away from me. My eyes were open, but I wasn't awake. I would finally wake up confused and in a state of panic.

The nightmares were always abstract, but horribly real. I was being attacked by an axe or crushed, possibly by two giant balls. Dad would eventually calm me down and I'd be taken downstairs for a cup of cocoa.

I was still having nightmares when I was seven or eight and I wet the bed for a long time, right up until I was eleven or twelve. Initially Dad would wake me up in the night and take me for a pee. He was particularly gentle with me because he used to wet the bed as a child and his mother had been very fierce with him.

When it became clear that the bed-wetting wasn't going to stop, he ordered a contraption to wake me up that looked like something from *Wallace and Gromit*: two sheets of wire mesh were sandwiched between the sheets and connected by crocodile clips to a steel box with a toggle switch and a big red light. If I released a tiny bit of pee, it would complete the circuit and the alarm would sound.

Sometimes it was too late and I'd already wet the bed, but mostly I had time to wake up and dash to the loo.

Years later, when I was living in Hove and paying my parents a visit, my dad took me down to the cellar to show me the bed-wetting buzzer again (you never know when you might need one). On the back it said 'Made in Hove', which Dad thought was significant, as if somehow my life had come full circle. I was just embarrassed by the memory of bed-wetting.

There was no central heating in the house when I was young, and on a winter's morning I would wake up, rush across the room to the fan heater, switch it on and kneel in front of it. It was so cold you could see your own breath and, if I'd wet the bed, a huge cloud of steam would rise from the bed when I pulled the bedsheets back.

My four brothers slept in two sets of bunk beds that Dad had constructed from beautiful Paranà pine and brass screws. He had varnished the wood, got hold of Nana Coogan's old steel bed springs, stripped them down and repainted them. He had then cut thick sponge into the right shape and Mum had stitched a sheet over the top to create a proper mattress.

We had Brentford Nylons on the bed, as advertised by Alan Freeman on television. They were fitted sheets, electric blue   so modern, a real injection of seventies colour – and oddly furry and warm. In the days before continental quilts and then duvets, we had sheet, sheet, blanket, blanket. The sheet was folded over the top of the blanket, very neatly.

Making the bed was a real pain in the arse. It was like being in the army. Kids with duvets don't know they're born. In those days 'go and make your bed' meant a good fifteen minutes of fiddling around that you were never going to get back.

I was on my own in a single bed because of the bed-wetting, and while I wasn't exactly isolated, I was slightly separated from my brothers in their bunks. I felt terribly self-conscious about wetting the bed; I'd get up in the morning and wash myself and my pyjama bottoms, then Mum would change the sheets.

I worried about it. I used to think, 'When is it going to stop? Oh my God, what if I'm still wetting the bed when I grow up?'

In the end, I learned to wake myself up from my nightmares. As soon as the axe attack started, I would distance myself from it. 'This is so awful,' I'd think, 'it can't be real. It must be a dream. This man is about to attack me, open your eyes.' Or 'Mum and Dad aren't dying, it's a dream. Open your eyes.'

I would wake up and realise I was lying in bed, staring at the ceiling, my brothers all fast asleep in their bunks.

Eventually both the nightmares and the bed-wetting stopped. But I had obviously been profoundly traumatised by my experience in hospital as a two-year-old.

★　★　★

In spring 1968, when Martin Luther King Jr was assassinated, Enoch Powell made his 'Rivers of Blood' speech and anti-Vietnam student protests were in full swing.

Meanwhile, in Middleton, I got lost at the local market. I was only two and I was supposed to be holding on to the side of my brother's pram, but I let go and almost immediately lost sight of Mum. All I could see were women's calves in tan tights and the hems of heavy overcoats, which I tugged on desperately in the hope that one might be my mother. But only the faces of strangers peered down at me.

I started to cry. I was petrified. I thought I'd never find her again.

A kindly old lady – she was probably fifty but seemed ancient to me – lifted me up and took me to the police station. I saw my mum at the end of a long corridor and ran as fast as I could to hug her, but when I arrived I started to hit her instead and shout, 'Why did you leave me? Why?'

I wasn't exactly a mummy's boy, but people would often say, 'Stephen is a bit soft.'

Kevin went to nursery, but I stayed at home. I wasn't ready for school, despite being one of the oldest in the year.

I was shocked when I was left alone at school for the first time. 'Mummy, where are you going? Don't leave me . . .' I felt tiny and alone. I burst into tears.

And then, at break, I stood in the playground, tilted my head back and drank the rain. Simon Bradley came up to me and said, 'You'll get worms if you do that.'

I burst into tears again.

★　★　★

I was terrified of tests and academic failure from a young age. The more I got myself into a panic, the less I was able to listen and concentrate. I had to keep asking my dad to explain things slowly so that I could grasp them.

For all his engineering knowledge, he was not a born teacher by any stretch of the imagination.

I lived in fear of the SRA reading cards that were used to test comprehension in primary schools in the late sixties and early seventies. I can still remember one called 'The Pond' in which you had to count how many times the words 'pond' and 'frog' were mentioned. I got something wrong and the teacher held it up in a horribly derisory manner in front of the entire class as an example of what not to do.

Everyone laughed at me. 'Have you seen what he's done?'

I thought, 'I'm a thicko.'

When I got home I told Mum I didn't want to go back to school the next day. She phoned the school and we both went in to see the teacher, who was incredibly nice and reassuring.

I was silently furious. 'You two-faced cow,' I thought. 'You're only being nice to me 'cause my mum's here.'

But, much as I was haunted by the idea of failure and humiliation, I didn't say a word. I didn't dare.

I wasn't a troublemaker, but I did get told off. On one occasion, my friend Brendan Tierney was talking to me during a music lesson and the teacher said, 'If you talk one more time I'll come and slap your legs.'

I told Brendan to shut up. The teacher saw me talking and called me to the front of the classroom to slap my lags. I was hot with the injustice of it, with anger and embarrassment.

★   ★   ★

In 1972, when I was six, there was a production of *The Wizard of Oz* at my primary school in which the teacher's son played the wizard. What were the chances of that? The same teacher, the one who thought I was thick, decided my skill set would be best applied to the non-speaking role of flying monkey number three. Of three.

She obviously knew I had something. A brown jumper. But I didn't even have that.

All the monkeys had to assemble a costume of brown jumper, brown tights, a brown balaclava and simple pumps. Brown fabric was sewn under the arms of the jumper to make it look as though we had wings. The only brown jumper I could find at home had two orange stripes down the front with wiggly lines in between. Instead of looking like a monkey, I looked like a monkey wearing a jumper. To make it worse, Dad then stitched huge plastic ears on to each side of the balaclava.

We were told to bring a plastic spider to school to throw into the cauldron. All we had at home was a rubber crab.

'I can't throw a crab in the cauldron!' I protested. 'Witches and evil people don't throw crabs into cauldrons. Everyone knows that . . .'

My sister Clare placated me. 'It's not a crab, Stephen. It's a special African spider that looks like a crab.'

'Are you certain?'

'Yes,' she insisted. 'It's well known than an African spider looks just like a crab.'

I was sceptical, but on balance satisfied. After all, why would she bother lying about something so stupid?

Someone from Granada TV filmed the play and one afternoon the school television was wheeled into our classroom on its stand so we could all watch the video together. I saw myself during the flying monkey song, sitting in the middle of the two other monkey boys. They were looking straight ahead and singing while my head was bowed. I was so embarrassed by my huge plastic ears that I couldn't look up. I was staring at my pumps for the entire song.

I wasn't a confident child. I couldn't ignore my plastic ears and look into the camera; I was terrified of being humiliated. And yet I was thrilled that the play had been filmed. I went around telling anyone who would listen that I'd been 'on television'.

CHAPTER 23

I was an unremarkable pupil. I wasn't a bad kid, I just got through school. I never got an A. I once got a B+, but normally I'd get C+. If I got a B, I was really happy. I was, in fact, astonishingly average. I didn't ever fully engage with my education although, as I went through grammar school, I did get fired up by subjects such as history.

And occasionally I read a book.

Anything by George Orwell or poetry by Wilfred Owen and William Blake. I found *Chaucer's Knight: The Portrait of a Medieval Mercenary* by Terry Jones quite exciting because he was challenging established orthodoxies.

My mum has kept all our reports in a drawer in the kitchen. I'm not surprised by what they say.

A report from St Thomas More from when I was seven concluded: 'Stephen does good work, but is a very slow worker. Grammar work is very good. Tables very good. Problems present some difficulty. Can do good work. C+.'

My dad, as I've mentioned, came from the generation where grammar was more important than literature or art. Shedding light on the human condition couldn't be measured. Grammar was either correct or it wasn't.

I had a decent education: I was lucky. My parents were in favour of comprehensive education and railed against the injustice of private schools and the grammar school system, but they were desperate for all their kids to pass the 11-plus.

Failing the 11-plus and going to the local secondary modern was a terrible judgement to put on a child. Most people perceived secondary moderns as simply containment, as if the kids who went there, rather than being educated, were just being kept in a holding pattern before they landed a local factory job, if they were lucky.

Grammar school, on the other hand, felt special. My Catholic grammar school conducted itself as a pseudo public school. We played rugby instead of football, which was probably regarded as proletarian, and uniform was strictly enforced.

I was the first child my parents worried might not pass the 11-plus and they made me practise mock tests at home like mad. If you went to grammar school, there were high expectations to achieve academically at a fairly young age.

I was always slow; I used to take my time and think about things. I never finished essays, because I spent so much time thinking about my story before I started writing. It was frustrating being told off for trying to come up with a good narrative. In 1975 or 1976, I wrote a story in my English exercise book that was eight pages long; I was given permission to finish it off at home and I relished the extra time. I loved writing it: there was a robbery and some boys were hiding down a manhole. The teacher was so surprised that I'd written eight pages instead of the usual three that he made me read it out in front of the class.

Writing creatively for the sake of it didn't appeal to me. I didn't have personal discipline; I failed English language O level not once, but twice. Pathetically, I didn't pass it until I was well into the sixth form. But I didn't know what the examiners wanted from me and I didn't think I had anything worth saying. I could write about a robbery, but if I was asked to write an essay about where I lived, I flew into a panic.

It would never have occurred to me that one day I might be nominated for an Oscar for co-writing a film. My ambition didn't stretch that far; I couldn't even describe Middleton, for God's sake.

Although I had a good, solid education, I don't think the 'one size fits all' education system really helps people like me. I was a daydreamer with a fertile imagination, but school did its best to make learning regimented. It took me a long time to fully realise that I might have something interesting to say.

It wasn't until I reached my thirties, in fact, that I properly began to have confidence in my own ideas. In a complete volte-face, everything that had made me feel insecure and inadequate suddenly made me feel authentic and enlightened.

★　　★　　★

I wasn't stupid, but I found it hard to focus on the matter in hand. It's no surprise that one of my school reports from primary school summed me up thus: 'A very pleasant child who is capable of good work. Often finishes last in class due to daydreaming.'

I liked to escape to a different world. I used to turn the chairs in the living room upside down to make dens. I played dead. I lived in a fantasy world without ever fully retreating from the real world. I was a bit ditzy.

The family used to laugh at me.

My auntie called me 'Stevie Wonder'. I'd no idea he was a famous soul singer; I'd never heard of him.

I used to overhear conversations in which the adults would say, 'What are we going to do with Stephen? He's away with the fairies.'

It was mostly affectionate, but I remember being upset by a birthday card I was given when I turned ten. It said, 'Tomorrow, I'm going to sort my life out.' I felt completely dumb, like I had something wrong with me.

My family used to watch *Some Mothers Do 'Ave 'Em*, laugh at Frank Spencer and say, 'He's just like our Stephen.'

Once they were watching *Harold and Maude*, one of my favourite films, and someone said I was like Bud Cort's attention-seeking character. The comparison bothered me. I didn't want to be perceived as odd, but I *was* a little odd.

It's fortunate that the slight oddness I had wasn't stamped

out of me. When I started working, I was able to nurture the oddness, to let my imagination wander.

But as a kid, I was more conflicted. I was both upset that they thought I was different, and glad that I wasn't like everyone else.

★   ★   ★

My career as an impressionist started early. From the age of five or six, I used to imitate the sound of car wheels screeching. Sometimes too effectively: Mum was always telling Dad off for driving too fast and on occasion she would tell him off when he was driving at a reasonable speed because she mistook my mimicry for real speed.

Most kids with a theatrical inclination put on quaint plays for their family. That didn't occur to me.

When I was twelve, I spent ages rigging up an elaborate structure in the living room. There were a couple of free-standing lamps in the room that were plugged into sockets but could be controlled via light switches near the door. In one of those sockets I plugged a hand-held tape recorder and in the other an anglepoise lamp, which I pointed directly at the doorway so that whoever entered the room would be dazzled by light. I made a Guy Fawkes dummy by stuffing an old jumper and trousers with socks, added a Frankenstein mask and sat it in an armchair with its back to the door.

The idea was that whoever walked into the room would flick on the light switch and be blinded by the silhouette of someone sitting in a chair. At the same time they would flick the other switch and trigger the tape recorder, so that the shadowy figure would appear to be talking to them. The creepy, pseudo-Cold War voice would say, 'Hello. Come in. Do exactly as I say. Sit down. Do not attempt to see who I am. Do not approach the chair. You are here for questioning. Who are you? Where do you come from? Who are you working for?'

I hid behind the curtains, waiting for someone to come in, excited by the potential theatre.

Mum walked in, flicking on both switches. 'Hello. Come in . . .'

She went over to the armchair, pushed the anglepoise away and pulled the head off the dummy.

'What's this?' she asked impatiently.

I stepped out from behind the curtain, deflated.

Mum looked at me, frowning. 'What are you doing?'

I replied, 'I was hoping to trick someone into thinking they were being interrogated.'

Another time, when I was nine or ten, I read about a man called Peter Cook who had been dubbed 'the Cambridge Rapist' and was given two life sentences after his arrest in 1975. He used to wear a balaclava with 'rapist' emblazoned on the front whenever he attacked women. I asked my mum what a 'rappist' was. She told me it was someone who frightens women and attacks them when they're walking home at night.

As well as not being able to pronounce the word properly, I had no sense of how awful the story was. So when my mum came home one day, I jumped out of the bushes dressed in black and wearing a balaclava.

I started shouting, 'Ha, ha, look at me! I'm a rapist!'

She was appalled and chastised me, telling me it was not a nice thing to say or do.

I, in turn, was miffed as my disguise had involved some thought and preparation. I genuinely thought she'd be delighted.

I was far more self-conscious around my dad. Mum was calmer and generally more tolerant of misdemeanours or morally questionable behaviour. But as soon as Dad came into the room, I'd stop goofing around. He wasn't big on praise. He thought criticism was a great way to learn. I have, to some degree, inherited it as a character trait and I hate it in myself. I've had to learn to recognise it and try to be effusive when I love something rather than be overly critical.

If ever I felt dissatisfied with the environment in which I was brought up, it was when I went over to friends' houses and witnessed their fathers goofing around with their kids. I felt jealous. I wished my dad would do that with us, with me. But he was very much a figure of authority.

If, on occasion, I acted the goat in front of him, he would tell me to stop. He thought that acting like an idiot was undignified, even if you were just being daft. He loved the Goons, the Two Ronnies and Morecambe and Wise, but they were *professionally* funny, as if they had been born that way.

He'd say to me, 'You can't get a job by fooling around and acting the eejit!'

He thought that making people laugh by being a fool was a very bad thing.

As soon as I got into Monty Python I knew he was wrong. You *could* earn a living from being daft.

My parents brought us up to be respectable, to be kind to people, to take personal pride by contributing to society in a traditional way. As it turned out, I've made my living from contributing to society in a very untraditional way. I have made a career by goofing around in exactly the way my dad disapproved of.

In its simplest terms, I have embraced my weaknesses and been liberated by laughing at myself. I have flagged up my imperfections and let Alan Partridge absorb some of my foibles.

All the things that were seen as not particularly attractive qualities are things I have utilised in my working life. There is method to it. It's almost like saying, 'You can be rude and swear and drop your pants and do things that are disrespectful and make a very good living out of it. Shining a light on the human condition by being ostensibly rude and disrespectful.'

My stupidity became my *raison d'être*. I discovered that I could mock myself through my characters and that as long as I was the architect, playing the fool gave me a certain sophistication. I was playing a trick on everyone: by being profoundly uncool, I ended up being the coolest person in the room.

Short-term fool, long-term cool.

It was exciting just by virtue of it being oppositional.

Mum told me that when I booked her and Dad into the hotel opposite the Lyceum in 1998, he was still incredulous that I had made a success of my fooling around.

Apparently he looked out of the hotel window, turned to Mum and said, 'When you think of what a bugger he was . . .'

The irony is that while Dad disapproved of my silliness, the rest of my family were always asking me to be a performing monkey.

I can't say I protested too much.

CHAPTER 24

As much as I am a product of my Catholic, lower-middle-class background, I am also a product of the television generation. I should emphasise that television watching was rationed in my home. We were never allowed to sit around all day in the holidays slumped on the sofa, watching television. Books were considered to be far more important and outdoor play was always encouraged.

We had a big house, fitted carpets, central heating and eventually ran two cars, but we were the last family in the neighbourhood to have a colour television. It was probably something to do with inverted snobbery. It wasn't budgeted for and Dad wasn't going to be hoodwinked into buying one.

Money was better spent on the *Encyclopedia Britannica*; the whole set cost about £500 in 1977, which is the equivalent of nearly £3,000 in today's money. Mum and Dad had to extend the mortgage on the house as they couldn't afford the books otherwise.

My dad, incapable of throwing anything out, was often given second-hand black-and-white TVs that he fixed when they broke down. There's still a photo in the lounge of two broken TVs placed on top of one another and, on top of those, a small working portable.

All my friends had rented colour TVs, which was the *sine qua non* of early seventies suburbia. By the end of the decade it was the video recorder. Those two developments bookended the seventies as the television decade.

There were only three TV channels, so they were touchstones for my generation – an intimate feeling of connection. Millions watched these shows.

If my dad was working in the attic, he would occasionally nudge the aerial while we were watching TV. An operation to correct it would immediately swing into action, made up of available family and friends. A chain would be formed down two stairways and the hallways, with me generally standing in front of the telly.

Dad would make small adjustments to the aerial and the question, 'How's that?' would be relayed along the chain to me.

'A bit better . . .' I would reply, and back the message would go.

The message would change. 'The picture's gone again!' or 'It's perfect, don't move it!'

By the time Dad received the message it was often too late and the aerial had yet again been moved from its optimal position.

It was a painful process, but crucial if I was to have my lifeline to this other world.

One of the most visceral pleasures of my childhood was opening the Christmas double issue of the *Radio Times* and circling the films and TV shows we wanted to watch. It was always an embarrassment of riches.

We only had one television, so if there was a consensus about watching a particular film, say *Ben-Hur*, that clashed with my preferred choice (James Bond), I would have to phone Brendan, Ged or even Paul Allsop. If any of them were watching Bond, I'd rush round and watch it at their house.

Afterwards I would run home, knowing that I would only miss the first five minutes of *The Guns of Navarone*.

I feel terribly nostalgic about the television I watched in my youth.

When I was very young, I loved *The Clangers* and *Bagpuss* – in fact, anything by the wonderful Oliver Postgate – and *Trumpton*, which was narrated by Brian Cant. I did a voiceover with him in 1990 and asked him to say 'Pugh, Pugh, Barney McGrew, Cuthbert, Dibble, Grub'. He was very gracious and I was thrilled.

There was a complete difference between the BBC and ITV. *Blue Peter* was informative and reassuring, with John Noakes like a favourite uncle. But the show had a whiff of imperialism about it. ITV's answer to *Blue Peter* was *Magpie*, which although always seemed a bit more rock 'n' roll was like a pretender to the crown. *Swap Shop* on a Saturday morning was presented by Noel Edmonds. Even as a child I regarded him as far too smug. He was completely trumped by Chris Tarrant on ITV's *Tiswas*. Tarrant's anarchy and irreverence made the BBC seem boring and po-faced.

The female presenters on *Blue Peter* and *Magpie* were posh and attractive. But I got excited about more grown-up and sexy shows such *The Persuaders!*, with Tony Curtis and Roger Moore, and *The New Avengers* with Patrick Macnee, Gareth Hunt and Joanna Lumley. To me they were the epitome of sophistication.

We all watched *Top of the Pops* religiously. If I saw a band on *Top of the Pops* that I really liked, I was always shocked by what they looked like; I'd only ever heard their music before, and maybe seen photos of them in the music press. I'd never seen them actually moving around.

Barry Norman's BBC film programme – *Film 75*, *Film 76*, and so on – was religious viewing. I learned about interesting movies from Norman, and of course the films he was reviewing then are now the iconic films of the maverick decade of creativity, covered in Peter Biskind's book *Easy Riders, Raging Bulls*.

As much as I enjoyed watching TV with my siblings, I have even fonder memories of sitting down with all my family to watch shows like *Porridge*. Now there's a false god of choice and people watch programmes on catch-up. Then, because you couldn't record television, it was a live event. When the show ended you knew it wouldn't be repeated for over a year, sometimes two. If you missed the show it would be crushing.

The immediacy of it brought it right into your home. You

knew that everyone who was like you was watching the same programme. It made the country feel small and intimate.

The ire now directed at smartphones, laptops, Facebook and Twitter was reserved for television in the seventies. Although it was known as the idiot box by some, TV was king.

When John Cleese ran into the hotel in *Fawlty Towers* you had to remember exactly what he was saying because you couldn't rewind the scene. Afterwards we'd go into the kitchen, someone would put the kettle on – we drank gallons of tea – and we'd have a post-mortem about our favourite moments. Unless you talked about it and kept it alive, it would be gone for ever. You had to commit it to memory.

I always looked forward to *Morecambe & Wise* and *The Two Ronnies*. My parents looked down their noses at *The Generation Game*, considering it vulgar, but they liked *The Good Life*, a gentle comedy with some moments of brilliance. I bought a box set of the series recently because it perfectly captured the suburban snobbery my parents laughed at. It held up a slightly exaggerated mirror to our world.

As a social document, a series like *The Good Life* is a more reliable portal into the mindset of the country than any news-reel footage or journalistic accounts.

A lot of TV comedies are rightly consigned to the dustbin of light entertainment history. *On the Buses*, for example, regularly had viewing figures of many millions in the early seventies but is completely unwatchable today. Its level of humour is Neanderthal.

Fawlty Towers and *Dad's Army* have both matured like fine wine. ITV sitcoms have almost all turned to vinegar.

One of the few good ITV sitcoms was *Rising Damp*. Leonard Rossiter's Rigsby was a Little Englander and a predecessor to Alan Partridge. Intolerant, inadequate, snobby and casually racist. The same adjectives could just as easily apply to Captain Mainwaring in *Dad's Army* and to Basil Fawlty. They have all failed in some way, which is at the heart of so much British comedy.

It separates us from the Americans, who, Larry David and Woody Allen aside, tend not to embrace noble failure quite so much in their comedy. As far as the Americans are concerned, you either win or you lose. Our ability to laugh at ourselves is to be celebrated. Bill Bryson writes about it in *Notes from a Small Island*. It's one of the things he loves about us: everyone likes to have a joke, even strangers.

Patriotism is hugely overrated, but sometimes it goes too far the other way and you're not even allowed to make observations of national characteristics. I love Britain. I love my country in a way that's not nationalistic or blindly patriotic. The Opening Ceremony of the London 2012 Olympic Games blew me away because everything I love about Britain was there on the screen in front of me. History, the NHS, music, cinema. It celebrated the culture of dissent and embraced the eccentric.

It was the first time I consciously thought, 'Oh yeah, this is my country too.' I wrote a long letter to Danny Boyle and writer Frank Cottrell Boyce admiring their work; they wrested the flag from blind nationalism and effectively gave us a licence to be patriotic.

Celebrating certain national characteristics has for too long been the preserve of racists, but it really depends on what you're celebrating. Self-effacement is one of the best things about Britain. We are very clear about certain things that differentiate us from the Americans: we don't admire people just because they've got money. In America, as long as you've got money it doesn't matter where you're from. It's a very Thatcherite stance.

At the same time, the old Tory class system in Britain means there is very little social mobility. So you are judged on your character.

I'm not a huge fan of period dramas that celebrate the old class system. Julian Fellowes is the epitome of Middle England values and of that selective revisionism that some people have about our culture and history. *Downton Abbey* is at best a simplistic fiction of a golden past and at worst a total distortion of facts. It's the kind of period drama that Alan Partridge would write.

I bumped into Julian Fellowes in 2013 and he was aghast that the BBC news had devoted time to discussing Hilary Mantel's follow-up to *Wolf Hall* and only two minutes on the baptism of our future king.

I was appalled that he was appalled.

I'm fascinated by British attitudes to certain things. We can be very negative, which, at its best, means we're not easily impressed. And certainly not by money. At its worst it can descend into a debilitating cynicism.

In England people judge the fact that I like classic cars; I must be a wanker because I occasionally drive a bright yellow Lotus that makes me feel like James Bond.

If the sun shone all the time, we might well be less repressed, less uptight. But we wouldn't be as funny. When I was growing up, mocking people with humour was a very roundabout but sophisticated way of saying 'I love you'. It's a peculiarly British sign of affection.

★   ★   ★

Seventies comedy is an easy target. People judge Les Dawson for his mother-in-law jokes, but in doing so they miss the point: it was all about Dawson not having the power. About him being disempowered, impotent. I admired the way Dawson, who also came from Collyhurst, wrote his way out of hardship. One of the great things about humour is that anyone can create it. It's free. For him, comedy was about survival. It was always a treat to watch *The Les Dawson Show* on the BBC, especially if a guest like John Cleese turned up.

Paul Calf owes his lineage to Les Dawson and Alan Partridge to John Cleese. One is intuitively melancholic, the other intellectually adventurous.

The BBC was my education. There was education at school, of course, but a sense of society, of a life outside my own, came from television. It was a smorgasbord of information and entertainment. We were definitely a BBC family – my parents were BBC1 while my brothers and I were the edgier, artier BBC2 – because ITV was too lowbrow. Not because we were intellectuals, but because Dad thought we should aspire to more than he thought ITV had to offer.

The BBC was accessible, entertaining and informative. My parents didn't have the values of the Oxbridge-educated people who ran it, but the output was aimed at people who wanted to be entertained and learn something.

The BBC educated my parents too. It made them more open-minded about the changing world around them. My dad didn't like Jon Pertwee as Doctor Who because he found him too effeminate; he was too much of a dandy in his velvet jackets and frilly shirts. Dad thought Sean Connery was far more masculine than Roger Moore. Slowly, however, he became less judgemental. Both my parents watched *The Naked Civil Servant* in 1975 and were suitably impressed by John Hurt's performance.

I have heard some great stories about the BBC. Terry Jones told me that when he heard that the BBC was about to erase the master tapes of *Monty Python's Flying Circus*, he smuggled them out of the building and stored them in his attic.

Years later, when Python became popular again, the BBC asked if they could broadcast the tapes.

The BBC may have had an element of left-wing bohemia about it, but it was shockingly short-sighted at times.

★   ★   ★

In the sixties, the BBC was committed to commissioning political drama for television in a way that is all too rare now. It offered, for me at least, a different way of looking at the world. I wasn't exactly drowning in Middleton, but those plays gave me a lifeline of sorts. Because my parents lived a modest life, there were limits on what we thought we ought to expect from life. Ambition certainly wasn't encouraged.

I was aware of 'important' television, which included work by directors like Ken Loach. *Cathy Come Home* was broadcast in 1966 to over 12 million people as part of the BBC's influential Wednesday Play series, and though I was too young to watch it, Mum told me the story: a young mother loses her home, husband and children because of the failings of the welfare state. Mum talked about how important *Cathy Come Home* was because it changed things; it led to Shelter, the homeless charity that was set up around the same time, being given massive support.

Kes, the film Loach made in 1969 about a boy and his kestrel, was a wonderful film that somehow managed to avoid the type of sentimentality I despise.

In my house the working-class experience was to be respected and not sugar-coated or denigrated. Which was just as well because the Wednesday Plays were radical and often wilfully controversial. I watched Dennis Potter's *Stand Up, Nigel Barton*, in which a coal miner's son wins an Oxford scholarship, Loach's *Up the Junction* and Jim Allen's doggedly socialist dramas. *The Big Flame*, about Liverpool dockers on strike, was also directed by Loach.

Allen was born into a Catholic family in Manchester and he worked on the docks and down the mines before he became a writer. His 1978 television play *The Spongers* was shot in Middleton, and I remember the excitement rippling through town when the cast and crew turned up. It is sadly as relevant now as it was then: a single mother on welfare is affected by local authority and government cuts until, in desperation, she kills her children and then herself.

With its echoes of *Cathy Come Home*, it was an attack on poverty in modern Britain, about the failure of the post-war vision that Labour had for this new world. It was very powerful,

but also disturbing and unsettling. I recognised the world Allen
was portraying: my grandmother lived on the housing estate
on which he filmed. Tragic though *The Spongers* was, it was
thrilling to be connected by geography and background to
something that was a pivotal piece of national television.

I was, like most teenagers, a series of contradictions. I was
becoming politically aware and didactic television fascinated
me. I understood that it had a place. And yet I was desperate
above all for glimpses of nudity. Even if it was only in black
and white on a small fuzzy screen.

CHAPTER 25

The morning after Nic Roeg's *Walkabout* was screened on the BBC, everyone in the playground was talking about Jenny Agutter's pubic hair. Twelve-year-old boys were absolutely thrilled to see a fully naked girl on the BBC. You could enjoy seeing a naked Jenny Agutter and at the same time be aware that the film had an idiosyncratic style.

Walkabout was exotic, arty and slightly forbidden, but also legitimate because it was on the BBC.

As an adolescent I developed a sonar for finding glimpses of female nudity. Often when my mum, Clare and Martin were watching something 'forbidden' on TV, I would sneak out of bed, crawl under the sofa on my belly, commando style, and pray that no one would notice me. The sofa had its back to the door, so no one could see me come in and I quickly learned how to enter the room with stealth.

It wasn't the most comfortable way to watch TV. I had to watch the screen sideways through someone's legs, but I didn't care.

Someone would inevitably ask, 'Is Stephen under the sofa? Stephen! Go to bed!'

If there wasn't any nudity or violence on the screen, they'd think, 'Out of sight, out of mind.'

I was always worried my cover would be blown, but it was worth it to watch those grown-up programmes.

In 1976, Harold Wilson resigned. There were riots in Soweto that led to the demise of apartheid. Concorde entered service, and Britain was experiencing the worst drought on record. It was the summer that never ended.

But for me, it was the summer of trying to see Susan

Penhaligan's breasts in *Bouquet of Barbed Wire*. Albeit sideways, underneath the sofa.

The series was risqué for its time. The boyfriend was sleeping with the mother-in-law . . . in fact, every possible permutation of family members sleeping with each other was explored, including a slightly incestuous father-and-daughter relationship that would cause an uproar now.

We might have been slow to catch on to the hedonism of sixties London, but by the seventies sex was reaching suburbia via TV sets. Television became a Pandora's box of sexuality. The Hammer Horror films always managed to incorporate sexual titillation against their Shepperton Studios Gothic backdrop. And of course if you watched a foreign film on BBC2 late at night, there was a fair chance you would see a woman not wearing a bra at some point. Particularly if the film was French. It was worth sitting through subtitles just to see a pair of breasts.

Television was where sexual liberation and feminism met misogyny in a perfect storm of toplessness. The symbolism of women burning their bras as an act of liberation was lost on me in my prepubescence. It simply meant that women would literally no longer be wearing bras, which seemed like a reckless idea but, on balance, a good one.

Later, I used to pretend to be looking at regular cinema listings in the local newspaper while scanning for inch-cubed adverts promoting a double bill of X-certificate films such as *Emmanuelle*.

I would stare at the ad, hard. 'That's got naked women in it. It's definitely not the sort of film my parents approve of.'

Emmanuelle at least seemed exotic because it was French. Soft porn films made in Britain in the seventies did huge business and yet most of them were rubbish. *Confessions of a Window Cleaner. Confessions of a Pop Performer. Confessions of a Driving Instructor.* A man glimpses a woman getting out of a bath. He sees her boobs before she sees him looking and, giggling coquettishly, covers herself with a towel. Bizarre.

It's even odder that fairly respectable middle-ranking actors such as Windsor Davies were prepared to appear in those films. But there wasn't much of a British film industry, so I suppose they had to go where the work was.

While I lived at home, I never snuck into the cinema to watch soft porn. As a student I might once have stuck my head round the door of the Cameo cinema in Manchester to watch a minute or two of a rude film. I didn't go in, partly because the place was full of the Dirty Mac Brigade, but also because I felt guilty. Part of me was still trying to be a good Catholic boy.

★   ★   ★

Mum and Dad would never have embraced my prurience. They had very specific ideas about things. They didn't like Benny Hill – not because he was sexist, but because, like Bernard Manning, they considered him to be rude and vulgar.

My early crushes were, somewhat inevitably, on female teachers. Brendan Tierney and I used to like Miss Beasley, who was like a dark-haired Diana Dors, with huge boobs and a big bum. She wore very heavy make-up, had an air of the dominatrix about her and looked wanton. She was very, very strict, but with a twinkle in her eye. Even at the age of seven, Brendan and I were excited by her.

We didn't quite know why.

'Would you like Miss Beasley to sit you on her knee?' Brendan once asked.

'Yes!' I didn't even have to think about an answer. I sensed it would be a thrill, but beyond that of course I didn't have a clue. I just knew she was unlike my mum.

Around the same time, I had a teacher called Miss Webster, who was also strict, but who had the same twinkle in her eye. She had ringlets that dropped past her ears and two pairs of glasses: hexagon-shaped ones with a purple tint and square ones with a green tint. Predictably seventies.

Miss Webster used to take us for PE as well. Next to her desk were white plimsolls with rolled-up socks stuffed into them, which she would wear in our PE lessons, with a whistle round her neck. I remember thinking she really ought to wash her socks occasionally.

I once watched her go out of a side door to say goodbye to a supply teacher with long hair. He picked her up and twirled her around and it dawned on me that she was a woman as well as a teacher. I tried to paint a picture of The Rolling Stones for her, but in reality it was just some men with drums and guitars and I had to write 'The Rolling Stones' at the top to explain who they were. My attempts to impress her were pathetic really.

For a shy seven-year-old, I was inexplicably bold. There was a really pretty eleven-year-old girl at school called Theresa. I had to know more.

'What's your second name?' I asked.

'Green. Theresa Green.'

All her friends were laughing, but I didn't know why. It didn't occur to me that I couldn't chat up a girl four years my senior.

★   ★   ★

When I was thirteen, a lad at school got hold of one of Paul Raymond's soft porn mags, removed the staples and gave a page to every boy in the class. I took the page home and hid it under my pillow. The content was pretty mild, but it was beyond exciting. And, of course, strictly proscribed.

I spent the next day at school thinking, 'I hope my mum doesn't change the bed sheets today. Please, God.'

The thought of my mum finding the magazine haunted me all day. All I could think about were the sheets. I thought about them every moment of every lesson. I tried to listen to the chemistry teacher talking about molecules, but I could only see the page of porn.

As soon as school was over, I went home and raced up to

my room. The bed was perfectly made. The sheets were crisp and clean. I lifted up the pillow. The page was gone. I tried to convince myself that I hadn't left it there. But I knew I had. I felt sick with nerves. It was like waiting for a bomb to explode.

Mum was normal with me.

And then Dad came home and they both went upstairs.

A few moments later, one of them shouted down, 'Stephen, could you come up, please.'

My throat constricted. I stood at the bottom of the stairs, delaying the inevitable by desperately trying to sound casual. 'What do you want?'

'Just come upstairs. We want a word.'

They insisted I went upstairs. There was Dad, holding the page of the soft porn magazine by a corner.

'What's this?' he asked, unnecessarily.

Mum looked at me. She was both angry and disappointed. 'Can you imagine how I felt when I found that under your pillow?'

I spluttered something about looking after it for a friend.

'You're supposed to be a Christian,' Dad continued, in a horribly disparaging voice. 'This woman is being displayed like a piece of meat. Go to the toilet and flush this down to the sewer where it belongs.'

It was a clumsy response to an adolescent's perfectly natural sexual curiosity.

My head hanging in shame, I ripped the page up and dropped it into the toilet. To this day I remember looking down at fragments of porn swirling round and round in the bowl. There goes half a leg. A bottom. A vagina.

Incidentally, Mum and Dad insist this didn't happen. Dad points out that he would never have told me to flush a glossy sheet down the toilet, as it would have seriously risked a blockage.

★   ★   ★

The seventies was also the era of Mary Whitehouse – the queen of the philistines. But someone to whom my parents neverthe-less gave some credence. 'She's a bit over the top, but she's got a point.'

The seventies was an altogether more conservative era. When I tried to take L. P. Hartley's *The Go-Between* out of the school library at the age of thirteen, I was stopped by the librarian.

'I don't think this book is suitable for you.'

The fact that it's a good book was irrelevant, because there was *sex* in it. The subtext was clear: don't give a teenage boy a novel with sex scenes in it because God knows what it might do to him.

Pretending sex didn't exist made it even more exciting. Michelle Eddisford, who lived next door and whose father, Maurice, used to wander into our house occasionally to play pinball, had a book called *The Girl Growing Up*. She asked if I wanted to look at it. Of course I did. We'd never have a book like that in our house. I was, ultimately, disappointed: it was full of black-and-white ink drawings of penises and vaginas, and offered the most clinical, diagrammatic, unsexy, joyless explanation of intercourse. It read like a Haynes car maintenance manual. The last thing it was going to do was make you feel precoital.

The truth is that although I liked girls, I was intimidated by them. When I was around nine, I scrambled over quite a high fence to get away from a girl who was determined to kiss me.

Everything about sex was awkward back then. When I was eleven, nearly twelve, I couldn't believe it when Mum said, 'Are you doing sex education at school? Is there anything you want to know about? Is there anything you don't know about that I can tell you?'

I was mortified. It was bad enough having to learn about it at school in a class full of giggling boys. Mum was only half offering, and I quickly squeaked, 'No. I'm fine, thanks.'

I was thinking, 'Oh my God, what a horrific conversation. I only just managed to avoid talking to my *mum* about *sex*!'

As my parents didn't allow us to watch sex on television, so they restricted the amount of violence we saw. I wasn't allowed to watch *The Sweeney* because it showed people with stockings on their heads wielding shotguns. Any kind of stockings were out of bounds in our house, whether they were on legs or heads. And of course anything taboo becomes more attractive.

As I've said, I longed to have a colour television, but it was ruled out for a long time. People in council houses rented everything without batting an eyelid. At least my maternal grandmother had a colour TV from Radio Rentals, and I was surprised to discover that a car I had admired on some show or another was bright red and not grey as I'd assumed.

In December 1975, I watched *Dr No*, the first Bond film to be shown on television, at my grandmother's house. I virtually wet my pants with excitement. At school I played in defence in football just so I could chat to the goalkeeper about James Bond and Bruce Lee. Instead of chasing after the ball, I'd hoof it down the other end so we could spend more time chatting.

My goalkeeper friend, Anthony Dixon, came round to my house with a View-Master and let me look at 3D slides of Roger Moore in *Live and Let Die*. We were beside ourselves. The glamour! The suits! The cars!

And of course I had a poster of Roger Moore (we share a birthday; but then I also share one with Cliff Richard, so it doesn't mean anything). It was probably an uncool thing for a boy to have on his wall, but to me, with his tan, open-necked shirt and safari suit, he oozed sophistication.

But then I was an unusual boy. Shortly after watching *Dr No* in all its Technicolor glory, I began to tape-record TV shows at home. I was a human video recorder in the days before they existed. I would borrow my older brother's cassette player, balance the microphone on a cushion in front of the TV and record my favourite shows. I then had the audio track of that show for ever. It was a serious business. If anyone started talking while I was recording, I'd get all shirty and pompous and growl at them, 'Ssshh! Stop talking!'

I recorded *Fawlty Towers* in this way, and *Ripping Yarns*, the BBC comedy series written by Michael Palin and Terry Jones.

I would listen back to the cassettes time and again. It was like capturing lightning in a bottle. Slowly and meticulously, I learned to do all the voices.

People were impressed and often said, 'You should be on the telly.'

I was called upon regularly to bring to life some aspect of the previous night's TV for a friend of my mum's or sister's. They'd be trying to describe the TV show but the effect would be lost.

'Stephen, did you see the show?'

'Yes,' I replied.

'Oh good,' they'd say, relieved. 'Do it for us.'

They knew they could rely on me to capture the essence of what it was that had made them laugh.

I would subliminally pick up voices. I had a voice stuck in my head for hours one night. And a phrase. 'The first man to swim the channel . . .'

I woke up my younger brother Kevin and whispered to him, 'Who's this?'

He mumbled groggily through his stupor, 'Ross McWhirter.' And then he turned over and went back to sleep.

Of course it was. I must have been watching him on *Record Breakers* and his voice had stuck in my head.

From a very early age, I had a photographic memory for voices. I had what is called 'a good ear'. I don't ever remember not being able to do it.

I used to bring friends home, sit them down and make them listen to my cassette recordings.

As they sat there patiently, I would describe the action: 'He's walking up a hill now. He's going through a door. He's just got into his car. He's driving . . .'

The bus from school went past my house, which made it

easier to lure my friends back. I think, otherwise, they might have found excuses to give my mimicry a miss.

I used to get the Monty Python records out to play to my friends too. I cherished vinyl comedy records because you could play them as many times as you liked, then analyse them and learn the lines off by heart.

We were incredibly careful when handling vinyl: we held each record at the edges with the palms of our hands and always replaced it carefully in its inner paper sleeve, turned the inner sleeve sideways and slid it slowly back inside the outer sleeve. Vinyl deserved reverential treatment.

CHAPTER 26

I was about ten when I discovered Monty Python. It was the comedy of anarchy. It was like punk: new and exciting and the kind of thing parents didn't understand. The Pythons were rude about Catholics and they parodied the Spanish Inquisition. It was the first time I'd ever heard about Catholics doing bad things; it made me start to question the idea that all Catholics were holy and wonderful.

As soon as I became aware of Python, I thought to myself, 'I want to make my living from this.'

But it was an unfocused ambition. I didn't have a plan. I wasn't well read, I didn't yet have a burning desire to write. It all struck me as scarily grown up and too much like hard work. I was lazy, a daydreamer, distracted, a bit feckless. But good at voices.

When I learned the sketches by heart, I had little or no idea of the significance or nuance of some of the references. Thomas Hardy, Marcel Proust, Jean de La Fontaine . . . they all went over my ten-year-old head.

I just knew it was different and odd and exciting. I'd watch my friends starting to laugh as I recited excerpts. It was a fantastic feeling.

I remember a particular sketch where the mother of the John Cleese character had just died and Michael Palin was playing the undertaker. What I loved so much about it was that it was pushing the boundaries of decency. The sketch ended with Michael Palin talking about vomiting the mother up into a grave, which is a really terrible image. My parents would have been horrified.

I know people tended to have favourite Pythons, much as

they had a favourite Beatle. But I liked each Python for different reasons: Michael Palin made you laugh when you weren't quite sure why, and I enjoyed the acidity of John Cleese.

My parents liked more orthodox comedy, such as *Fawlty Towers*, which started on BBC2 in September 1975. The very idea of it was intriguing – John Cleese had a new sitcom in which he played a boorish hotel owner.

My brother David talked about it before it was broadcast; he always tipped me off about new shows. In 1979 he told me about a new BBC2 show called *Not the Nine O'Clock News*, rightly predicting that everyone would be talking about it. I owe him a debt.

I bought the scripts for *Fawlty Towers* and, later, *Ripping Yarns*. It was easy to get hold of them then. The *Fawlty Towers* script had a photo of Basil Fawlty's hotel on the front cover and was full of dialogue to covet.

I remember certain scenes from it even now.

The two old ladies saying, 'Don't do anything we wouldn't do, Mr Fawlty.'

And Basil saying, under his breath, 'Just a little breathing, surely.'

It was full of really fantastic, bleak humour.

'The Germans' episode – which is very funny, outrageous and rude – is a favourite.

> BASIL: 'Now, would you like something to eat or drink before the war . . . ning that trespassers will be tied up with piano wire?'

He can't stop mentioning the war and has to quickly change 'war' into 'warning', but then makes it worse by mentioning an appalling act for which the Nazis were infamous.

'The Germans' episode was only thirty years after the war, and yet here I am, misty-eyed about an episode that was broadcast over forty years ago.

There was an edginess to the comedy which I loved because you never knew what was coming next.

When I see those episodes now by chance on TV, there's a wonderful *joie de vivre* about them. It's fantastic to see John Cleese in his thirties, his talent maturing at the right moment.

Of course, *Fawlty Towers* is now cloaked in a haze of nostalgia, but it works on so many levels for me: Alan Partridge owes so much to Basil Fawlty; it's the BBC at its best; it's familiar and comforting.

Watching *Fawlty Towers* or *The Good Life* is the closest I can get to touching the past. When I catch glimpses of those programmes on TV, I can see myself watching them in the living room in Middleton as a child; us all sitting around, laughing; the safe, comfortable place I grew up in.

It's incredibly evocative. It reflects back the world I lived in, because the world I lived in loved those programmes too.

★   ★   ★

The next time a TV show really hooked me was in 1982, when I was in the lower sixth. *The Young Ones*, which launched Ben Elton's career as an alternative comedy writer, felt more relevant to me than *Not the Nine O'Clock News*; I was studying A-level Government and Politics, and the references in *The Young Ones* were really current. I liked the fact that I got those references as well as the fact that I got the humour.

I probably felt a little smug.

I was surrounded by students who were into mainstream television, film and music, and here was a series that made me realise I wasn't alone. I felt like one of those people who have an illness and when they discover it's a condition that lots of other people have, they can suddenly deal with it because they are not on their own.

I remember waking up the morning after the first episode of *The Young Ones* and thinking, 'These people speak the same language as me. They are talking about the stuff I'm thinking about!' It's dated now, of course, but at the time it felt very punk rock in its mocking not only of the establishment in general and Thatcher in particular, but also those who opposed it.

Political polarisation in comedy is always fruitful.

Unlike the Pythons, none of the actors – Rik Mayall, Ade Edmondson, Nigel Planer, Christopher Ryan and Alexei Sayle – had been to Oxford or Cambridge. If Python was posh punk, then *The Young Ones* embraced anarchy and was as silly as it was funny.

I did an impression of Kevin Turvey in *A Kick Up the Eighties* before I really knew who Rik Mayall was. Then I found out that not only had he been to Manchester University, but he also used to do stand-up comedy in the foyer of the Royal Exchange Theatre in Manchester. He was a brilliant, exciting, talented young comedian who had spent some of his formative years in my city.

When I was young, being a comic wasn't the career option it is now. It's what old blokes like Les Dawson did. Nobody of my generation thought, 'I want to get into comedy.' But knowing that Rik had spent time in my city made me feel that there might just be a way into his world.

★　★　★

Dad had a traditional sense of humour that involved terrible puns, and often he would tell a funny story that just didn't land. When Martin was seventeen and I was twelve, we started to mock the clean, traditional sense of humour that Dad embraced, in which there were no dirty jokes and no swearing, sometimes even sniggering as he was telling some unhip joke.

Yet Dad had real soft spots for *Hancock's Half Hour* and *The Goon Show*, which really were the last hurrah for radio comedy. He would play them on vinyl, his enthusiasm drawing me in until I too became a fan.

Tony Hancock plays a version of himself in *Hancock's Half Hour*, which is something I have done a number of times.

Hancock had that discontentedness that comics tend to have. A disquiet. Feeling at odds with the world. Frustrated. That feeling that you could have been a contender and that it's other people's fault you're not. Feeling that the world owes you a living. Aspiring to have a greater intellect – that is Hancock to a tee. Wanting to be more noble, civilised, learned.

There are things about me that are both ridiculous and simultaneously quite noble. I can be both those things at the same time. Alan Partridge is one manifestation of that and I am another.

Ray Galton and Alan Simpson, the scriptwriters who worked with Hancock between 1954 and 1961, were such wonderful writers, as were Dick Clement and Ian La Frenais, who wrote *The Likely Lads* and *Porridge*. Jeff Pope and I share an affection for those comedies, which I hope is evident in *Philomena*.

Anyway, Galton and Simpson went on to write *Steptoe and Son*, a gritty black-and-white sitcom about two working-class rag-and-bone men. Wilfrid Brambell played the dirty old Tory father, Albert Edward Ladysmith Steptoe, and Harry H. Corbett played the lefty son, Harold Albert Kitchener Steptoe.

We used to do that kind of television so well; I miss it. Galton and Simpson's comedy was so sad, poignant and full of pathos that it often pushed me to tears. The pilot episode in particular stands out. 'The Offer' was a two-hander set in one room. Harold threatens to leave; he wants his own shop with his own name above the door. Albert argues that he already has his name above the door: '. . . and son'.

Steptoe senior says that if his son leaves he can't have the horse, so Harold tries to take the cart. But he can't move it; he can't physically leave. He bursts into tears.

Albert comforts him. 'Go in the morning. I'll make you a nice cup of cocoa.'

Harold agrees, but you know he's never going to leave.

It's heartbreaking and funny at the same time.

I met Galton and Simpson about twenty years ago, at the Sony Radio Awards. They said *Knowing Me Knowing You with Alan Partridge* on Radio 4 was as good as anything they'd ever done.

I was quite young to hear that kind of compliment from writers I respected so much. I was firing on all cylinders and had very little introspection or self-doubt; I was like a hyperactive child, wanting to consume work, sex and life voraciously.

But I wasn't stupid. I was speechless after talking to Galton and Simpson. It remains one of the best compliments I've ever been paid.

CHAPTER 27

Although, by eleven, I was becoming aware of a world beyond Middleton, I wasn't yet ready for secondary school. I was still wetting the bed. I still wanted my mum all to myself when I ran home from school at lunchtime.

I was so petrified of starting grammar school that I skipped the first few days. I was worried about the new subjects I'd be learning. I was worried I'd get lost. I was daunted by all the big, smelly teenagers in uniform, who looked like apes. I had to talk myself into going. At least I could catch the bus with friends from primary school. And I had my new, cool Terylene blazer from a shop in the Arndale Centre.

Most kids who went to Cardinal Langley Roman Catholic High School in Middleton had black wool blazers that smelled of damp dog when they got wet. Some kids had blazers with red braiding sewn on by their mothers that looked home-made and cheap. It was easy to spot those who had home-made blazers and those who had the real thing. The wool blazer boys always had ink on their fingers. They were Just William, Billy Bunter types. Old-fashioned.

I spurned a wool blazer in favour of this sharp-looking blazer that you could roll into a ball and watch spring back into shape. Terylene was a wonder material; housewives loved it because it was so easy to wash, dried quickly and never creased. Although if you had put a match anywhere near my blazer, it would no doubt have melted.

I'm surprised Dad didn't make me wear a DIY blazer; I must have talked Mum into splashing out £13.50 for the synthetic one.

I often wore hand-me-downs from my brothers, but on this

occasion I was allowed a new blazer, a new tie and a proper school sweater. It must have cost my parents a small fortune.

The Terylene blazer boys could afford a slight swagger. I certainly felt a bit James Bond in mine. I wore nine-hole Dr Marten boots; nine holes were just the right measure of rebellion, they were ever so slightly punky. Boys with eleven holes were taking it too far.

Cardinal Langley was a prestigious grammar school, and it sometimes felt like it secretly wanted to be a private school. Or Hogwarts. The boys were separated into six houses. I was in Rigby, like my two older brothers before me. You had to earn points for your house by doing well at sport and generally excelling and, at the end of the year, the winning house was awarded a shield. I was so proud when we won. There was a slight kinship with other people in your house, even if you weren't best friends.

The school was run by De La Salle Brothers. The first De La Salle Foundation in England opened in 1855, five years after the restoration of the Catholic hierarchy in Britain. The Brothers are, generally speaking, in favour of teaching the poor; when comprehensive education came along, my school had the option to assume private status, but it was against the ethos of the Brothers. So, in September 1979, when my younger brother Kevin joined the school, the school turned from a single-sex grammar school into a co-ed comprehensive.

And yet, when I started in 1977, Cardinal Langley was still old-fashioned and patriarchal in so many ways, and my first two years felt very *Tom Brown's School Days*. It was run by Brother Thomas, a headmaster with a soothing Irish voice who commanded everybody's respect. He gave us a welcome talk on the first day and addressed us all as 'gentlemen'.

His nickname was 'The Boss', but he never raised his voice and preferred to punish the boys by giving them chores like cleaning windows rather than the strap or the slipper. He was humane.

In the few decades since the late seventies and early eighties, education has changed virtually beyond recognition. What would seem barbaric now – namely, corporal punishment – was the norm then. And a strict Catholic boys' school was at the extreme end of eighties education. Even when I started, Cardinal Langley still hadn't quite left the Victorian era behind. It was a gloomy building, with wooden benches and Bunsen burners and cross-country runs in all weather.

I was lucky to have two older brothers in the school. People knew I was one of the Coogans and it offered some insurance. But it didn't stop a boy in the fourth year from punching me in the face just because I answered him back. My lip was bleeding and I burst into tears. When I told the teacher he admonished the boy lightly, but nothing more. Generally, however, the teachers didn't hold back when it came to punishment.

★   ★   ★

My generation was the last to experience corporal punishment, which was outlawed by Parliament in 1987 but slowly fell out of fashion before then. I lost count of the number of times I was slippered. And by 'slipper' I mean a plimsoll with a hard sole. We used to be given on-the-spot geography tests and if we got less than three out of five, the slipper would appear. Each time, a line would form of around ten kids, waiting to be whacked. If you forgot your PE kit, you'd get the slipper. If you forgot your biology homework, you'd get the slipper, twice. One teacher drew a chalk cross on the bottom of the slipper so that everyone knew you'd been punished. I was often to be seen walking around with a white chalk cross on my backside.

Only the strap had to be signed for and a reason given for its use; the slipper could be used arbitrarily.

I had a fight once with a tough kid from Langley council estate. The kids from the estates were tougher than us, but clever too – we all had to pass the 11-plus to get into the grammar school. This lad was a boxer and he punched me, perhaps because he didn't like the look of me or maybe because I'd made a smart comment. Bravely – stupidly – I grabbed him by the hair, pulled his head down and kneed him in the face. He was smaller than me, so he got slippered once and I got slippered twice.

In the first year – now known as year seven – our form teacher used to drag us around the classroom by our hair. But that was nothing compared to the strap. It was made from weighted leather and was so potentially brutal the teachers weren't allowed to raise it above their heads. It was designed to cause pain but not injury, to leave a red mark but not a welt.

Sometimes you had to hold your hand out for the strap. Other times you had to bend over, holding your breath and clenching your buttocks as you anticipated the thwack. Then you would blink really hard and bite your lip to stop the tears. Sometimes I cried. Not because I was upset, but because it really bloody hurt. I can vividly recall the pain now and it still makes me wince.

My dad's cousin's husband worked at the school and he strapped me once. I was on the field when I shouldn't have been, but I think he did it to show no favour. And then I saw him over Christmas, acting as though nothing untoward had happened.

Dad used to say the slipper was character-building. Perhaps it was, for some people. For the emotionally vulnerable I imagine it was soul-destroying. I found it a bit of both. There's no doubt some teachers got off on it. Since the guidelines for the use of the slipper were non-existent, it's fair to say that those who employed it regularly for minor misdemeanours were suspect.

Clearly my home life wasn't like Billy Casper's in *Kes*, but my school wasn't a million miles away from his in many ways. We were expected to be tough. In my first year we had to do six-mile runs. Mostly I came in the top ten of the hundred boys who took part in the run, simply because I had stamina and refused to give up. We went along dirt tracks, across the canal, up to Tandle Hill Country Park, then we had to run up to the monument on the hill, kiss it and run down the other side. Once I lagged behind and found myself on the wrong side of the canal. I couldn't find the bridge; I was stranded. I burst into tears. I walked and walked in one direction until eventually I found a bridge.

For the last stretch we'd be running like zombies, splashing through puddles, covered in dirt, snot streaming down our chins. Always thinking, 'Keep going. Just keep going . . .'

When we got back to the games area, we would collapse on the tarmac floor of the indoor court. We'd lie there, exhausted, our slender bodies throbbing and steam rising off us like race-horses. And then for the communal showers. Some boys were already hairy and man-like, others smooth as an eel. I was somewhere in the middle. And yet there was no embarrassment about nudity; we just jumped in the showers.

If you forgot your PE kit, you would have to borrow a rugby shirt that stank of another boy's sweat. And you got the slipper. Unless you paid a fifteen-pence fine, in which case you would be let off. When it was my birthday one year I came to school with some of the money I'd been given and I paid the fine for all the boys who had forgotten their PE kit. I was a hero that day. All the boys kept saying, 'Thanks, Coogan!'

It wasn't only about a need to be liked. I liked to put a stick in the teacher's spokes, to deny him the pleasure of giving the boys the slipper.

Luckily, I didn't have to pay for friendship. I was friends with a flashy kid who lived on the council estate. His dad was a scrap metal dealer and they lived in the best house on the estate. This boy was smart, confident and cool. I was neither smart nor cool. I wasn't into hanging around with the sporty, popular types, who were too pleasant and polite. I wanted to be cool and interesting, in a kind of unconventional way. Much as I hoped the flashy kid might improve my image, he proved a transient friend.

I was separated from Brendan Tierney when I went to Cardinal Langley. Brendan was one of non-identical twins, and while his brother passed the 11-plus and went to grammar school, Brendan failed and went to the local secondary modern.

I kept my friendship going with Brendan, despite him being at another school and despite my family always mentioning the time he had climbed on top of our TV when he was five. It felt a bit like he'd been given the short straw by going to a school that wasn't great. But he hasn't let it hold him back; he's incredibly well read now, much more than I am.

I still saw Brendan at weekends. We'd go out on bikes, hang around in the woods, listen to music together. He rang up one day and said he had a question for me.

'Stephen, I'm thinking of becoming a heavy rocker. Do you want to join me?'

'Bren, I can't do that,' I said. 'It would be a betrayal of everything I've always loved, which is punk rock. But I'll still be your friend.'

Brendan told me recently that when his family had booked a holiday at Pontins in Brean Sands in 1980, he had dreaded telling me. I had been, he said, a terrible closet snob. One day I had asked him if he was going anywhere that summer, and when he told me I apparently let out a huge laugh. 'For God's sake, mate, you don't get people with Jags going there.'

★　★　★

I have remained lifelong friends with a handful of school friends, including Brendan and Mike Taylor. I met Mike on the first day of secondary school. He wore big National Health glasses and was quite short, but tough. He was from Oldham and had a proper old Lancashire accent. When I first met him, he used to say 'thee' instead of 'you' and 'thine' instead of 'yours'.

'What's wrong with thee? That's thine . . .'

It's a way of talking that has all but disappeared. Mike doesn't talk like that now, obviously, but I found it a comforting, old-fashioned way of speaking. I love a Lancashire accent. It's more forgiving and musical than, say, the more guttural Yorkshire or the lazy nasality of central Manchester and Salford.

I didn't mess around – I preferred to charm the teachers – but Mike messed around all the time. He would crawl under all the desks until he got to the teacher's desk right at the front. And there he would sit, under the desk, waving to the rest of the class and pulling faces while the Latin teacher marked books.

We were both in the school rugby team and played regularly against local public schools. We were frequently thrashed by Manchester Grammar. Little fascists.

I wasn't very fit or tough, but I was allowed to join the rugby team because I could entertain everyone with funny voices. I liked the camaraderie of a team game, but I didn't relish jogging on to the field when it was so cold that the ground was frozen solid. At least when it was muddy you had a soft landing.

I played flanker, so I had to run off the edge of the scrum. The scrum collapsed on me once and nearly broke my back. And I've still got a small scar on my lip from doing a tackle from behind: I was diving through the air and grabbing an opponent's legs when a stud hit me on the mouth. This lad's stud hadn't been properly filed down and it was like a blade. There was blood everywhere.

I managed to say, 'I think I need a stitch, my lip has opened right up.'

The teacher practically laughed at me. 'Don't be soft, it's just a scratch.'

So on I played, with blood streaming down my shirt. I wasn't a tough rugby-playing type, but I have fond memories of getting splattered with mud as the adrenalin flowed. It was oddly satisfying.

Mike remembers me playing out of position and lost in a

dream world until I got the ball. Then, suddenly, I would become totally focused and committed to tackling.

Once we played against Marple Hall School, whose rugby teacher was called Keith Harding. He occasionally appeared in a long-running TV series called *Superstars* in which famous sportsmen such as Kevin Keegan and James Hunt participated in a range of events. And what did I do? I had a fight in front of this minor celebrity. Ged McBreen wrung his muddy shorts out in my shoes and we started throwing punches at each other.

I disgraced the school.

And for that I was given a talking-to and then slippered by Mr McPollen, the games teacher. It wasn't done in anger; it was a formality, like an execution. I was bad and I had to be punished.

★ ★ ★

The conservative brethren wore habits; the more liberal ones wore suits. Others were lay teachers who just happened to work at our school. We were taught some archaic dross, but our school was more progressive than the local convent school, which warned its female pupils not to shine their shoes. After all, they didn't want boys seeing a reflection of their knickers in the leather. Potty.

There was always a smart and robust sense of humour at our all-boys' school.

Mar Jones was a Russian physics teacher who bore an uncanny resemblance to Rosa Klebb, one of James Bond's fierce Soviet enemies in *To Russia with Love*. One afternoon she was performing an experiment with magnets and iron filings on the workbench to demonstrate magnetic fields.

When the filings didn't behave as she thought they ought to, she said, 'That's strange. I don't understand why this is happening . . .'

One of the boys proffered an explanation: 'Maybe it's the knives in your boots, miss.'

The rest of the class was helpless with laughter.

She furrowed her brow. 'Knives in my boots?!'

Unlike us, she wasn't a James Bond aficionado.

I particularly admired David Hennessey, who taught history and religion. He was an intellectual who had come down from Oxford to our school because he was taking up holy orders from someone on their deathbed. I could tell he was punching below his weight. He was about twenty-six, super-smart, provocative and prematurely greying.

Looking back at my reports, I can see that I must have driven Hennessey to distraction. An early report refers to me as a 'lively class "theologian"', the following year my religion exam result is 'disappointing', and the year after that I am 'capable of mature thought on complex subjects'.

In the third year, my general report for the Christmas term said: 'This report is rather disturbing. I think Stephen is now old enough to stop playing at this work. His French particularly has slipped steadily downhill since he started. No one doubts his intelligence – the remedy is in his hands.'

I was, in truth, probably more interested in asking awkward questions than learning fluent French. When we were on our way back from a religious retreat in the fifth form, I kept trying to push Hennessey to engage with various debates.

'Brother David, isn't it wrong of the Church to teach sex only as an act of procreation and not as something from which to gain pleasure?'

It was late at night and he was driving the minibus. 'Oh, please, Stephen, not now.'

But, when he wasn't tired and distracted, Brother David – or 'Bro David', which now sounds weirdly ghetto – would talk about the Church in Latin America aligning itself with Marxists to fight dictatorships. He wanted us to discuss the moral issues of the Church engaging in armed resistance and he seemed genuinely interested in my thoughts.

I was more used to conservative Catholics: when General

Franco died in 1975, our parish priest held Mass for him. He may have been a fascist dictator who violated human rights, had people tortured and stole babies from socialist women and gave them to right-wing families, but he was a devout Catholic.

Bro David was a breath of fresh air. In an old religion exercise book I still have, I've written: 'Armed resistance might be justified against a repressive fascist regime.'

In the margin he has written: 'Violence begets violence.' And then, 'Just underlining my orthodoxy in the hope of landing a sinecure in the Vatican.'

He had a sense of humour, and he talked to me as an equal. He talked to all of us as adults. He seemed at ease with himself and I looked up to him. I wanted to be like him when I was older: smart, laconic and charismatic.

Martin Wilde taught us maths and games. He gave us extra maths lessons so that we would get the right grades. He was withering and he mocked our incompetence, but he was funny too.

My English teacher, Miss Lewis, was Jewish. She randomly taught us Jewish songs such as 'Hava Nagila' in the middle of English lessons. She used to say Christian prayers with us, always avoiding the word 'God'.

I quickly learned that my impressions gave me a certain kudos at school. A few months after I had started Cardinal Langley, my brother Martin, who I hero-worshipped, started dragging me up to the sixth-form common room to do impersonations. He wore effortlessly cool clothes and was the best-looking of us Coogan boys. He wandered around school like he owned the place. I sometimes felt I was walking in his shadow, so I liked being asked to perform in front of six or seven of his mates. It was as though he thought his coolness would be enhanced by showing off his brother.

'Check out my kid brother, he can do all these voices.'

I stood there and did Edward Heath, Margaret Thatcher and James Callaghan, who was prime minister at that time.

Everyone laughed and said, 'What a funny little thing he is.'

And then they'd tell me to bugger off.

By the time I was fourteen, my housemaster and art teacher, a long-haired, amiable Scouser called P. B. Murphy, was asking to hear my impressions of him.

One day he said, 'Why don't you take house assembly this morning, Coogan?'

P. B. Murphy was always talking about how precious and precarious life is. He'd mention a fatal accident and go into far too much detail: 'They were killed terribly, their necks broken, lying dead in the road. Life is so precious.'

I would stand up in assembly and impersonate him, exaggerating the way he talked: 'I read something in the news today about a family being completely decimated, chopped up into tiny pieces, blood trickling down the road, bits of their bodies lying everywhere, heads rolling into gutters . . .' Pause. 'How precious is life?'

I then went around the hall, talking about God and straightening the ties of older boys, because that's what P. B. Murphy did. He was very laid-back. He gave me a licence to laugh at him.

He helped me organise two school trips to the Motor Show at the NEC in Birmingham. The first was in October 1978, when I had just turned thirteen, and the second was in 1980.

I was always the most car-oriented sibling. Whenever I played with my Matchbox Superfast track when I was younger, I would do a car chase really slowly while doing all the voices.

'C'mon Jack! Where are you?'

'He's over here!'

'Quick! Let's head him off!'

My family laughed at me because I'd keep playing and replaying the car chases until they were as I wanted them. Sometimes they weren't aesthetically right or the drivers said the wrong things.

While my brother David was into Airfix models, my focus was always on the free Matchbox cars you could send off for after collecting sufficient tokens on cereal packets.

Cereal packets played a large part in a child's life in the seventies. I could never quite believe that tokens could translate into a free Matchbox car. Somehow it was like cheating the rules of life. I would sit at the kitchen table, carefully cutting out the tokens and dreaming of the morning I would hear a dull thud on the mat in the hallway.

Sometimes I was still lying in bed when the post came. As soon as I reached the top of the stairs and saw the brown manila envelope, I knew that a shiny car in a vivid primary colour was waiting for me. Even now, vivid metallic colours remind me of Matchbox cars.

On the way home from school I would often stop off at John Menzies. I'd go straight to the toy department and stare at the rows of cars in their colourful cardboard boxes. I'd stand there for five, even ten minutes, wondering what it would be like to have enough money to actually buy a toy car. I would also wander through the Arndale Centre, looking at Action Man toys and thinking, 'This is what rich parents buy their children.'

I made friends with a boy just because he had some Action Men, which were essentially dolls for boys. My parents never bought us Action Men, partly because of the expense and partly because it was a branded toy. We would have to make do with some cut-price impersonation of an Action Man that didn't have grippy hands or realistic hair.

Meanwhile, this boy had all these expensive toys and he was always playing in his garden. Every time I walked past he'd ask if I wanted to play with him. Eventually I agreed and at some point he gave me three Action Men. I couldn't quite believe it. I thought he was mad.

★　★　★

P. B. Murphy let me get away with murder and gave me special dispensation when it came to homework. He would call me into his office to talk about what had been on TV the night before. He liked engaging with me and, like Brother David, talked to me as an adult.

My classmates would say, 'You jammy bastard, how did you get away with not doing your homework?'

Murphy would simply say, 'Bring it in next time.'

And yet the threat of the slipper always hung over us. There were two brethren at school known by the kids as Batty Bates and Bully Bates. Batty had big ears and was rotund; Bully was stocky and, well, a bully. Both had fought in the Second World War and were much older than my dad. Bully Bates carried a slipper in his inside pocket and if you were running too fast down a corridor he'd hold his arm out, shout at you to bend over and whack your backside with the slipper.

And then there was P. K. Murphy – not to be confused with P. B. – who had a terrible temper and threw chalk at us. Once he threw the wooden board duster at a kid, missed and hit the kid behind. The kid's head split open and P. K. Murphy was banned from using a board duster. As a badge of his inadequacy, he was only allowed to use a limp rag.

Thereafter, he would admonish pupils by defiantly dusting their heads with the rag, as if to say, 'They can take away my board duster, but they can never take away my ability to annoy pupils at will.'

CHAPTER 28

Everything changed when Cardinal Langley became a co-ed comp in 1979. The best part of girls joining the school was not their nascent sexuality, but the fact that they couldn't be slippered. And if they couldn't be slippered, we boys couldn't be slippered either. The Brothers didn't think it was right to slipper the girls, I suppose because they recognised the potentially sexual element to it. Whereas slippering a boy couldn't be titillating at all. Hmmm . . .

I don't remember being slippered after girls started at Cardinal Langley, though I could be wrong. But the strap didn't entirely disappear. In the fifth year we had a new teacher, an Indian chap called Mr Mohammed. His English was far from fluent and a bunch of us fifth-form boys used to mock him cruelly.

He came up to me on one occasion and accused me of talking when I hadn't said a word. He refused to listen.

'Go and get the strap.'

One of the other boys volunteered to go and get it. 'I'll go, sir! You just have to sign for it.'

Mr Mohammed turned to me. I held my hand out. He clearly hadn't used the strap before. He looked nervous. The strap whacked my hand and I just stared straight at him, my hand steady. I didn't flinch at all. I just kept on staring.

He lost his temper and started hitting my body with the strap.

'You idiot! You cheeky boy!'

I grabbed the strap from his hand and flung it across the classroom.

'You're in deep shit, sir. That is assault.'

He swore at me. He told me to sit down. He wanted it all to

stop. Even though my hand was smarting like hell, I felt sorry for him in the end.

The school's new comprehensive status also meant, of course, that the 11-plus was dropped. There was a definite feeling that 'thick kids' had been let in the school, and merciless teasing went on. An older boy, one of my brother's friends, walked past a classroom of slow readers, put his head round the door and yelled, 'D-O-G, dog!' The teacher shouted straight back, 'O-U-T, out!'

It wasn't very PC, but then each incoming year had to put up with teasing of one sort or another. On my very first day at secondary school, a group of thirteen-year-old boys came up to us.

'Do you have periods?'

'Yes,' we answered.

They burst out laughing as we stood there, clueless.

I never smoked at school, but I liked the frisson of getting on with the ne'er-do-well boys who hung around the toilets with cigarettes dangling casually from their mouths. I was slightly friendly with Gregory Mounfield, whose brother Mani is in The Stone Roses and Primal Scream. Gregory was tough, with fingers made yellow by persistent smoking.

He spoke quietly, as if passing on secret information, like a shady character from a Dick Tracy comic book. I'll never forget when he sidled up to me in July 1981, looking around furtively as if he might be overheard, and said, 'There are going to be riots in Moss Side on Wednesday.'

'Really?' I said. 'How do you know?'

'Oh, I know.' He smiled to himself as he strolled off for yet another cigarette in the school toilets.

Two days later, Moss Side exploded into forty-eight hours of mayhem.

I was about to turn fourteen when girls started at Cardinal Langley. We had hardly been exposed to any since primary school and suddenly the school was swarming with all these eleven-year-old prepubescent girls. I was scared of them. They were in a school overwhelmingly dominated by boys and they were on the verge of becoming young women. Theirs was a strange kind of power.

Some of them were mouthy. One girl punched a boy who was four years her senior and he went flying. She was thirteen, scary and had very large breasts. Scary and sexy. She would punch you if you got in her way. In fact, Pauline Calf was based on her: a predatory, tough and fast-speaking female.

★   ★   ★

It was also around this time that nuclear reactors melted on Three Mile Island, Rhodesia became Zimbabwe, and the previous winter of discontent led to the election of Margaret Thatcher, our first female prime minster. More importantly, I put my hand inside a girl's bra for the first time.

I had taken the local girl to the woods over the road from my house and snogged her in the long grass while Brendan snogged the girl's best friend nearby. We were both thirteen and we felt on top of the world.

Occasionally, when Mum and Dad went on holiday, my brothers would have a party at the house and everyone would smoke and drink too much. When I was fourteen, a nineteen-year-old girl snogged me for a bet. It was my first proper kiss. Much as I was blushing, I thought I'd gone to heaven.

From the age of fifteen, I would use the front room to snog girls and have a bit of a grope. There was a tacit understanding that no one would come in. Sometimes I'd go in with a girl and find one of my brothers in there. The disappointment was quite crushing.

Girls weren't usually drawn to me, because I lacked confidence. I wasn't macho or bullish; I hero-worshipped sophisticated guys with cigarettes always on the go. While James Bond was someone to aspire to, John Wayne was crass and slightly vulgar, and

Sylvester Stallone was just some meathead boxer who held no appeal at all.

I met Bernadette Jones, my first proper girlfriend, when we were both in the fifth form at Cardinal Langley. The Jones girls were all gorgeous. At one point Kevin, Brendan and I were all going with a Jones girl of a similar age to each of us. I'd go round to their house and pass a brother in the hallway. Everyone knew the Coogans and the Joneses, both respectable families with six kids apiece.

The Jones house, in the private housing part of the Langley estate, was another essentially lower-middle-class home with two lounges, a television room and a music room where you could be alone if you were lucky. Bernie was into David Bowie and we listened again and again to *Hunky Dory*, even though it had come out in 1971. Her love of Bowie impressed me; it made her seem exotic and enigmatic.

In 1982, when we were still in the fifth form, Bernie and I went to a religious retreat at St Cassian's Centre in Kintbury, near Newbury – a trip organised by Brother David. It was very happy-clappy; we made the sign of peace and hugged each other, we broke bread and drank beer. Even we sixteen-year-olds. The brothers wore sandals, but with jeans and chunky jumpers instead of dog collars. It was all incredibly liberal; I even asked Brother David about the joy of sex as he was driving us back.

When I got home, I said to my dad: 'Some people think that when you die, God is going to have a big list of all the things you did right and all the things you did wrong. That's nonsense. God is so merciful, he's not like that at all. He's not going to be standing at the gates of heaven with a list.'

Dad said, 'Well, I'm not sure about that. I certainly think you have to account for your actions.'

But the brethren at this retreat were really radical. Revolutionary. They said, 'God loves everyone equally. He loves Myra Hindley as much as he loves the Virgin Mary.'

For a while, I was swept up in this movement. They called themselves the Charismatics. It was all beer, hugs and tambourines. I remember one service where they all held hands and danced around the altar, singing. Afterwards my mum and dad said, 'It's a bit much.' I blush when I think about it now. I much prefer the mournful, reverberant Gregorian chanting in a cathedral.

Anyway, Bernie and I sat together at the back of the van, huddled under a coat, kissing and cuddling. It was the best part of the four-day retreat. We didn't ever have sex though; we were both Catholic and her dad was a headmaster at another local school.

Bernie and I started going out after I saw her at a concert and we got chatting. It was around the time of Haircut 100, Fun Boy Three, The Human League and Heaven 17, and the fashion for women was big skirts and big baggy jumpers. Nothing figure-hugging. It wasn't a flattering period, sartorially speaking, and yet she looked so gorgeous, with piercing blue eyes. She was so clever too, with impeccable exam results. I was hypnotised by her. She was completely out of my league.

I was going out with the most beautiful girl in the school and I was miserable because all I could think about was everyone else being in love with her too. I only went on the religious retreat because I was paranoid about someone copping off with her. I knew I'd lose her at some point and that made me even more miserable.

It was like walking around with a Ming vase in your arms, and being terrified of dropping it.

When Bernie dumped me, she immediately went out with one of my best friends. They were inseparable.

I was devastated. I didn't know how to deal with it. I felt like my whole world had fallen apart.

It was January 1984 and it was straight after I'd crashed my car by going through a red light and driving into the side of a bus. I was the loser who crashed his car and was then dumped by his girlfriend. Years later, when I left drama school, I ended up going out with Bernie's sister, who was equally gorgeous. My brother had been out with her too; it was a bit of a merry-go-round.

I didn't lose my virginity till I was nineteen. I met a dancer who I had absolutely nothing in common with. She just had a body that I wanted to have sex with. And, by this point, I very badly wanted to have sex.

I would try to be witty and she'd look at me blankly: 'You're mad, you! You're mad!'

She thought I talked in riddles.

All she could think of saying was, 'You're mad. Come on, you can have sex with me now.'

I'd drive her home. On the way I'd find a dark country lane and we'd have sex. The windows would steam up and, after I'd dropped her off, I had to wind them down to air the car while I drove back to mine. Salad days!

CHAPTER 29

By the late seventies, I was beginning to learn about the popular culture that existed outside the mainstream. I was becoming aware of people who were clever and irreverent. They weren't just rude and vulgar, but rude and clever. Rude and posh. I was drawn to anything that was arty and mildly subversive.

I occasionally read one of the copies of the *NME*, *Melody Maker* or *Sounds* that were lying around the house. David and I had a huge crush on Kate Bush; she was so mysterious, beautiful and other-wordly.

But mostly I listened to my brother Martin's records. The Beatles, Genesis, Fleetwood Mac, Carole King, David Bowie, T. Rex, Roxy Music, The Adverts, The Damned and The Clash.

We both thought the music most people liked – Abba, The Bee Gees – was rubbish.

I was a complete snob, as was evident in the letter I sent my sister Clare, mocking the French teacher's love of disco.

I liked Blondie, but they were successful too quickly and, despite being a fantastic pop band, didn't quite cut it. Debbie Harry, however, was always cool. Every boy had a poster of her on his wall. I also had posters of a Lamborghini, Farrah Fawcett-Majors, as she was then, her husband Lee Majors, and Roger Moore in a safari suit.

I used my brother's cassette player to record music off the television. Tony Wilson was the first person to have the Sex Pistols on TV, in his regional show, *So It Goes*; Joy Division also performed 'Transmission' on the show, and I played it over and over, thinking it was really interesting.

I couldn't get enough of 'My Perfect Cousin', and I liked the fact that The Undertones performed in the same scruffy clothes they hung around in. They were angular and awkward in their anoraks and jeans, back when working-class kids were skinny.

When I brought home a copy of *Never Mind the Bollocks, Here's the Sex Pistols* in 1979, I had to hide it inside a Val Doonican sleeve. I knew my dad would say that the use of 'bollocks' was crude and provocative for the sake of it. I could only afford to buy it by going halves with Ged McBreen; we each had it for a week at a time.

I was almost as geeky about music as I was about comedy. I used to listen to lyrics and sing along. It was a way to escape into my head; I would sit with an album sleeve and study the lyrics. The most interesting bands didn't have pictures of themselves on their album covers. Being mysterious was part of their allure.

In the days before the Walkman or the iPod, you didn't listen to music as you walked down the street. You sat in a chair and listened. Sometimes the gatefold sleeve would include lyrics; other times you had to guess what they were singing about. I still get a thrill from googling lyrics.

The local nutcase, who was thin but prone to violent outbursts, would steal records to order from the local record shop. You'd tell him what you wanted and he'd go and steal it for you and sell it to you for a quarter of the price. He stole a red vinyl version of 'King Rocker' by Generation X in 1979. And 'London Calling' by The Clash. He charged me twenty-five pence for both, which I paid for with my paper-round money.

He once accused me of looking at him in a funny way, which of course I denied. But not before I was 'gobbed' (punched in the mouth so as to make it bleed).

I was obsessed with punk and then electronic music. Martin, ever the cool big brother, played the electric guitar and dyed his hair. I looked up to Martin and copied him, to the extent that if he bought a jacket, I'd buy the same one.

He sometimes sent me to buy a record if he couldn't be bothered.

'Stephen, do me a favour. Go down to Boots and buy me "Hong Kong Garden" by Siouxsie and the Banshees.'

I remember standing in the lounge putting the needle on the edge of the 7 inch and hearing 'Hong Kong Garden' for the first time. I still get goosebumps when I hear the oriental-sounding electronic xylophone kick-starting the song. It's one of the most remarkable intros to a song I've ever heard.

In the seventies and eighties, people were desperate to have some kind of identity. You were a mod or a rocker, into ska or northern soul. It was far more tribal than it is now. People from different tribes didn't really mix. You couldn't like heavy rock and punk, or disco and punk. Which is why I could never accept Brendan Tierney's offer to become a heavy rocker.

I liked punk because it challenged the status quo. I thought I was clever and different and edgy because I played *Never Mind the Bollocks* at top volume, singing along to 'Bodies' with wild abandon. I would have been mortified if they'd heard me.

★   ★   ★

My brother Martin could play electric guitar really well. He had a huge record collection and was already forming a band in the sixth form. As lead singer and songwriter of The Mock Turtles, he would later have a top 20 hit with 'Can You Dig It'. But he was a rock god years before he went on *Top of the Pops*. He was always one step ahead.

Throughout the seventies, he was really into guitar-based music. And then, at some point in 1978, he made an announcement: 'Guitars are dead. Rock music is dead. It's all about synthesisers now. The future of music is going to be electronic.'

He started going to a new wave night at a club called Pips in Manchester. He told me about one regular who had dyed ginger hedgehog hair, glittery eye shadow and a lightning bolt drawn across his face, a look that was undermined by a broad Yorkshire accent. He was known as Ziggy Arkwright.

It became clear that the ten-minute drum and guitar solo of rockers was self-indulgent and tired. Also on the shitlist were Marshall amps, favoured by rockers. Significantly, Buzzcocks used HH amps because their high-end tinniness was the antithesis of the Marshall sound.

The X-Ray Spex song 'Germfree Adolescents' perfectly encapsulates that era. It was androgynous, nuanced and provocative, while rock had become Neanderthal and smelly. Most rockers were spotty and didn't have girlfriends.

I was still listening to *Never Mind the Bollocks*, and Martin would shake his head. 'That's so out of date, Stephen.'

He was listening to 'Warm Leatherette' by The Normal – nihilistic, emotionless, industrial music. And to John Foxx, the original lead singer in Ultravox.

It was the soundtrack to a bleak, faceless existence, anticipating a depressing, robotic future.

Martin was, of course, right about the music: soon I too was listening to Kraftwerk, The Human League and Jean Michel Jarre.

I even grew my hair longer on one side than the other and crimped it in honour of The Human League's Phil Oakey. I wore eyeliner, foundation and blusher. A double-breasted shirt, black stretch denim jeans and winkle-pickers. I thought I looked like the enigma of all enigmas.

It's strange how very close that look is to total twat.

I started writing really awful lyrics, asked two girls at school to be backing singers, and found a bass player and a drummer. I played the DX7 keyboard and did lead vocals. We looked like a provincial Human League, which meant we looked like The Human League.

Astonishingly, I won the school music competition one year with that band.

As I adopted this snobbish attitude towards popular culture, so I had this idea about nothing commercial having any value. In 1978, when I was twelve, I refused to go to the cinema to see *Grease*, even though all my friends went. As I wrote to Clare, I loftily considered it 'commercial rubbish'. If lots of people liked something then it must be dreadful.

I didn't – and don't – understand the fuss about the *Star Wars* films either. Still less, their devotees. I wish they'd fuck off to a faraway galaxy long, long ago (I've deliberately muddled the words, I want to annoy them). What a colossal waste of time.

I already knew that culture slightly hidden from view, or underground – in other words, something you had to find for yourself – had to be better.

★   ★   ★

Rejecting the mainstream and singing 'Bodies' loudly, albeit when my parents were out, was my way of quietly rebelling. I wasn't a naughty kid, just a normal teenager kicking gently against the establishment.

Mum and Dad weren't hard to rebel against. There was a fantastic headline in the *Onion*, the satirical online news magazine, in 2000: 'Parents' record collection deemed hilarious'. My parents' collection was truly atrocious.

As Martin perfectly recalls, 'They loved the snide versions of legitimate music.'

They weren't into Crosby, Stills and Nash, they were into The Seekers. They weren't into Joni Mitchell, they were into Mary Hopkin and Judy Collins. Cliff Richard was Elvis without the rudeness, the sneer and the sexuality. Elvis himself was vulgar, unrefined and dangerous, but Mum quite liked 'Summer Holiday'. And Nana Mouskouri.

They liked all the artists who had guest spots on *Morecambe & Wise*. Anything that had an unashamed, middle-of-the-road feel.

I asked Mum once, when I was growing up, if Dad had ever

liked any kind of pop music. She said he thought The Beatles had some good tunes. That was it.

My parents didn't understand Martin. It was OK for him to introduce me to bands such as T. Rex and Roxy Music, the slightly artier, androgynous side of glam rock. Coming home with his ears pierced and hair dyed blond at the front was not OK.

By this time he was at college in Manchester and working in a clothes shop on a Saturday. One time Dad told him not to come home again with 'that hair'.

I heard Dad's raised voice from my bedroom. I stood in the hallway and leaned over the banisters so I could hear exactly what was being said.

My brother, aged seventeen, was crying his eyes out as Dad shouted, 'What's wrong with you? You look like a girl!'

'I'm just expressing myself!' he yelled through the tears.

It must have been hard for Dad to understand. He worked hard to maintain a respectable home, and there was his son wearing an earring and eyeliner and bleaching his hair blond, like he was a woman.

★   ★   ★

I found ways of rebelling that were more unusual. When I was eleven or twelve, my sister bought me a movie make-up set from her first trip to America. It was the wax skin and bloody glycerine used to create fake wounds.

I went to the post office to collect the family allowance with two vampiric puncture wounds on my neck.

'I think you've cut yourself,' said the postmistress.

'Yes, I know,' I replied, with a *Village of the Damned* stare. I collected the ten pounds and returned home, flapping my arms like the wings of a bat.

On another occasion I fashioned a wax, skin-coloured crater between my eyes, which I filled with small pieces of tissue doused in the glycerine blood, creating a perfect bullet wound. My sister's blue eyeshadow helped create that dead look.

I draped myself over the sofa in the living room, eyes open and vacant . . . waiting. Eventually my dad walked in.

'Stephen?'

I tried to play dead, but bottled it. Instead I continued to maintain the lifeless stare as I replied, 'Yes?'

He stared at me for an instant.

Then he said, 'You're warped,' and left the room.

Dad, being an engineer, was very particular about things. He didn't like two-seaters: they were driven by selfish people who could only give one person a lift. He would shake his head at people who drove into their driveways forwards. They knew that they'd have to reverse onto the road at some point, which was dangerous.

There were also rules regarding the phone. We all had to answer with these carefully scripted words: 'Middleton, 1234. Who's speaking, please?'

We weren't allowed to just say 'hello'.

Dad would criticise cops in television dramas who answered the phone by just saying 'hello'. He thought they were slapdash and unprofessional, which was only compounded by their frequent failure to lock their car doors.

Can you imagine John Thaw in *The Sweeney* answering the phone by saying, 'Hello, Flying Squad, 1, 2, 1, 2. My name is Jack Regan, how may I be of assistance?'

I thought it was a mildly aggressive way to answer the phone. When I first left home at eighteen, I thoroughly enjoyed picking up the phone and saying 'hello'.

It's an extension of how cross Dad used to get whenever he saw a cop on a TV drama walking away from his car without locking it. Later, when I could drive, I used to really like not locking my car.

CHAPTER 30

I have been pathologically late all my life. My school reports often drew attention to my lack of punctuality: in the summer term of my third year, the general report states that my punctuality record is 'appalling. It is easily the worst in the class.'

I'm amazed I ever got to school on time. School started at 9 a.m. and the bus left at 8.40 a.m. I used to get up at 8.30 a.m., pull on my uniform, comb my hair, maybe brush my teeth, and run down the stairs two at a time. My cornflakes were always soggy because they'd been laid out in a bowl with milk at 8 a.m. Mum didn't have time to feed each child individually, so getting to the table on time was up to us.

If I was lucky, I would make the bus. Otherwise I knew that if I ran fast enough I could catch it three stops on because it slowed down as it drove through the shopping centre. I had to climb over a wall and run across two bus lanes to catch it. I would do that with alarming regularity.

Clare, as the eldest, was sometimes called into the garden to help Dad out with some project or another at one in the morning, and she often fell asleep on the sofa. But she had a different childhood from me. I was one of the three little ones and we had to be in bed by 10 p.m. at weekends. Probably at 9 p.m. on a school night. Although I sometimes sneaked out of bed and crawled under the sofa to watch television, bedtime was regulated for us little ones, especially when we were younger.

I would overhear my parents saying, 'What are we going to do with the three little ones? Have they gone upstairs yet?'

If they could hear us making a noise, Mum would stand at the bottom of the stairs and shout up to us, 'If I hear one more peep from you, I'm going to come up and give you a damn good hiding.'

If we carried on making a noise, Mum or Dad – mostly it was Mum – would come upstairs.

As soon as we heard her coming up the stairs, one of us would turn the light off and all three of us would leap into bed, pull our duvets up and pretend to be asleep.

Mum would burst into the room, turn the light back on, grab a piece of Matchbox Superfast track, pull the blankets off and whack us in our beds. Sometimes we'd start laughing and maybe Mum would end up laughing too. Then she'd get annoyed with us for making her laugh, whack us some more and go back downstairs.

The yellow plastic track was bendy rather than rigid, but it hurt, even through our pyjamas. It wasn't nice, but it didn't feel barbaric. Corporal punishment was the fabric of life back then. It was legal and widely used. It was just bad luck that you'd been caught.

'Spare the rod, spoil the child' was the received wisdom; if you don't discipline your child properly, you'll end up with an unpleasant human being.

I can't imagine hitting my daughter, but we live in very different times.

Besides, the Superfast track wasn't nearly as painful as my school's preferred punishment of either the slipper or the strap.

★   ★   ★

We could never be sure what would tip Mum or Dad over the edge. Sometimes I expected to be in real trouble and for some reason I got away with my bad behaviour.

In the early eighties, when we were making one of our regular trips to see my rich uncle Peter in Ireland, my brother Brendan trapped his finger in a highly sprung, heavy deck door on the ferry. As soon as the ferry had docked, Peter sent a marine engineer on board to investigate and Brendan was consequently awarded £5,000 in compensation.

He goaded me in the dining room one day: 'You haven't got any money. You're broke and I've got £5,000.'

I was furious. I pulled the pin out of the fire extinguisher and sprayed it at him across the room. He hid under the table and begged me to stop, but I carried on covering him with foam.

Mum came in and asked what I'd done. I explained that Brendan had goaded me and so I had let the fire extinguisher off. She tried to reproach us both, but she kept laughing.

Dad came home and heard about the fire extinguisher. He didn't reprimand me for letting it off on Brendan; instead his response was practical.

'If there was a fire straight after you'd let it off, there wouldn't have been an extinguisher available to put it out.'

★　　★　　★

I spent the first ten years of my life deifying my father. As a child you could ask him why the sky was blue and he invariably had a satisfying answer, because as well as being a devout Catholic, he also read the *New Scientist* every week. For a long time I thought everything Dad said was the law. He wasn't to be questioned. It took me a long time to realise that he was fallible and that there were people out there with very different but equally legitimate points of view.

People who know our family always say that you can tell a Coogan, but you can't tell him much. Or, 'Something you'll never hear a Coogan say: "Oh, that's interesting. I didn't know that. Please tell me more."'

The men in the Coogan family are very assertive in terms of knowledge. If we don't know it, it's probably not worth knowing.

It was from my father that I learned how to be oppositional and question received wisdom. Probably to the point of insanity, certainly to the point of irritation. It's healthy to have that mindset to an extent, but for a while I took it too far. It's a very British trait; everyone has a negative opinion to share. If you ask someone to extrapolate on something they love, they inevitably become tongue-tied. Everyone is eloquent in their criticism and ineloquent in their praise.

And, like everyone, Dad was full of contradictions. He could be wrong about things. Although he knew why the sky was blue, he was a terrible teacher. When Martin was learning the clarinet, Dad, who could play the sax, would offer to help. But he quickly lost patience and often ended up giving him a 'clout'.

As much as he was a Victorian-style dad, he was also human. The first and only time I saw him burst into tears was in June 1979, when there was a fire in the house. Most of us were oblivious to the fire raging upstairs, as we were downstairs watching *Nancy Drew* on television; we had stored a pile of mattresses and pillows in a cupboard, and a hot pipe melted through a wire, causing it to spark.

Brendan, who was nearly nine, ran into the living room. 'There's smoke upstairs!'

The girls' bedroom, which Gerry and Tina shared now that Clare had left for university, was a raging inferno. The heat had even blistered the paint on the living-room door.

We phoned the fire brigade.

Dad, in his boiler suit from doing DIY, told us to form a chain with buckets to try to put the fire out. The polystyrene tiles on the ceiling were fizzing as they melted. White plastic stalactites decorated the hallway above us.

The air smelled bad and we couldn't stop coughing. Dad was in such a panic that he opened the bedroom door, hoping to flush the fire out with water. Instead the influx of oxygen into the room shot the flames right out into the hallway and set fire to his hair and beard.

He slammed the door shut and extinguished his burning hair.

'Everyone! Out of the house now!'

We all stood in the back garden, watching flames shooting out of the top of the house.

The first fire brigade arrived, pushed a ladder up to the bedroom window, smashed the window and drenched the room.

My dad had spent the best part of two decades rebuilding the house from the inside out. And now he was slumped against the wall in his boiler suit. He burst into tears.

As Dad cried, Mum kept on saying, 'Everyone is safe and that is all that matters.'

I wasn't upset by the fire, but when I saw my dad weeping I started to cry.

He was a mere mortal after all.

★   ★   ★

Dad wasn't very sociable in the traditional sense. He never went to the pub. Before wine arrived in suburbia, Dad might have the occasional half-pint of shandy or a sweet sherry at Christmas.

And yet he was a member of Round Table, a social organisation for young families that also raised money for charity. One of the more admirable rules stated that you had to leave at the age of forty. It scares me to think I'd have been kicked out ten years ago.

It now sells itself as 'The Original Social Network', and I suppose in a way it was. It's not, as people often think, anything to do with the Freemasons – thankfully. Fraternal organisations or any groups that help their own above all else bring out the rage in me, as well as in my dad.

Round Table was a non-elitist, fairly egalitarian and slightly patriarchal organisation that gave young family men the chance to socialise, raise money for charity and help the community. It was patriarchal in the sense that only men could join, but the focus was very much on family days out. Dad would often organise a fair with coconut shies and treasure hunts – I remember having butterflies in my tummy as we searched for clues.

One of my earliest memories was going to a Round Table fair in 1969, when I was three and a half, and hearing Peter Sarstedt's 'Where Do You Go To (My Lovely)?' through the speakers as a hovercraft floated around the field. It stopped and two children were picked out of the audience to take a short trip. They randomly picked me and my brother Martin. We climbed into the gull-wing door of the hovercraft and took off across the field. The world felt full of possibility in that moment.

My dad has a sister who is twenty years younger than he is; my grandma had her when she was forty-seven. In 1969, Patricia was sixteen years old. For the fair my dad – and this seems unbelievable when I think about it – built a platform so that she could sit on it in her bikini. In front of Aunt Patricia was a pool of water. You had to throw a ball at a plate and if you hit the plate dead on, it would release a mechanism and *kung!*, she would tip into the water. Naturally, these being the days preceding political correctness, men were queuing up all afternoon to throw a ball at the plate.

Occasionally Mum and Dad would go to a Round Table dinner. My dad is always late – I've inherited it from him – and at some point in 1973 they were so late for the bus that they missed the dinner altogether and ended up going to the cinema instead. They came home telling us all about Roger Moore in *Live and Let Die*. I felt jealous and betrayed. I didn't care that it was a last-minute decision.

'You know how much I like James Bond,' I said, petulantly. 'You don't even share my enthusiasm for 007 and yet you've gone to see *Live and Let Die* on a whim and all you can do is talk about it in great detail and laugh about it and say how enjoyable it was, and I haven't seen it.'

Which just made them laugh more.

CHAPTER 31

I used to run all the way home from school at lunchtime just so I could sit and watch the news with my mum while everyone else was at school. I wanted her all to myself. One lunchtime in March 1976, we watched Harold Wilson announce his resignation. Shirley Williams, who was still a Labour MP at the time, was mentioned as a contender and Mum was excited. She'd always liked her style, her straight-talking nature and her strong sense of social justice. Mum thought we might have a female prime minister, and the fact that she was a Catholic was the icing on the cake.

Two years earlier, Mum had walked into the bedroom and pulled back the curtains.

'Harold Wilson is prime minister for a second term!'

I blearily said, 'Hurray!'

But I was nine and only vaguely aware of the general import-ance of politics, rather than the specifics of each political party. By the time he resigned, I was far more au fait with which party was 'good' and which was 'bad', even though my dislike of the Tories at that point did, to some extent, mirror my slightly dim view of Protestants.

There were endless conversations in our house about the Irish being bullied by the English. For all my parents' conservatism, they didn't embrace the establishment. They were never flag wavers and only had time for the Queen because she handled herself with dignity and did things for charity.

My parents used to say, 'We think there should be a united Ireland, but what the IRA do is wrong. Violence is wrong.'

I was aware of the Black and Tans as I was growing up. The way those former soldiers were sent to Ireland by the English government to assist the Royal Irish Constabulary was terrible. We were never to forget what murdering thugs the British had been towards the Irish.

By the time a woman made it to Number 10, three years after Wilson's resignation, I was thirteen and fully politicised. My family loathed Thatcher even before she was elected. There was no delight in her being the first female prime minister, because she wasn't about community, which my parents believed in, and she didn't back the unions, and the unions protected working-class people. My siblings and I knew that the Industrial Revolution had started in the north and we were proud of being northern, of industry, of the unions. It was all tied up with supporting Labour.

Dad, who left Labour to join the SDP at a certain point, was never anything short of furious with Maggie. 'Thatcher and her cronies have this appalling "I'm all right, Jack" mentality, which means they only care about themselves.'

On 4 May 1979, Margaret Thatcher became Britain's first female prime minister. The previous week, Brother David Hennessey had talked to us about the election.

'Mrs Thatcher will be prime minister this time next week, boys.'

I was incensed. How could he say such a thing? I wanted Labour to stay in power.

Somebody in the class said, 'I think it's good there's going to be a female prime minister.'

There were lots of little Tories in my class. In fact, I was in the minority. My parents, as liberals, were also in the minority in their parish. My dad, despite his passion for decency, can be very damning about politicians. Before William Hague stood down as foreign secretary, Dad said, almost with pity, 'The poor chap. He is a bit of an Aunt Sally.' It's an economical but devastating criticism of the man.

★   ★   ★

When we went to Ireland in the school holidays, Dad would argue about politics with his younger brother, Peter. In the seventies, Uncle Peter was found on a list of potential IRA targets. A panic button was fitted in his house and he had to vary his routes to work. But he was a successful entrepreneur who ended up as the head of a bank, and I couldn't help but think, 'Uncle Peter has got the life I want. He's got a big house, nice cars, land, a mischievous sense of humour.' He always made me laugh. He was cheeky and a bit cocky. Not like my dad at all.

Uncle Peter would drink whiskey and go on about how awful the Labour Party was. The drunker he got, the more he'd infuriate Dad by saying things like, 'You should kneel down and pray to Margaret Thatcher every morning and thank her for saving your country.'

We'd often hear raised voices as we were drifting off to sleep.

I found out when I was making *The Look of Love* in 2013 that Thatcher had invited Paul Raymond to Downing Street. She was willing to overlook the fact that he was a tawdry porn baron, simply because he was generating so much wealth.

I felt slightly – only slightly – sorry for Thatcher in her old age. She was detached from any kind of reality, even before dementia fully set in. Denis Oliver, her chauffeur of fourteen years, revealed something really telling after her death: whenever he made a joke, it would go straight over her head. She had no sense of humour at all.

There was a real sense of impending apocalypse in the 1980s. Before the Berlin Wall came down in 1989, I think we all felt that nuclear war might really happen. Dad marched with the Campaign for Nuclear Disarmament and took me to a meeting with Bruce Kent, who was the general secretary. Dad thought nuclear weapons were immoral. He was very clear on what was moral and what was immoral. He often held up the Geneva Convention as a measure of decency in a brutal world.

When I was about twelve, I used to sit up with my dad into

the early hours having rigorous intellectual conversations about morality.

There is a fine line between imbuing your children with the values you hold to be true and indoctrination. Perhaps it's inevitable that you can't have one without the other.

But I liked having those kinds of moral maze discussions. They helped me to understand that while there are plenty of people who take all their views off a political shelf, as though they were buying a job lot of them, life is actually more complicated than that.

I always had time for the late Tory MP Alan Clark because although he was a right-wing xenophobe, he also cared passionately about animal rights and would hang out on the docks in Dover with all the animal-loving crusties and hippies. I loathed his politics, but I admired the fact that he thought independently.

Duality is, I think, generally a good thing. Otherwise – and this is to simplify hugely – you're in danger of sounding like George Bush when he said, 'Either you are with us or you are with the terrorists.'

CHAPTER 32

I stayed on at Cardinal Langley for my A levels. Although I had done well at religious studies, maths and physics at O level, I decided to study English, British government and politics, art and design, and general studies.

Despite taking three attempts to pass O-level English language before I finally got a B, I got a B first time for my O-level English literature and actually enjoyed A-level English. Shakespeare immediately made more sense to me than almost anything in the Bible.

Every Sunday I would listen to this supposed wisdom from the Bible and the Gospel, and so very little of it had resonance for me. Occasionally I'd hear a passage from the Bible that was illuminating or had wisdom, but there wasn't much in the way of enlightenment for me. Shakespeare, meanwhile, embraced ambiguity, nuance and contradiction in his writing.

And I fell in love with William Blake. He seemed to think differently about the world, and in doing so gave me permission to think differently, in much the same way as Monty Python. When I read 'The Garden of Love' in the sixth form, I was surprised that someone as spiritual as Blake was so openly disenchanted with the Church.

Because I admired my parents and everything they stood for, it always felt churlish and disrespectful to disagree with them. But Blake was criticising the institution for being bereft of spirituality and, in doing so, legitimised the distrust I was beginning to feel. I was shocked that a revered poet had articulated my point of view so perfectly.

It was part of a slow dawning in my late teens that respectable, intelligent people could have a different point of view.

Top: In Venice in 1991 with my slightly more handsome brother Martin, on the set of a Mock Turtles video shoot.

Above: Lizzie and me in 1991. I'm trying out a character.

An early publicity shot.

My arse on display in Achill Island in County Mayo. I was on a road trip with Martin Murray.

Top: The Dum Show poster with, left to right, Patrick Marber, Stewart Lee, me, Simon Munnery and Richard Herring.

Above left: A letter from my agent, Jan Murphy, detailing a £31.50 fee for *The Krypton Factor*.

Above right: John Thomson and me after winning the Perrier in 1992.

Above: Attempting to save the day in *Alpha Papa*.

Right: Frank Skinner and me during our Edinburgh show in 1990.

Above: Patrick Marber as my husband Spiros and me as Pauline Calf in *Pauline Calf's Wedding Video* in 1994.

Right: Patrick Marber wondering how much he should fine me for being late.

Opposite: Me and Armando Iannucci.

Over: Winning two BAFTAs for *I'm Alan Partridge* in May 1998.

That there is something valid, in fact desirable, in being disrespectful to any type of establishment institution.

Still, despite being impressed by the likes of Blake, the story of my education hadn't really changed since primary school.

The summary of my summer term in the lower sixth is, in fact, all too familiar: 'There are some indications that Stephen needs to organise himself better: both for exams and for school work generally . . . Stephen's absences and late arrival in the morning are a matter of concern and are, perhaps, a reflection of his poor organisation.'

I only managed to get an 'E' for my end-of-year English exam. 'A fair result. Unfortunately, Stephen is still too easy-going in regard to essays and revision.'

When I left Cardinal Langley, I was given a blue folder that I had filled in when I'd first arrived at the school in September 1977. I'd listed my interests and hobbies as 'compose music; listen to music (all types); hiking; bike riding; youth club, etc'.

My final assessment says that I was reliable, cheerful, sociable and a leader. My determination, sensitivity and ability to work hard all fall under the '?' category.

Beneath this final assessment is a box about personal qualities for the teacher to fill in. 'Extrovert character. Well accepted by staff and pupils. Good musically. Willing to "have-a-go". Contributes to house activities.'

The very final comment made on my school report sits in a column of its own and appears in handwriting so small that you have to peer closely to decipher it.

'Destined to go far in the entertainment business.'

★　★　★

All my school reports refer to me as 'Stephen', and my family have never referred to me by any other name. But when I was nineteen I changed my name to 'Steve'. I vehemently dislike the diminutive 'Steve', which makes me sound like a garage mechanic, but I thought 'Stephen Coogan' scanned badly.

I could live with 'Steve Coogan' and I was determined to keep my family name: I always thought that if I became successful, I would want my family name to be recognised.

PART THREE

CHAPTER 33

I had no idea what I might do after my A levels. I didn't know who I was.

In the final term at Cardinal Langley, I considered several possibilities and ended up sitting the executive officer exam for the Civil Service simply because it sounded like a sensible, grown-up job. And it paid around £7,000 a year, which sounded like a good wage.

I didn't even know what the job entailed, but I thought, 'How hard can it be? You'll have to put on a suit, but you're not stupid. Surely you can make a go of it . . .'

I failed the executive officer exam.

Then they phoned me to say I had got in because they'd lowered the entry threshold.

By which time I had decided I didn't want to be a civil servant after all.

I briefly considered being a teacher. For my parents' generation, becoming a teacher was an aspiration; it was achievable, it wouldn't mean reaching too high.

I didn't think I'd be a good teacher, so I applied to Lancaster University to read Politics.

But my heart wasn't really in studying Politics. I was interested in it, but in a social rather than academic context; naturally left of centre, I had developed a kind of knee-jerk left-wing idealism to face down the Little Englanders at school. I became more outspoken and radical than I might otherwise have been, simply because they irritated the hell out of me.

When Michael Foot became Labour leader in the run-up to the 1983 general election, the Little Englanders suddenly had ample opportunity to mock.

'You really think *he* should be prime minister? With his donkey jacket and his walking stick?'

I liked the fact that Foot was a principled politician, but I only defended him half-heartedly. Under his leadership, Labour got its lowest share at a general election since the 1920s; it really felt like fighting the Tories with one hand tied behind your back and both your legs strapped together.

In an age before it discovered spin, the Labour Party was all about comb-overs, brown kipper ties, Terylene trousers and working men's clubs.

Not fully committed to Lancaster, I also applied to all the drama schools in London.

I thought, 'I may as well. I think I've got something.'

Generations of comedy have always replaced each other. The Goons were replaced by *Beyond the Fringe*, which was then replaced by the Pythons, after which came *Not the Nine O' Clock News* and then *The Young Ones*. As sure as night followed day, a new generation was bound to emerge. It was just the way of things.

I was aware that some of my contemporaries would be part of the next wave of comedians without yet knowing it. It was a moment I remember with great clarity: I was sitting in the refectory area of the sixth-form common room.

I thought to myself, 'I'll do whatever you're supposed to do and see what happens.'

I also thought, 'I can't do anything else. And I don't want to be a bloody civil servant.'

With money saved from my part-time job at the petrol station, I got the National Express coach down to London about five times in my final term at Cardinal Langley. I then had to pay for each audition: it was £11 for the Central School of Speech and Drama and £15 for LAMDA.

I stayed at my aunt Patricia's house in London, which turned out to be a learning curve in itself. Patricia, who was a TV make-up artist, invited a few neighbours around, a couple of whom happened to be the producers of an ITV drama called *Dempsey and Makepeace*.

I didn't bother standing up to shake their hands, because I didn't know that you ought to get up when someone comes into the room. I didn't show due reverence to these ostensibly sophisticated, confident people.

I had been brought up to be well mannered and polite, but not remotely metropolitan.

It didn't occur to me at the time that naivety can also be a strength. Teenagers find it much easier than adults to think, 'Well, why can't I?' about so many things. It's not really entitlement as such, more a kind of bluster.

At eighteen, I was a fairly typical contradiction of confidence and self-doubt.

It didn't help that, because I'd stayed on an extra couple of months in the sixth form, I felt like a dimwit.

It was that term that I auditioned for Hamlet and my younger brother Kevin got the role instead. I played Polonius. I can't deny that I was a bit gutted. On a very minor level, Kevin and I were like the Milibands. But with much less at stake.

Jane Hazlegrove was Ophelia. She was in *Coronation Street* while she was still in the sixth form and she's been in *Casualty* for years now.

I went out with her for a while. She's a lesbian now.

Not being cast as Hamlet really wasn't a big deal. I didn't take any of it that seriously; I remember getting told off by the director for playing the piano in the rehearsal space.

I was, however, serious about drama school. I certainly felt anxious and uneasy about the auditions. It was a world I knew only from a distance, from watching television and going to the cinema and from the once or twice I'd been to the Royal Exchange in Manchester to see a play. Actors such as Tom Courtenay and John Thaw were northern and had been to drama school, so it wasn't necessarily beyond my grasp.

I wasn't uncultured or ignorant, but I was naive in so many ways.

I was of course aware that arty people existed, but I hadn't been among them or seen them up close.

I was immediately apprehensive about the other students at the auditions, most of whom exuded an innately bohemian, cosmopolitan confidence.

At the audition for the Central School of Speech and Drama, everyone seemed to be called Sebastian or Julian. While I was waiting, a bloke with Byronic hair, a long overcoat and a statement scarf strode in, thrust his hand into the principal's, shook it manfully and said, rather loudly, 'You know my father? He works for the BBC World Service.'

'Ah, yes,' responded the teacher, clasping the applicant's hands with both of his.

More bollocks was spoken, with sackfuls of confident laughter.

That bloke cast a fine silhouette and had swept into the audition. I had trudged in, with bad posture. I sat there looking at this walking cliché, my shoulders sagging, despondent, thinking to myself, 'I'm not in this club.' I was a petulant child having a silent tantrum. 'It's not fair, because I think I'm good at impersonations and I've got a fertile imagination, but I don't know anyone at the BBC. I haven't been to fucking finishing school.'

My thoughts were interrupted by a bouncy girl in dungarees, her hair in a ponytail, her manner excessively friendly.

'You must be Stephen! Come this way. Have you had a long journey?'

I didn't come from a demonstrative, effusive family and I didn't know how to respond. It seemed I was out of my depth in myriad ways. Or at least that's the message I was receiving.

I felt like Frank Spencer drowning in a sea of Mr Darcys.

★   ★   ★

I auditioned for all the London drama schools and was knocked back by every single one, apart from RADA, who offered me a recall.

The truth is, I didn't know what I was doing at those auditions.

When asked why I wanted a place at their drama school, I would reply, 'Because I do impressions at school. People say I should be on the telly.'

The panel would look distinctly unimpressed. The late Edward Hardwicke, who played Dr Watson in *Sherlock Holmes* on Granada TV, was on the RADA panel. When I said I did impressions, he looked at me and said, with something approaching disdain, 'We *all* used to do that.'

I felt utterly deflated.

I was out of place. Northern, provincial, state-educated. I hadn't read the relevant books, nor was I interested in Stanislavski and his quest for some kind of psychological truthfulness. I watched telly, I was good at voices, and people were always telling me I should be on the telly. That was the sum total of my reasoning for wanting to be an actor.

★   ★   ★

My A-level results were disappointing. I didn't get the grades because I didn't put in the work and so I decided to return to Cardinal Langley to do resits.

When I told my English teacher that I wanted to go to drama school, he shook his head.

'That's a shame,' he said. 'If you'd got into Cambridge, you could have joined Footlights and you'd have been away.'

It was like the die was cast and the odds were stacked against me. Every time drama school was mentioned, there would be a puffing-out of air and a slumping of shoulders. It was the antithesis of the American dream/delusion that anyone can grow up to be president.

The implication was clear: it wasn't going to happen for me. I had the talent, but I was never going to get the break. Unless you knew the right people, you'd never get on, especially when you weren't from the right background in the first place.

While waiting to resit my A levels I signed on and, during a visit to the job centre, noticed a simple card: 'Actor/actress required.'

I asked about it. The job-centre person said, 'It's not a proper job, it's just profit-share.'

I didn't care. I wanted to meet Andrew Mulligan, whose name and number were on the card.

It turned out that he had moved to Manchester from Oxford to set up a regional theatre company. He had no money, but he was very clever.

Years later, when I mentioned Andy to Patrick Marber, he told me that at Oxford University Andy was the director of his generation. Everyone wondered what had happened to him; he was expected to pursue glamorous directing jobs in London, but instead came to Manchester to work with real working-class people.

Or, in my case, a real lower-middle-class person.

I went along for an interview and Andy asked me what I thought about politics and art. I wanted to please him, so I said, 'Oh, I think they are intrinsically linked. It's *very* important to be political.'

I was bluffing, but I sensed he was pretty left-wing, probably one of those good old-fashioned militants, and I was willing to say whatever I thought he wanted to hear. I probably mentioned Jim Allen; Jim's son David had given me a copy of *The Spongers* and at some point I watched it with Andy.

Whatever I said did the trick, because Andy asked me to join his company and I left school a couple of months after going back to do the resits.

The company was very much of its time. It had a truly terrible name that sounds even more Stalinist now than it did then: Greater Manchester Theatre Company.

We did straightforward adaptations of plays, including C. P. Taylor's *The Magic Island*, about a bloke who lives in a cave. We took it around schools and showed it to six- and seven-year-old children, who laughed at me playing this bogeyman.

The theatre company reflected the politics of the time, and 'inner-city deprivation', a shocking by-product of Thatcher's first five years in power and one of the main buzzwords of the eighties, was a central theme. It's remarkable, in fact, how that deprivation has since more or less disappeared from the inner city and in its place we have shiny new city centres and rings of neglect on the outskirts.

Andy sent me out to wander around the Miles Platting housing estate, taking photos on an SLR camera. Everything was boarded up and it was incredibly depressing, almost dystopian; in fact, just a decade after it was built, the estate was earmarked for demolition. We used the images to devise a play that we then took around adult education centres in the north-west. There were only four of us doing this DIY theatre: Andy, me and two young women.

One was an eighties political cliché: a militant lesbian vegan in dungarees who spent all her spare time on the picket line, supporting the miners' strike. I had total sympathy with the miners, but her constant talk of the picket line irritated me in much the same way the Little Englanders had done at school.

I used to wonder what those miners thought of this daft lesbian in fingerless gloves warming her hands around their brazier.

I loathed Margaret Thatcher with as much gusto as this woman did, but I mistrust anyone who has absolute moral certainly about anything. It's irritating that such people feel they have *found the truth*. It's a reductive, simplistic world view. But she wasn't a nasty person, just too earnest for my liking.

★   ★   ★

Each day I caught the bus to Hulme, rehearsed with Andy and the two young women in a private space in the library, ate fish and chips at lunchtime and returned to my parents' house in the evening.

Andy ran the theatre company like a boot camp, breaking us down before building us back up again. At nineteen, I was still terribly self-conscious and more than a little graceless, but Andy refused to indulge me.

There wasn't time. If he told me to pretend to be a fried breakfast, I had to get on with it.

The exercises were often quite brutal; he liked, for example, to use a drama-school exercise in which you play a character who has no dignity. He taught me that you have to lose all inhibitions if you want to be an actor. You can't worry about looking like a dick.

He would say, while pushing his glasses up his nose, 'I don't know why you bother coming here to rehearse if that's the best you can come up with. If you don't want to be seen making a fool of yourself, then you shouldn't be doing this sort of thing. Stop worrying about what people might think. Just do it or fuck off.'

Occasionally, at the end of an explanation or instruction, he might add, 'It's as simple or complex as that.'

I thought it a fascinating way of breaking everything down: you could choose to see things in two different ways. It may sound obvious, but those revelations matter when you're nineteen.

It was a steep learning curve, but slowly my confidence grew.

Of course, in typical Stockholm-syndrome fashion, I wanted to please Andy most of the time. Sometimes I felt so exposed that I objected, but it was worth the pain.

He believed in me when no one else did.

I recently saw him for the first time in thirty years – he now writes very successful young adult fiction – and we reminisced about the eighties.

Among other things, he reminded me that he had helped me prepare for my audition at Manchester Poly, now Manchester Metropolitan University, where I'd applied to do a diploma in theatre after my London knockbacks.

Clearly I hadn't thought carefully enough about my earlier auditions in London. No one had been around to give me advice, and I'd been too vague during the auditions about why I wanted to go to drama school.

Andy knew I had to stand out from the other candidates. He suggested starting with two standard speeches – typically Shakespeare followed by a modern piece – and ending with Duncan Thickett doing a bad audition.

Duncan was, at this stage, a nascent character, a little voice that had started out in my head and grown into an inadequate fool. I hadn't consciously thought about developing a character, I just used to do him in rehearsals to make Andy laugh. He was, I suppose, my first foray into the comedy of embarrassment, which I would later revisit with Alan Partridge.

I rehearsed in front of Andy, and as he drove me to the audition I was as anxious as I'd been during my visits to London. It felt like my last real chance to get into drama school.

I read from Shakespeare's *Pericles, Prince of Tyre* in a Cockney accent, standing on a chair like a market trader, followed by a speech from Arnold Wesker's *Chips with Everything*.

After the Wesker speech, I left the room, knocked on the door as Duncan and asked if I had come to the right place for my audition. I walked back in with my papers and immediately dropped them all over the floor.

I kept saying, in a ridiculously overconfident way, 'I just want you all to relax and enjoy my audition.'

The panel was crying with laughter.

The voice teacher, Alex Clement, then asked me to repeat a specific phrase after him in a variety of accents.

I stood there and said, 'Come upstairs and have a cup of tea,' in Mancunian, Scouse, Cockney, vaguely posh and cut-glass accents.

Then, in a cut-glass accent again, I had to repeat, 'I put some money in the bank today.'

Alex pulled me up on my flat vowel on the word 'bank', but otherwise said my accent was impeccable.

When I had finished, Alex looked at me. He knew I was going back to RADA for a recall, and he didn't want to risk losing me. 'We normally operate a recall system here, but we're going to offer you a place straight away.'

I was amazed that they had broken the rules to offer me a place on the spot.

Andy, who had been waiting for me in the pub over the road, remembers me walking out of the audition looking shell-shocked.

Flushed with excitement, I went home and told my mum. Perhaps I was right after all. Perhaps I had something.

★   ★   ★

Despite the Manchester Poly offer, I couldn't ignore the RADA recall. Once again I did the formal pieces followed by the Duncan Thickett routine, curious to know how RADA would respond. They sat rather formally in a line, looking at me with poker faces; after the easy-going atmosphere at Manchester Poly, it felt sterile and slightly hostile. One of the principals clearly liked what I was trying to do, but I needed the whole panel on my side.

I rehearsed one scene with Rosemary Leach and another with an actor called Lucy Maycock who now works in Oxford. I remember sitting on the stairwell in RADA and chatting to Lucy, who had just come down from Oxford. I secretly hoped she and I would become friends at RADA.

I mentioned her to Patrick years later and he remembered her. He seemed to have known everyone at Oxford, whatever college they were in.

Rosemary Leach was lovely. She put her arm round my shoulder.

'Don't worry,' she said. 'You'll get in.'

She was wrong. I didn't.

I wasn't surprised not to be offered a place. I got a rejection letter that said something along the lines of, 'You made the final hundred, but you didn't make the final thirty. You're quite good, but you're not good enough.'

My dad was so impressed he actually framed the rejection letter.

Of course I would have gone to RADA had I been offered a place, but part of me was glad to stay in Manchester. I had warmed to the people on the panel at the poly and, frankly, after all the rejections I needed their validation.

I thought, 'I want to be with these people who think I'm good. Fuck the others.'

CHAPTER 34

The high of being offered a place at Manchester Poly did not, inevitably, last. I still felt out of place. I tried to be enthusiastic, even signing up for yoga and buying special blue tights. But there was no escaping the fact that the southerners who got on to the theatre course with me were fellow London drama-school rejects who seemed to have more confidence than talent and were shockingly poncey.

There was the odd exception: Gary Sneddon was in my year at college and he did really good impersonations. He still owes me money because I paid his rent for a year. Or maybe we're quits. Martin Murray, whom I met in the first year and who remains one of my best friends, invited me, Gary and another friend, Alan Francis, to his parents' house in Wales. I drove us there in my dad's Volvo. We were on the M56, going fast, when Gary and I had an argument. I got so cross that I reached across and punched him in the face. He punched me back. I barely took my foot off the accelerator. I don't even remember what the argument was about. Something trivial, no doubt.

Generally, though, the students and teachers were all equally pretentious. There was a Geordie tutor who was just the kind of self-righteous, subsidised-theatre person I couldn't stand. He thought he was Bertolt Brecht, or at least he dressed like him.

And he kept trying to make me perform Brecht even when I made it clear that I wasn't interested. He would dismissively tell me, 'Well, you had your chance and you blew it.'

I didn't care. I didn't get Brecht and I didn't know how to do it.

I did, however, like Martin Nestor, the anti-structuralist tutor who was always smoking roll-ups and who had cried with laughter at my audition. Decades later I met students doing the same course and apparently Martin Nestor would entertain them with a detailed description of my audition, which I still find hugely touching.

Martin was the maverick poet of the drama teachers. He didn't fuck around. He was a mix of Oliver Reed, Ian McShane and Alan Bates. Like someone who took time off from writing poetry to build another drystone wall.

He wasn't afraid to give us short shrift if he thought we were performing badly.

He'd say, 'I didn't believe what you were doing then. Do it again.'

If he praised you, it actually meant something. He threw me a few morsels and it made me feel good.

But the theatre course was, in the end, too prescriptive for me. I was repeatedly told to read Stanislavski and Chekhov, and I cared for neither. Most of the other students had a pretentious, pompous love of theatre that left me cold. They read all the books on the syllabus, whereas I read none. I didn't think that a theatre course should be so inflexible, that a rejection of Stanislavski should imply a lack of interest in acting. My approach was more populist.

Even when I tried to fit in, no one seemed to notice. I did a piece from Alan Ayckbourn's play *Just Between Ourselves*, which I thought was really well crafted, and yet the casting agents that turned up from London paid it no attention. They were interested only in floppy-haired students ready for their Merchant Ivory moment.

It came as no surprise that my report at the end of my first year echoed those handed out at school:

ATTENDANCE AND CONDUCT:
All the staff were impressed with the improvements this term – until the final week. Your essay was inexcusably late, and despite the fact that the ideas were clearly expressed

(i.e. it was good work) I sense it is far below the standard you could achieve with more thought and preparation. You also let down the entire third year and the school at the Library Auditions. (I am still receiving complaints about them, which I could well do without.) Stephen – get your priorities SORTED OUT – and FAST. You are wasting your talent and everyone else's time otherwise. A.T.

'A.T' was Alex Taylor, a harmlessly camp tutor who once said to me, 'Ooooh, Steve, I can see your knickers through your tights!'

I do remember being in trouble for letting the school down, but I must have blocked out the reason. I possibly didn't show up.

There's a line elsewhere in the report that speaks volumes about how the course worked: 'General comment from all staff – don't confuse mimicry with acting or your work will remain superficial.'

★   ★   ★

Despite the tutors' persistent negativity, I managed to take my 'mimicry' and spin it into something more mature and sophisticated. Most people go to college hoping to get a decent job once they graduate; I was performing or getting paid work nearly the whole time I was there.

I wasn't even intending to make my live debut as early as I did.

Martin Murray, who, incidentally, was the lead guitarist in The Mock Turtles and who many years later played the priest at the start of *Philomena* and a paparazzo in *Alpha Papa*, was in a covers band who played at a Law Society revue at the end of my first year. Gary Sneddon – the guy I punched in the car; we were still friends – and I went along. There was an open mic slot in which students were performing appalling sketches. Everyone was booing and it was completely shambolic.

Gary and I were on the side of the stage, waiting for Martin's band to come on.

Martin said, 'Why don't you two get onstage and do your Zippy and Bungle impersonations?'

I didn't want to.

I genuinely tried to resist, but Martin coerced me. He literally dragged me to the microphone.

Our confidence grew as the students started laughing really loudly, really quickly.

We had saved the night!

Well, what had come before was so shabby, it didn't take much. The audience was grateful for anything.

When we walked offstage to applause after five minutes, I was on a huge high.

I thought, 'I've never had an experience like this before. Everyone in the room was listening to everything I was saying. And *laughing* at everything I was saying.'

It was the summer of 1986 and I was hooked.

CHAPTER 35

The theatre course at Manchester Poly has some celebrated alumni – Bernard Hill, David Threlfall – and of course it's where Julie Walters famously met Victoria Wood at an audition in the spring of 1971.

It's also where I met Simon Greenall, who gave me my first break and then went on to play Michael the Geordie in *I'm Alan Partridge*, and John Thomson, with whom I was to win the Perrier Comedy Award in Edinburgh in 1992.

Simon was in the third year when I was in the first year. He was well dressed, clean-cut, quite well spoken. He was also unique among students in that he was never in debt.

Like most students, I had to keep shifting my debt from one account to another, paying off the old debt before the bank came after me. If you had zero money in the bank and no debt, it was a cause for celebration; you felt rich simply because you weren't in debt.

I didn't, of course, move my debt to Barclays. The big banking issue of the mid-eighties was the bank's involvement in South Africa. The British student population put huge pressure on Barclays to withdraw from a country where apartheid was still legal and, in March 1987, it ended investment in South Africa.

I don't think the bank had a Damascene conversion; I doubt they were responding to moral outrage, rather they realised that the student activists would one day have money and they wouldn't invest it with Barclays if it appeared to condone apartheid.

To quote Bobbi Flekman from *Spinal Tap*, 'Money talks and bullshit walks.'

Anyway, word got around to Simon that I was doing impersonations in the college cafeteria and he turned up one day to
listen. He was doing some comedy for Radio Manchester and in
early 1986, in the second term of my first year, I was the only
first-year to be invited to contribute alongside three third-years.

Julie Taylor, Pierce Quigley, Simon and I met up and wrote
and performed in a series of comedy sketches and then
performed them for a show called *The Buzz*, which was hosted
by Phil Caldwell.

One of the sketches I wrote was an advert for an imaginary
board game called Revolution that was all about toppling fascist
dictatorships. It was a welcome distraction from my drama
course and, better still, I got paid fifty quid by BBC Manchester
for services as a sketch-show artist.

The Buzz was my first ever professional engagement. It started
a ball rolling; by the end of my first year – and after my
triumphant appearance at the Law Society – I was doing a few
impersonations at a cabaret night in a pub bar.

Simon and I worked well together. We sent sketches off to
Colin Gilbert at BBC Scotland, responding to an advert he'd
taken out in *The Stage* simply saying 'sketches wanted'. We were
nothing if not ambitious: in the early eighties, Colin was a
producer on *A Kick Up the Eighties*, which gave Rik Mayall his
first TV break, and a few years later he created *Naked Video*,
which starred Helen Lederer.

Simon wrote a sketch that I slightly embellished and it ended
up on *Smith & Jones*. When I heard Mel Smith and Griff Rhys
Jones doing this sketch, I thought, 'Oh my God, I'm *nearly*
connected with a TV show.'

Simon also wrote some of the material that I eventually used
in my stand-up act in 1987, including a brilliant sketch in
which Nato bombs Trumpton.

I didn't think about it much at the time, but this first experience of writing with Simon was a blueprint for the way I
would eventually work, collaborating with one or more writers.

Writing alone is too solitary, too lonely. I like dialogue. Unless I can articulate my thoughts to another person, they'll just remain jumbled up inside my head.

In the meantime, I was trying to get my Equity card. I figured out that stand-up was my best way in because Equity was pretty much a closed shop: you couldn't get paid work unless you were a member, and you couldn't become a member unless you'd had paid work.

When I submitted my Equity application and said that I'd been paid £50 by Radio Manchester, the Equity representative went straight to the BBC and caused a furore about them paying a non-union member with cash. Which tells you everything you need to know about the closed-shop mentality of the unions and the failure of the Left.

Phil Caldwell got himself into a panic and washed his hands of me.

And instead of getting my Equity card as planned, I was blacklisted for a while for being a sort of mini acting scab.

★ ★ ★

When Simon left college, I gradually lost touch with him. A decade later, we were auditioning for the part of an ex-army Geordie handyman whom Alan Partridge would befriend in *I'm Alan Partridge* because he was vulnerable and weak. Simon popped up on a tape – we used to watch auditions because Armando Iannucci, Pete Baynham and I were writing and too busy to meet everyone – and I recognised him immediately.

I didn't tell Armando or Pete that I knew him. I wanted to work with Simon again and return the favour, but it was important that Armando and Pete liked him independently. When they both said he was the best candidate, I admitted I knew him and that he had given me my first break.

It's still strange to think that I've known Simon since I was eighteen; perhaps that's why we have effortlessly developed an on-screen rapport that has become part of the Alan Partridge narrative.

After we met up again in the mid-nineties, Simon went on to have a phenomenally successful career in advertising as the voice of the Russian meerkats in comparethcmeerkat.com. Luckily for me he still acts and was pleased to reprise the role of Michael in *Alpha Papa*. It would've been a little odd doing an Alan Partridge feature film without him. I'm really happy how it worked out.

★   ★   ★

In my third year, I lived in a house with some first-year students at 40 Mauldeth Road West in Withington. I was the oldest bloke but I was given the smallest room and in it was an ungenerous single bed. I had no one to blame but myself: I'd pretty much run out of friends because I never did any washing up or housework.

One weekend, my student housemates – Andy Spearpoint, who became vocalist of New Fast Automatic Daffodils in 1988, Johnny Moran and Neil Gallery – threw a party.

John Thomson, who was also a first-year, turned up.

We had a kind of impression off in which he did Bruce Willis quite well and I dazzled him (his words, not mine) with my two versions of Sean Connery: as a young man circa *Dr No* and as a more mature man.

John and I hit it off straight away; he was like a younger brother who could really make me laugh. We hung out in the Black Lion bar in the basement of the Withington Ale House, drinking and having impersonation competitions, much as Rob Brydon and I would do much later over very expensive meals in *The Trip*.

John and I also used to drink in the Parrswood pub, opposite college. It was here that an early incarnation of Paul Calf materialised.

I would make other students laugh by pretending to be this drunk bloke hurling inarticulate abuse at all the privileged, poncey students who were thriving on subsidies provided by the hard-earned taxes of the working man. Apart from anything, it was a good way to vent the frustrations I felt about some of the other students.

Paul Calf was also based on the guy who drove a stacker truck at the chemical plant in Rochdale where I had worked in the summer of 1985, just before starting drama school. During breaks, I would sit on my own in the corner reading the *Guardian* while they were all leafing through the *Sun* and playing cards. They would glance over at me with a look that said, 'Who the fuck is *he*?'

I wasn't beaten up because I could do a good impersonation of Sylvester Stallone in *Rocky*. They loved it.

One lunchtime I was in my corner, laughing at an article in the *Guardian* by Hugo Young, a stalwart writer for the paper at the time.

One of them looked across at me. 'What are you laughing at?'

I said, 'Oh, it's just an article.'

He said, 'Read it out.'

I read out this nuanced observation of the prevailing political machinations of the mid-eighties, which was greeted with a bunch of faces reminiscent of Easter Island statues.

And utter silence.

Finally, one of the men said, 'You think that's funny, do you?'

'Well, to me it is.'

Again, silence.

Mick, the hard man, piped up and threw me a lifeline. 'Do yer Rocky.'

I contorted my face, affected a deep baritone with a speech impediment, got down on my knees, pretended to be battered and bruised and screamed, 'Adrian! Adrian!'

One particular guy who worked there *really* didn't take to

me. He was dense and aggressive and he curled his lip at me. He was always saying things like, 'I bet you can't wait to get to drama school and put your fucking tights on and get the arse fucked off you by a bunch of poofs.'

He also had a slight speech impediment which meant I could impersonate him very easily. Although they all held me in contempt for wanting to be a poofy actor, they loved the fact that I could impersonate their slightly stupid workmate. And in turn he couldn't beat me up because all his mates thought I was funny.

Paul Calf was a combination of both this bloke and the locals in the Parrswood pub, but he didn't yet have a name. He was just the drunk guy in the pub who hates students.

★　★　★

After I graduated, I stayed in touch with John and regularly went back to college just to see him when he was in his second and third years. Much like Simon, he has been in and out of my life since then; we won the Perrier together at Edinburgh in 1992 and, in 1993, he played Fat Bob in *Paul Calf's Video Diary*.

John's star really took off later in the nineties with *The Fast Show* and *Cold Feet*. Around that time I asked him, when the old BBC was still in Wood Lane, if he'd do one more: *Paul and Pauline Calf's Video Diary*.

But he didn't want to be Fat Bob any more.

I said, 'Please, just one more time. I'm asking as a friend.'

He looked me in the eye and said, 'No.'

He didn't mess me about, he didn't keep me waiting. But I was hurt.

★　★　★

Other than meeting Simon and John, the best thing about being at college was living in a flat and being able to have sex freely.

I no longer had to have hurried sex in my dad's car and then wind down the windows to release the steam.

I fell in love with two women while I was a student, both of whom I met when we were all working as stagehands at the Royal Exchange Theatre in Manchester.

Rosie Blackshaw was a few years younger than me and I was slightly obsessed with her, even after she had moved in with the actor Adrian Scarborough. Whenever I phoned her and heard their joint answer-machine message, I used to petulantly say to myself, 'Who the hell is this Adrian?'

But I got over it and the brilliantly talented Scarborough worked with me on *Coogan's Run* and continues to be one of our finest character actors.

The other stagehand I fell in love with was Trisha Budd. She was a year or two older than me and went on to become an art director for Aardman Animations.

Although neither relationship lasted that long, both Rosie and Trisha stick in my mind as first loves.

Working at the Royal Exchange was another welcome distraction from my course. It was – and is – a fantastic theatre.

I was in charge of the revolving stage when Harriet Walter starred in *The Merchant of Venice*. One night I took off my headphones and didn't hear my cue to switch the lever that revolved the stage and put the actors in the right position. The actors were all waiting about onstage, wondering what the hell was going on, until someone nudged me. I got away with it by claiming it was a technical fault.

I was also a stagehand on Nic Hytner's 1986 production of *Edward II*. I used to watch with curiosity as a handful of the audience walked out each night when Ian McDiarmid appeared to have a red-hot poker shoved up his arse.

The following year, I was a Greek spear carrier in a Royal Exchange production of *Oedipus* by Sophocles. It starred David Threlfall, who had graduated from the theatre course at Manchester Poly around a decade before me. Alongside the other spear carriers, I had to stand stock-still onstage as the audience came in. Every night we had to concentrate really hard to avoid fainting. We weren't allowed to move, so there was a real danger we might black out; we weren't even allowed to rock on our heels, like police officers do to keep their blood flowing.

The casting director had turned up at college one day to find some suitable spear carriers. The audition was simple: we rolled up our trousers to see who had the best calves.

I might not have had the floppy hair that was de rigueur among poncey actors, but at least my calves were OK.

CHAPTER 36

My tutors expected me to get work experience at the Royal Exchange, but they were less supportive of the regular work I was building up as both a stand-up comedian and a voiceover artist for local radio ads. Although I had got on to the course on the basis of my impressions, I was then widely regarded as being lowbrow for doing voiceovers for Yorkshire Bank.

As far as the people who ran the course were concerned, earning money wasn't the path to true art.

I was at drama school during the height of the militant Left, and at times I felt like I was surrounded by a sort of Stasi-in-dungarees: 'You *will* read Stanislavski and Bertolt Brecht, you *will not* do voiceovers for Piccadilly radio.' I felt like I was living in East Berlin and nipping over the wall to do voiceovers.

On one occasion I was even taken aside by two drama students who sternly told me I was not supportive of the group. My activities outside college were, in fact, counter to the spirit of the group and were not about the pure art of acting.

My brazen ambition didn't help. In my first year at college, I heard about a local woman who wrote for *Spitting Image*, the hugely successful satirical television puppet show on ITV. Co-created by Roger Law and Peter Fluck in 1984, it was an institution; 10 million people regularly tuned in to watch the puppet of Margaret Thatcher using the men's toilets, Norman Tebbit dressed in leather or the Queen supporting CND.

Spitting Image was never perfect, but 60 per cent of it was funny and it felt as though everyone was watching it. It was one of the last programmes we watched as a family.

I sent the local woman a letter asking if I could help. I

enclosed some short dialogue for Margaret Thatcher, Norman Tebbit and Michael Heseltine that was risibly bad. Unsurprisingly, nothing came of it.

I was momentarily hurt that this was not to be my big break, but decided to focus on stand-up. I didn't earn much, but the voiceovers paid well and funded the comedy.

By 1987, when I was in the second and then third year of my course, I was performing in various venues in and around Manchester.

I often had to support indie bands because there was a dearth of places to perform in Manchester. I did gigs at the Greenroom in Whitworth Street and sometimes supported The Mock Turtles, my brother Martin's band. The Greenroom also ran buskers' gigs, where people would turn up to play guitar or sing or perform comedy. It was properly exciting; anything could happen.

The gigs rarely lasted longer than twenty minutes but they gave me time to try out my increasingly surreal impersonations. I often juxtaposed famous people with unusual situations: Ronnie Corbett in Vietnam, Sylvester Stallone as a social worker, Robert De Niro meeting Alan Bennett, Terry Wogan possessed by the devil in *The Exorcist*.

I deconstructed *The Sweeney*, and in 'A Question of International Revolutionary Politics' I did David Coleman discussing the Chilean *coup d'état* of 1973 as though it was a sports event.

I was doing unusual, odd, daft comedy just to test the water.

Stand-up gave me a real buzz, but I was initially only doing it to get my Equity card. I got my card at the end of 1987, then, in 1988, when I was in my final year at college, I slowly started to get offers to appear on television. This guy at the Greenroom – I can't remember who, perhaps a scout – thought I might be able to get a slot on a London Weekend Television talent show called *First Exposure*. Hosted by Arthur Smith, it was a way for up-and-coming alternative comedians to get on TV.

In early 1988, I got the train down from Manchester to audition for *First Exposure*. I found my way to an upstairs rehearsal room in Kennington, south London, and stood nervously in front of yet another expectant panel. I did the same impressions I'd been doing in venues in and around Manchester and they immediately asked me to go on the show. They even offered to pay my train fare back to Manchester, although they weren't paying for any of the other comedians' travel expenses.

I'm not sure if they thought I was unusually funny or they simply felt sorry for me because I was still a student.

First Exposure was recorded several months later, in May 1988. I had my own chinos and Doc Martens, but I 'borrowed' a dogtooth sports jacket from the costume room in the basement of the drama school and a polo shirt from my dad.

My family watched the show at home in Middleton when it was broadcast. It was strange, I think, for them to see me on television when not long before I'd been sneaking under the sofa to watch late-night programmes.

I felt sick with nerves before walking onstage in my half-borrowed clothes. At least I wasn't daft enough to try anything new; I was just dipping into the best bits of the material I'd endlessly refined in small northern clubs.

Afterwards Juliet Blake, the producer, came up to me and said, 'I hope you're ready for what's going to happen to you.'

I was shocked, but then I'd only performed in the north-west before. I'd never, at that point, done a gig in London. As far as Juliet was concerned, I'd come from nowhere.

I also met Geoff Posner for the first time at that *First Exposure* recording. He had directed *Not the Nine O'Clock News* and *The Young Ones* and would later direct several of my TV shows, including *Coogan's Run*.

He came up to me and said, 'We stopped doing *Saturday Live* because we thought we'd exhausted all the talent. Are there more people like you up north?'

I didn't really know, or care. *Saturday Live* was the Channel 4 comedy show that made stars of Ben Elton, Stephen Fry, Rik Mayall, et al. And Geoff thought I was good enough to join them.

★ ★ ★

I went back to Manchester on a high. I was twenty-two, I looked even younger and I had just made my first appearance on television.

I had also done an audition for *Spitting Image*.

My first proper agent, Sandy Gort, had seen my dream advert in the *Stage* at the end of 1987: 'Voices required for *Spitting Image*.'

I sent off a cassette tape with a selection of my impressions and was called down to London. The late Geoff Perkins, a producer on the show, showed me around the studio. It was strange to see Neil Kinnock and Roy Hattersley lying deflated on a shelf and several puppets of Thatcher, each with a different grotesque expression.

I had an informal chat with Geoff and then went home.

In the days before the mobile, all the news at drama school would come via the pay phone in the corner of the canteen. There was often someone yelling, 'Is so-and-so here? Can you go and get him/her?'

Students hung around the canteen for hours, partly because they were so fond of Elsie and Margaret, the dinner ladies. If former students went back to college, it was to see those two and not the tutors, to whom they mostly had an ambivalent attitude.

One day, someone shouted my name across the canteen. This time the phone call was for me.

It was Sandy, beside himself: '*Spitting Image* want you.'

I couldn't believe it. I was stunned into silence.

I found out later that John Lloyd, the *Spitting Image* producer also famous for *Blackadder*, had worked his way through thousands of taped auditions. He was listening, throwing a tape in the bin, listening, putting a tape to one side. Endless bloody listening.

He arrived at my tape and stopped in his tracks. At the same time, Juliet Blake had told Geoff Perkins to watch my *First Exposure* appearance.

John Lloyd rang Geoff. 'I think I've found the new voice for *Spitting Image*. You won't have heard of him . . .'

Geoff: 'Is he called Steve Coogan?'

John: 'How . . . ?'

Curiously, they had both found me separately.

Back in the canteen, I returned to the table and sat down with my student friends.

I said, still incredulous, 'I'm the new voice of *Spitting Image*.'

They looked at me, as shocked as I was: 'You jammy bastard . . . I suppose you'll be all right then.'

★   ★   ★

By my final year, I knew it was all to play for.

There was a girl at drama school called Fran Ryan whom all the boys fancied.

She said to me, 'It's no good just being talented. You need to have a talent for having talent.'

In other words, you need to know how to deploy that talent when the opportunity presents itself. Fran's advice really stuck with me. I decided not to go on holiday in case anything happened. I wanted to be available for any opportunity that might come my way.

Even before I started at *Spitting Image*, I was summoned by some pretty heavyweight television people.

David Liddiment, who was head of entertainment at Granada TV at the time, had seen me do a play at college as well as one of my local stand-up shows. He contacted me and we met in the Parrswood pub.

He wanted me to be the warm-up for a Granada TV sitcom called *Watching*, with Liza Tarbuck. I didn't do it in the end, I can't remember why; the point is that I hadn't even left college and I was on his radar.

As well as my theatrical agent, Sandy Gort, I had a voice agent who found it easy to get me work; I often bunked off college to do voiceovers.

I had a state-of-the-art pager that made one beep for my voice agent and a different beep for my acting agent in London. I could never tell the difference, so I ended up ringing both of them every time it beeped.

After that I had a text pager, which I clipped attractively to my belt. The text would run along the screen: 'Phone your agent now' or 'You need to be at this address for this time.'

You had to phone a messaging service to reply. It was painfully slow compared to the way we text now, but it felt revolutionary at the time.

Having two agents was complicated, but useful in unanticipated ways. When I needed an overdraft, I asked the voice agent if he would write a letter to my bank assuring them that I would earn good money when I left drama school.

The letter said something along the lines of: 'Based on Steve Coogan's current earnings from voiceovers, he should be earning in excess of £8,000 a year once he leaves drama school and pursues a career in comedy.'

The bank were impressed, said they looked forward to seeing me on television and gave me the overdraft.

★   ★   ★

And still the tutors, Martin Nestor and one or two others aside, refused to take me seriously and paid little or no attention to my graduation show in the summer of 1988.

One of the pieces I chose to do was from *The Vortex*, the Noël Coward play that caused a sensation in 1920s London for its unapologetic look at posh people taking drugs and having sex. I wanted to perform the play according to the drama-school rules of How You Act, but I fell at the first hurdle.

To get into character, I was told to put pictures of my family on the wall and imagine what it was like to be sad. But I wasn't into method acting and I preferred to do it in a different way.

When I look in the mirror, in costume, and see somebody else, I start to become that character. Paradoxically, starting with the exterior aspects of a character helps me then go back inside and find out who that person is.

As a student, the more I thought about the process of acting, the worse I became. I was a square peg being knocked into a round hole and I felt cowed by my college tutors into towing the line.

I didn't have a clue how to do a straight, posh role in *The Vortex*. I realised, with dismay, that drama school is about overthinking *everything*. There were some great people there who could talk the talk, but couldn't walk the walk. I, meanwhile, couldn't talk the talk, but I could walk the walk if you didn't tell me how to do it.

I then played Wall in an ensemble production of *A Midsummer Night's Dream*. It's a small role, but I played him as Duncan Thickett and it worked perfectly.

Still no one paid any attention.

The casting directors knew nothing about comedy and were interested only in the good-looking, privately educated students. All the focus was on the Celestia Foxes, wrapped in their pashminas; I didn't have floppy hair, I didn't speak with a posh accent and I did stand-up instead of serious theatre, so I was routinely ignored.

There seemed to be an inordinate number of female casting directors who in my mind's eye smoked cigarettes in long holders, though I'm sure none of them did.

There remains a huge problem with equality of opportunity in this country. There are, without doubt, privileged, privately educated kids who are incredibly talented, but it is also beyond doubt that anyone from such a background is going to find it easier to get into the world of acting than those who go through the state system.

The odds are stacked against you if you come from a modest background; you need exponentially more talent and determination to make it. If you are moderately talented and very privileged, you'll find it easier. It's just a mathematical paradigm.

I'm reliably informed by a Conservative friend of mine that when the Eton-educated David Cameron became prime minister after a blip in which PMs were state-educated, there was a general feeling that 'normal service has been resumed'.

Yuk.

I'm afraid it applies to the acting world too. There was a brief hiatus when the angry young men of the 1960s came along, working-class playwrights and actors who explored the underbelly of Britain. Before that, theatre was all about people coming in through French windows in Noël Coward plays.

But there was no point in me being chippy about my lower-middle-class background. I didn't really care what anyone else thought. I had secured a job as the new voice on *Spitting Image* before I'd even graduated. I had my foot in the door. People were already talking to me.

I even had a part in a film in my final year. Paul Greengrass had seen me on TV, thought my impersonations were funny and had given me a small part in his first feature film, *Resurrected*. I liked him hugely and worked with him again a decade later on *The Fix*.

So I knew it didn't really matter about casting directors who knew nothing. I just went where the work was.

I just couldn't wait for the course to end. I knew I was going to swim while others would inevitably sink. I wanted to be thrown out into the world because I knew I would make things happen.

CHAPTER 37

In the summer of 1988, after I'd been on *First Exposure* and graduated, people started saying I should do gigs in London. And then, when I initially went down to London, they said I couldn't join the capital's comedy circuit because I'd already appeared on television.

For a while I carried on doing gigs in Manchester. A guy called Tim Firth held an event in Salford called Poet's Corner to try to encourage southern-based comedians to travel up to Manchester. He resisted booking me at first, saying he preferred London acts. Finally, however, he relented and gave me an open spot.

I knew exactly what I was capable of. I always killed an open spot because I was on top of my material. I was hard on myself too: if the audience didn't demand an encore then I had failed. Firth watched me bring the house down and gave me some paid bookings, but I still had my eye on London.

Persistence paid off in the end. I managed to get open spots at the Comedy Store and Jongleurs, two of the most popular venues in London at the time, killed them both and got encores.

And then I did the Tunnel Club, at the southern end of the Blackwall Tunnel, which was run by the late Malcolm Hardee. Everyone knew that to be accepted on the London comedy circuit, you had to survive the Tunnel Club. But it was a brutal rite of passage.

As soon I tried to do my nuanced observations, the audience threw plastic beer glasses at the stage. And then a chair.

The heckling was relentless.

'Fuck off!'

'You're shit!'

'You're fucking shit!'

'Get off!'

I ignored them, but changed tack. I did the characters from *Rainbow* – Geoffrey, George, Bungle and Zippy – in a sweary, scatological, sexual manner.

When they started laughing, I returned to my usual material.

As I left the stage, the audience started shouting again.

'More! More!'

Malcolm came over and asked if I'd do another one.

'No,' I replied. I'd won.

★　★　★

Around this time, I bumped into Rob Newman on an escalator in the Tube. He'd just graduated from Cambridge and was an emerging impressionist.

He said, 'You're the new voice on *Spitting Image*, aren't you? Fuck, I want that gig! I thought I had it in the bag as the edgy new impressionist on the block and now you've turned up out of nowhere.'

No one could put me in a box. They couldn't quite work out who I was.

But not everyone was as generous as Rob.

Many didn't think I'd done my time. At the tail end of alternative comedy, I'd come down from Manchester wearing a shiny suit and I no doubt looked like a misfit. An *arriviste*. I was openly ambitious and certainly didn't shy away from commercial work.

My voiceover work had, by this time, graduated from local radio to television ads for high-profile brands such as Ford. Sometimes I would earn as much as £20,000 for a voiceover, which would then be used repeatedly. I didn't like doing them, but the more you did, the more often you were asked back.

I hardly had any outgoings either, because I was still renting a cheap flat that was really little more than student digs.

Just five months after graduating, I was able to buy myself a brand-new Mazda MX-5. I went straight back to Manchester Poly and knocked on the door of the canteen.

Elsie appeared in her blue overalls, hairnet on. As I drove her around Didsbury, she sat in the passenger seat, grinning. She looked at me fondly and said, 'Look at you! Aren't you doing well!'

I floored it, drove back to college and dropped her off. She was still grinning when I left her. She's dead now, sadly, but I still think of her fondly; John and I were both there for her retirement party.

Always having in excess of £15,000 in the bank was a big deal. It was a small fortune. I spent my money in typical bachelor fashion: I bought a sports car but not a washing machine. I used to drive to the launderette once a week with my washing in the passenger seat of my Mazda.

I'm often made to feel self-conscious about my love of fast cars. I have several classic cars in the garage and part of me always feels contemptuous of them because they are a luxury, an indulgence. But as addictions go, liking fast cars is fairly benign, and they connect me with my childhood in a very simplistic way. I buy cars that date back to the period I grew up in, that remind me of the times I would lie in bed and wait for the heavy thud of a Matchbox car in a padded brown envelope dropping through the letterbox and on to the doormat.

The truth is that most people who like cars are white, overweight and right-wing, and I want nothing to do with them or their base values. I like talking to genuine car enthusiasts who are as encyclopaedic as I am; it's sometimes a relief not to have to talk about what I do for a living.

I'm aware it's profoundly unhip. Every time I buy a car magazine and read it on the train, I feel very aware of people looking at me as though I'm an idiot. It's just very . . . lowbrow.

Part of me is very simple. I have these profound thoughts

and then I'll spend hours looking online at a white MGA with leather seats and I know that if I bought it, it'd make me happy. I don't think I'll ever tire of being able to buy the cars I loved as a child.

I have rarely felt guilty about earning good money; my Catholic upbringing taught me to be generous. Once I got very well paid for a gig and I gave the money to my sister, Clare, to buy a car for her family. I always pick up the tab, unless the person I'm dining with is super-rich. I take a very dim view of people who are tight; if you're lucky enough to earn good money, share it around a little.

I didn't, however, always behave well. I was so busy doing corporate gigs, often being paid several thousand quid a pop, that I sometimes got into trouble.

One night I tried to squeeze in two gigs.

The first a corporate gig, the second a left-wing, right-on gig. The corporate gig was delayed and delayed. I had to make a choice, so I went with the people who were paying me the big cheque, not the trendy lentil-eaters.

I phoned the young female organiser of the right-on gig from a call box in the pub – that's how long ago it was – and told her I couldn't make it.

She was bilious: 'You're a cunt. I'll make sure you never work on the circuit again.'

★ ★ ★

I also performed at Edinburgh for the first time in the summer of 1988.

LWT invited me to be one of their showcase acts at the festival and my agent said they'd fly me up from Manchester. I was baffled. Why would I fly such a short distance? I'd only been on a plane once before, to France, and yet in my head I felt like I was virtually in the jet set.

In the end, I got the train.

I stayed at the Caledonian and felt uncomfortable when a man old enough to be my father addressed me as 'sir'.

Within a year or two, of course, I'd completely adjusted to being called 'sir'.

At the time, it was all new and exciting. And I was so naive. I had the following conversation with someone:

Him: 'Have you been to the festival before?'

Me: 'Yes.'

Him: 'When?'

Me: 'In 1979.'

Him (surprised): 'Gosh, that's a long time ago. Which shows did you see?'

I gave the least arty, edgy response possible. 'I was here with my dad. We saw the Military Tattoo.'

I went to an LWT party at the hotel and a pre-Tiananmen Square Kate Adie was there alongside Melvyn Bragg. I had to keep reminding myself not to look too desperate.

I remember thinking that anything could happen. It was a period of real flux in my life. It felt as though my career was in perpetual fast-forward.

Spitting Image was looming and there was talk of an invitation to appear on *Sunday Night at the Palladium* with Jimmy Tarbuck.

Also, crucially, I was starting to meet the people who would later shape my life. I met Doon Mackichan briefly in 1988, who I went on to work with on *On The Hour* and *The Day Today*.

Around the same time I bumped into Patrick Marber. He was doing a reasonably good act on the circuit and was memorably moody.

I had, of course, no idea he was to become my mentor, and the man who would push me to bring Alan Partridge to life.

CHAPTER 38

I started work on *Spitting Image* in the autumn of 1988. I moved out of my rented flat and back in with my parents in Middleton.

Every Saturday I caught the 6.30 a.m. train to London, arrived at Molinare Studios in Soho at 10 a.m. and left at 6 p.m. Sometimes the show was recorded in a Birmingham studio, which was more convenient for me at least.

My Young Person's Railcard meant that my return train ticket to London only cost £21. My *Spitting Image* fee quickly rose from £350 to £1,000 a day, but I carried on using my railcard. I managed not to feel guilty.

Anyway, the show went out on ITV on a Sunday at 10 p.m. and the majority of the sketches were recorded a week ahead. Because it was broadly topical, we would also react to news at the last minute, recording sketches on a Saturday for the following day's show. *Spitting Image* pre-dated rolling news, so week-old sketches weren't an issue, but at the same time topical jokes were applauded. I don't think people could believe we were so quick off the mark.

Sometimes we recorded a sketch with two different punchlines for the following weekend's show and the producers would wait to see how that particular news story unfolded during the week. Alternatively, the puppets would be live in the studio and we would do the voices as the show went out. Or a sketch would be pre-recorded with a guide voice that sounded nothing like, say, Neil Kinnock. And then I'd come in and do Kinnock's voice, knowing that the guide voice had set the tempo.

I was the youngest and most inexperienced voice actor on *Spitting Image*. Chris Barrie, who voiced Ronald Reagan and

Michael Heseltine, had already been on *The Young Ones*, *Smith & Jones* and *Blackadder*. Kate Robbins, who voiced Queen Elizabeth II, Thora Hird and Sarah Ferguson, had been on *Mike Yarwood in Persons*. And Harry Enfield, who voiced Denis Thatcher and David Steel, had already made a name for himself with Stavros and Loadsamoney.

We all did dozens of different voices, sometimes swapping over. I started off doing Douglas Hurd and Jeffrey Archer and progressed to Stephen Fry, Ben Elton and Stan Laurel before voicing more politicians, including Geoffrey Howe, John Major, Neil Kinnock and Paddy Ashdown.

I kept thinking to myself, 'I'm on the inside. I just have to not fuck it up and my life will probably now be completely charmed.'

A never-ending stream of people commented on my age, saying things like, 'You've got *this* far and you're still only twenty-two! You're really going to fly.'

It was quite hard to deal with. I believed my own hype for a while. I was naive and cocky, which isn't a great combination. You always think you're going to be the youngest and most exciting person in the room. Years later, I would watch young comedians come through and recognise the cockiness of youth and the flush of self-assurance. It's like watching someone who's just learned to drive, but who hasn't yet had a bump.

★   ★   ★

Each time a new figure appeared in the public arena, all the *Spitting Image* voice actors had to do mini auditions to see who would be best suited to take him or her on. I jumped up to the microphone every time like an eager puppy, but I was also conscious of the fact that some of the voice artists had a limited repertoire.

It was awkward being the new boy who could easily pick up most voices. Not only that, but I'd stand up and nail a voice and then listen to the others having a long discussion with the director about getting the nuances of the voice right.

The director would indulge them and then finally say, 'I think we're going to go with Steve.'

I had to sit in silence through the entire process just so that I couldn't be accused of muscling in.

Once, when Chris Barrie wasn't available, I had to do his Neil Kinnock, which was inferior to my Kinnock. I couldn't do my Kinnock for the sake of continuity, so I had to do an impression of Chris doing an impression of Kinnock. It was a caricature, albeit a funny caricature.

The one politician I couldn't do was Thatcher. Steve Nallon was brilliant at doing Maggie for *Spitting Image*; he adjusted his performance as her voice became deeper and less grand during her eleven-year premiership. Although I couldn't quite capture Thatcher myself, I could do an impression of Steve's impression. Sometimes someone else's impression gives you the key: I really improved my Ronnie Corbett after I heard Rob Newman do him.

Most of the time I have a good ear and I can pick out the characteristics of someone's voice. My technique is a bit like looking at a caricature by Gerald Scarfe or Ralph Steadman in which the politician's nose is hugely exaggerated: maybe you hadn't noticed the size of the politician's nose before. Wogan's voice, for example, is very sing-song. So to do an impression of him, you go from a high to a low register. It's the same for, ahem, Rolf Harris.

As a child I listened back to cassettes again and again, but as an adult I don't practise voices. Around 70 per cent of the time I just hear a voice and repeat it. It's like having a photographic memory of some kind. Sometimes I can instantly do a voice: I hear it replaying in my head, then reproduce the voice while capturing the attitude at the same time. You refine it as you go along, concentrating on the person's verbal tics.

By the end of my time at *Spitting Image*, I started to notice that the writers were trotting out the same sketches. Or a sketch that had been ditched would be dressed up and resubmitted a year later. I would always remember a sketch.

★   ★   ★

On 9 April 1992, on the day of the general election, John Thomson and his flatmate Zoë Ball had an election party in Manchester. Neil Kinnock lost to John Major and the evening descended into a wake.

I went into *Spitting Image* the next day, already angry at the idea of being condemned to another four years of bullshit, so when a fellow cast member asked me if I was secretly glad as Labour would inevitably have raised income tax, I went crazy.

I got on my soapbox about tax avoidance and it all went very quiet and uncomfortable. I said she should be ashamed, coming as she did from Liverpool, a place of cripplingly high unemployment and deprivation, a place that had suffered the most from Conservative rule.

We were told to take a break to calm down.

It wasn't very nice of me to have yelled at someone I worked so closely with, an otherwise very pleasant person who used to make me laugh a lot.

I left *Spitting Image* the following year; I had been there for six years, during which my life had completely changed.

I had both my feet in the door.

CHAPTER 39

In the time I spent as a *Spitting Image* voice artist, I went through a kind of extended metamorphosis. I had just graduated when I started the show in autumn 1988 and, by the time I left, I was getting letters of complaint from Radio 4 listeners convinced that Alan Partridge was real.

Between *Spitting Image* and the birth of Partridge, I had a tricky road to navigate. I was hyper-aware that alternative comedy was in opposition to the mainstream and yet I had a foot in both camps. I had set out to be an actor but became an impressionist because it was a means to an end. Similarly, I wanted to be a clever alternative comedian, a Stephen Fry or a Ben Elton, but I wasn't in a position to turn my back on mainstream entertainment.

I wanted to do the kind of comedy I watched, but at the same time I wasn't about to look a gift horse in the mouth.

As I was leaving college, I got my first London agent, Jan Murphy. Sandy Gort was a great agent, but he was based in Manchester, whereas Jan was based in central London and had more contacts.

Jan introduced me to Kenneth Earle. Kenny was like Mr Showbiz, a real old-school manager with a wood-panelled office in Regent Street. He wanted to get me straight on *The Des O'Connor Show*. When I pulled a face, he said that perhaps if I did *Friday Night Live* – the new version of *Saturday Live*, presented by Ben Elton – I could do *Des* next.

I was confident enough at twenty-three to say that I didn't really want to do *Des*.

Kenny didn't understand why I'd rather be associated with

Ben Elton than Des O'Connor. I could see him thinking, 'Fucking hell, mate. I'm not in that game.'

Much as I didn't want to do *Des*, I decided to get as much experience as I could. I went where the work was.

Some encounters were better than others; I was lucky enough, for example, to work with some of the last music-hall comedians.

I did a corporate gig with Ken Dodd that seemed to go on for ever. Dodd is a brilliant live performer. He came from the music hall and managed to make the transition to television, a move that eluded many of his peers. He is famously addicted to performing – he is still touring in his late eighties – and has always said he only feels alive in front of an audience. I understand that addiction; it's a particular curse of comedy. When you are onstage and the audience are laughing, you feel surges of adrenalin. It's like a fix. And so, inevitably, the silence of your dressing room post-gig can be deafening.

I also did *The National Lottery Live* with Bob Monkhouse, who was very funny in person. I had never really liked him as a TV performer, but I found him to be a genuinely nice, generous-hearted man and a comedy super-fan. He had a near-encyclopaedic memory of other comics' material.

He came up to me at the Lottery show and said, 'I remember this routine you did . . .'

It turned out the routine was from several years earlier. He quoted my material back at me and I was stunned. It was word-perfect.

He then gave me a good gag for Tony Ferrino, the Portuguese singing sensation I was doing on the Lottery show.

Bob: 'I'll say to you, "Tony, it's great to meet you." You say, "Bob, it's an honour and a privilege." I'll say, "It's an honour and a privilege for *me*!" And you'll say, "That's what I meant."'

So he gave me a joke to do at his expense and it got a big laugh.

Ken Dodd and Bob Monkhouse were from another era. I was

glad to have crossed over with that world as it was disappearing, but only because I knew I could step away from it.

At the same time, I was never keen on being overtly or loudly left-wing in the way that Ben Elton and his peers were. I tried to be vaguely political on occasion, but never in a straightforward way; David Coleman discussing Chilean politics as though it was a sporting event was probably the closest I got.

There was a small fire in my belly and I felt huge antipathy towards Thatcher and Reagan, but I was undeniably an armchair lefty.

I had been very purist at drama school. It was about ideas and attitude and being vaguely anti-establishment. As soon as I started to earn money I changed my mind.

I thought, 'This is quite nice.'

The holier-than-thou bleating of my college peers on the left didn't help much.

I was also becoming increasingly aware that some of the people who were laughing at my work were right-wing, and I realised that I could make people laugh when I didn't agree with their politics. I didn't want to create enemies, so I thought it might be best if I wasn't angry any more.

I said to myself, 'I don't want to foster discord. I'll just concentrate on being funny rather than not liking the establishment.'

I wanted to be adventurous, but without alienating anyone politically.

For a while I got high on the material success of it. I was doing what I wanted to do and earning a bloody good living. How could life get much better? I wanted to make a living and have a career. Even if it meant sidelining my politics. It wasn't about any kind of Thatcherite dream, it was about taking the opportunities that were on offer.

I had to go where the money was.

★　★　★

In October 1988, two days after my twenty-third birthday, I did *Sunday Night at the Palladium*.

I sanctimoniously said to myself, 'Keep your distance from these guys. They are yesterday's people.'

Much as I felt awkward about being on the show, it was a chance to be watched by millions of people on national television. It would have been bizarre to turn it down.

The show was quite glamorous: Kylie Minogue, Robert Palmer and Shirley Bassey were also on the bill. And Jimmy Tarbuck was very nice to me backstage.

He said, 'Kid, how old are you? If it happens for you, it's a great life. If it doesn't happen for you, it's still a great life. The only real advice I can give you tonight, kid, is: 'Get on, hit them, get off.' You get no prizes for hanging around.'

He was right. You should always leave the audience wanting more, tempting though it might sometimes be to bathe in the glow of their applause.

As the curtain came down for the commercial break, Tarbuck came up to me while I was still onstage and thrust his hand into mine. I felt incredibly self-conscious because I didn't want anyone to see me shaking hands with a supporter of the Conservative Party who was also a very high-profile member of the establishment.

Again, I wanted the exposure, but not the association.

Nor could I deny the thrill of being on television. I rang my mum on a payphone during the commercial break. 'Mum! Did you see me! I'm going on again at the end, for the curtain call!'

My family were delighted. There was a sense of, 'Gosh, our Stephen's on prime-time telly!'

Mostly my parents were baffled by my early success.

I did a gig at the 500-seater Davenport Theatre in Stockport in early 1989 for which I must have cobbled together an hour of stand-up, including Duncan Thickett as my support act and various impressions.

I invited Mum and Dad to the gig and they were amazed that the show sold out.

Mum was as shocked as she was impressed. 'I can't believe all these strangers who don't know our Stephen are queuing around the block for him.'

★　★　★

In 1989, the year after I graduated, I was still following the work and the money. I just had to get out there, get my foot in the door and, when I got some purchase, do the work I wanted to do.

Accordingly, my CV for that year is a little strange. I appeared alongside John Sessions on *Ten Glorious Years*, which marked a decade of Thatcher being in power, and I still have a letter from my agent showing that I was paid £31.50 for appearing on *The Krypton Factor*. There was an observation round in which contest-ants had to spot continuity errors in a sketch; the sketches were written by Paul Abbott, who of course went on to write *Shameless*, and I acted in them.

At least I was savvy enough to know that shaking Tarbuck's hand on national television had to be tempered with performing at small, out-of-the-way venues such as Stand and Deliver. Between 1988 and 1990, I did some of my first stand-up gigs at Darren Poyzer's comedy club in Ashton-under-Lyne.

These home-made, below-the-radar gigs were the lifeblood of comedy in the north-west in the mid to late eighties. Darren, a cook on HMS *Sheffield* before it was hit by an Argentinian Exocet missile in the Falklands, paid £30 or £40 in cash for each gig. You had to get changed next to empty beer bottles and you didn't have long to get the audience on your side. It was character-forming stuff.

Henry Normal and I used to perform in the theatre bar in Ashton-under-Lyne to about twenty people. I had first bumped into Henry two years earlier, when he was doing his punk poetry gigs at the Greenroom in Whitworth Street, and we used to see each other all the time at small, underground venues, supporting indie bands, playing at student gigs or upstairs rooms in pubs.

Once I had got to know Henry, I realised he was the right person with whom to run Baby Cow, the production company we set up in 1999. Protestant work ethic, disciplined, methodical and diplomatic. I am none of these!

I toured with lots of interesting people in 1989: Simon Munnery, Stewart Lee, Richard Herring, Patrick Marber. Sometimes we'd be on the same bill as Jon Thoday, who had co-founded Avalon the previous year and who tried to be my manager for a while. And I had a few gigs with Richard Thomas, who went on to compose *Jerry Springer: The Opera*.

In the summer of 1989, I went back to Edinburgh and did a double act at the Playhouse with Mike Hayley, who had also been on *First Exposure*. It was called *Coogan and Hayley's Seaside Special*, and our publicity said that we wanted to create 'a show that proves you can be radical – but still wear a sweater'. We had investment in the show and there were adverts on the back of buses in Edinburgh.

Mike and I shared a flat right behind the Playhouse with an older American comedian called Will Durst. The *Marchioness* disaster, in which two boats collided on the Thames and fifty-one people died, happened on 20 August and I remember Will trying to write material about it before realising it was way too soon.

Mike and I wrote some sketches together and I did Duncan Thickett. I'd come onstage as Steve Coogan, leave after doing a series of sketches with Mike, and return as Duncan Thickett as a failing stand-up. Duncan always drew a big laugh.

The *Scotsman* reviewed the gig on 25 August:

> Coogan, a voice behind some *Spitting Image* puppets, has an unrivalled repertee of impersonations ranging from Ronnie Corbett's squeak to Roy Hattersley's slobber which

should rightfully put Mike Yarwood and the like out of business and into premature retirement.

Published two days earlier, the *Herald* review was a little more probing:

> With a little more work, Coogan's stand-up creation, Duncan Thickett, an unconscious icon of Northern gormlessness, could go on to rival Harry Enfield's Stavros and Loadsamoney in capturing a nation's imagination. But the question of whether or not that happens will only be resolved when Coogan and Hayley decide which audience they want to attract, family or adult, alternative or mainstream.

There it is again: alternative or mainstream. I was still not part of the circuit and I was definitely regarded as a lightweight. I only bothered with the Comedy Store or Jongleurs. I'd do two shows on a Friday and two on a Saturday, and pocket £500 in cash. I was certainly never short of work – perhaps because I was so willing to cast my professional net wide. If I was worried that it left me open to gentle ridicule, I was right.

At the end of 1988, for example, I supported Kit & The Widow at the Lyric Hammersmith for five weeks, providing light relief in the middle of their show. My routine was to finish the gig on a Friday night and drive all the way to Hull every weekend in a battered Vauxhall Chevette to see Maggie Jones, the sister of Bernie, my first true love.

Kit & The Widow were a double act who performed songs in the vein of Flanders and Swann; their audience was populated by posh theatre people who considered them a bit racy and who liked their witty songs. It was about being clever as much as funny.

Kit Hesketh-Harvey, the singer, and Richard Sisson, the pianist, would introduce me thus:

'Here he is, in his Burton suit.'

I didn't quite understand why it was funny. As far as I was concerned, Burton was a good shop where you got quite nice, shiny suits.

If people asked me where I'd got my suit from, I certainly wasn't embarrassed to say.

In his 2001 autobiography, Frank Skinner recalls comedy-circuit dressing rooms in the late eighties and early nineties: Eddie Izzard would be discussing how some rooms suited comedy while others didn't, while I would be 'getting all excited about a new pair of tan-leather driving gloves'.

Those dressing rooms were verging on the anarchic; at the Comedy Store I frequently saw female comics pissing in the sink in the dressing room to avoid the long walk through the crowd. In fact, both female and male comics, myself included, would piss in the sink. It was the act of being OK and accepting of this environment that meant I was able to be spat out the other side relatively unscathed. I was still very naive at this time, I can't deny this.

CHAPTER 40

I recently found a dusty box of random mementos dating back to the eighties and early nineties. It's always unnerving looking at visual evidence of your life, not least when you don't know what you might find.

I found my Youth Hostel Association membership from 1981, in which my face looks like a smacked arse. It's shocking how young I look, but preferable to photos from the nineties in which I mostly look chubby, pallid and unfit, a direct result of no exercise, a bad diet and too much alcohol.

There's a photo of me youth-hostelling in France in the eighties in obscenely short shorts. Another shows my old friend Mike Taylor diving into the sea from the top of a forty-foot cliff in 1985. I remember standing on the edge of the cliff for twenty minutes before I was brave enough to follow him.

My Filofax from 1988 lists gigs and voiceover sessions, meetings with my bank manager, random lists of earnings and one entry that simply says 'lunch with Geoffrey Perkins'.

A sheet of negatives reminded me that Bruno Tonioli taught me to walk like a woman when I first started doing Pauline Calf.

He would show me how to walk with a braggadocio that I lacked: I had to suck my tummy in, push my bum and fake tits out, put my shoulders back and my chin down, put one foot in front of the other and sway my hips from side to side.

But the key to it was when he said, 'OK, Steve, you've got the technique and now I want you to forget about everything I've taught you. Do it again but without concentrating too hard on the technique. And, as you walk along, you should be pretending you're a woman and thinking, "I want you to fuck me."'

I bumped into Bruno at an airport years later and he couldn't stop laughing. 'Can you believe what's happened to me, Steve? I'm famous and rich. It's ridiculous!'

I also found a handful of photos taken on the set of *24 Hour Party People*, in which I played Tony Wilson, a genuine eccentric and a legend in his own lifetime. I couldn't bring myself to look at them. More than any other film I've done, *24 Hour Party People* made me realise what I might be able to do with my life, what might be possible.

In 1986, I did a gig at the Hacienda just a few hours after I'd been a pallbearer at my grandad's funeral. Someone in the audience threw a glass at me. Two of my best mates, Ged and Mike, happened to be standing right next to the guy and they jumped on him. Dave Allen, son of playwright Jim, was also there. I could see them from the stage, fighting next to one of the iconic Hacienda pillars painted in black-and-yellow diagonal stripes.

When I did *24 Hour Party People* in 2002, I was amazed to see that the set of the Hacienda had been so faultlessly recreated. I stood on the stage, looking out at the black-and-yellow pillars, and thought, 'I performed on the real stage fifteen years ago and someone threw a glass at me. And now here I am on a replica stage, playing the guy who opened the club.'

It was a perfect moment.

I haven't watched *24 Hour Party People* for a decade because it seems so real to me. It's part of my identity. Watching it would be like looking through those old photos. I don't want to go there, not yet.

Finally, at the very bottom of the box, I found an undated Christmas card from Frank Skinner. Inside it says, 'I miss you, you cunt. Merry Christmas from Frank.'

Back in 1989, I often used to stop off at Birmingham on the way to London and do a gig at the Bearcat Club, where Frank Skinner hosted a night.

He always gave me a generous introduction along the lines of: 'This guy's fucking brilliant. You're going to love him. He makes me laugh, anyway . . . Steve Coogan!'

I'd do my show and then I'd hang around and watch Frank. He was funny full stop. He was quite old-fashioned in some respects, and his material was sometimes a bit coarse, but he always transcended it with an irresistible charm. He felt familiar, like an old friend.

I assumed that the content of his material would stop him from ever appearing on TV. It seemed such a shame that this properly funny guy would be consigned to the shadows. How wrong I was. As soon as postmodernism kicked in during the early nineties and *Loaded* magazine was launched, comedians like Frank were in favour again. He was suddenly the right man at the right time.

What impressed me most about Frank was his work ethic. He was always working, always writing things down. He really pushed himself, endlessly trying out new material and seeing how far he could go.

My attitude in turn was, 'Everything is going to happen for me now. I've done all the hard work. Surely someone else can pick up the baton and just do it all for me.'

Of course it never stops being work. If you want to do well, you have to do the work. There is no way round it.

There is a Zen saying by Lao-Tzu: 'Before enlightenment: chop wood, carry water. After enlightenment: chop wood, carry water.' Not someone I was in the habit of quoting as a child – he wasn't on the telly.

Slowly, my laziness started to impede me. Frustration began to creep in. I didn't want to be known as the man who did funny voices. Peter Sellers had the same issue for a while; being a good impressionist can be a curse as much as a blessing.

But I didn't know how to move away from impressions.

I was like a rabbit in the headlights. Everything had happened too quickly.

I shone so brightly that, in retrospect, it was inevitable burnout would follow. Although, in truth, laziness was as much of an issue.

I rang my agent Jan in 1990 and said, in a panic, 'Why am I not getting any work? I thought everyone liked me? Where's the noise gone? What's happening?'

She said, 'Darling, they've seen you. They know what you do. You're an impersonator. You do funny voices and you're very good at it.'

I said what I always say. Only perhaps, in this instance, I was slightly more petulant. 'I want some acting work.'

Her response was unequivocal. 'If you want to do something different, love, you're going to have to pull a rabbit out of a hat.'

★ ★ ★

When I worked at *Spitting Image*, I used to mess around between takes doing funny voices. I did Duncan Thickett, my first real character, and Gavin Gannet, who later became Gareth Cheeseman. Gavin was a yuppie with slicked-back hair and a double-breasted suit. He was very Thatcherite and would lecture everyone about how good he was at business. He wasn't very subtle; he was more of a caricature than a character study.

Jon Glover, who did the voices of the Duke of Edinburgh and Oliver Reed on *Spitting Image*, used to encourage me to do Ernest Moss, a health and safety officer who complained in a broad Lancashire accent about people not following proper procedure. There is a tiny bit of my dad in Ernest Moss: they share a preoccupation with the minutiae of technical engineering.

When Harry Enfield joined *Spitting Image*, he would look at me and say in a withering tone, 'Are you doing your funny characters, Steve?'

Everyone else was laughing at me, but Harry wasn't. He's

been very nice to me since; back then I was no doubt rather obnoxious.

Anyway, I suspected the ace up my sleeve was Duncan Disorderly, the drunk who hates students.

I went into the wig cupboard at Granada and nicked a streaked-blond feather-cut, a hairstyle that had been very popular with certain men in the eighties and immediately felt right. I bought a stick-on moustache, borrowed a jacket with rolled-up sleeves from one of my brothers and added a thin tie, slip-on shoes and white socks.

By 1990 it was already a dated look: Duncan was still wearing a Bryan Ferry jacket just as the world was turning its attention to grunge. He was *Miami Vice* meets Rochdale. With a fag dangling from his mouth and a Ford Capri outside.

Just before John Thomson and I performed at Edinburgh in the summer of 1992, Patrick Marber suggested I change Duncan Disorderly's name.

Again, I nearly missed a trick.

In early 1993, I started doing sketches on *Saturday Zoo*, an alternative variety show on Channel 4 hosted by Jonathan Ross. For the first show, John Thomson and Simon Day did a sketch in which they played two gay Hollywood men gossiping, while Patrick Marber and I did a lame sketch.

I was holding Paul Calf back, being precious about him.

At the end of the show, the photographers swarmed around John and Simon. Patrick leaned over to me, nodded at the pack of photographers and said, 'There you go. It's all over, mate.'

Patrick and I were both humiliated, and my blood ran cold. I thought I'd been in the driving seat. I immediately knew I had to stop messing around and put Paul Calf on the next week.

Meanwhile, Henry Normal and I wrote and rehearsed every week to make sure we had five minutes of rock-solid material every Saturday. Paul Calf was then given the Patrick Marber polish.

And the viewing figures spiked every time Paul Calf came on.

Suddenly people in the street started shouting 'bag o' shite' at me.

Paul Calf's catchphrase was catching fire.

Paul Calf was instantly recognisable. He was yesterday's man playing catch-up with the new world. The classic pub bore. In a period of near-obsessive political correctness in which you could get a dirty look for opening a door for a woman, Paul Calf got away with everything. He was postmodern just as it was becoming a buzzword. In 1994, a test copy of *Loaded* magazine had Paul Calf on its cover, alongside the slogan 'For Men Who Should Know Better'.

Loaded became emblematic of everything that was tired about postmodernism. But when it first came along, it was like punk. There was a strangulation of ideas at the time, and *Loaded* was a breath of fresh air. It was a totally legitimate and authentic response to the zeitgeist. It's important sometimes to take everything, throw it up in the air and see where it lands.

Although I'd created a postmodern character, it took a while to fully understand the postmodern vibe.

Someone saw Rob Newman do a stand-up gig in which he said, 'I hate working-class people. I wish they'd fuck off and take their scaffolding with them.'

I was shocked; I thought it was a terrible thing to say. I didn't understand what he was doing. Around the same time, Nick Hancock was booed by freshers for saying that he couldn't stand poor people because they make you feel guilty for having a few bob. And he patted his trouser pocket.

He had to stop mid-show and say, 'Why are you booing? Do you not understand irony? Is the only conversation you're having still along the lines of what A levels you did?'

Rob and Nick were postmodern first. It only slowly started to dawn on me; I wasn't the sharpest knife in the drawer at that time. I was keen and enthusiastic, but I wasn't as smart as Rob Newman, who was really tapping into the zeitgeist.

In the end, I grew to despise everything postmodern for

covertly legitimising appalling attitudes that we thought we had got rid of. But the timing was perfect for Paul Calf because people liked to laugh at his outmoded way of thinking.

He was a release because he'd say things like, 'I'm a radical feminist. I think you have to be these days if you want to get your end away.'

Of course, in much the same way I'd initially been appalled by Rob's routine, not everyone got Paul Calf.

I was doing a gig in a student union and this guy kept shouting, 'Sexist!'

I pulled my Paul Calf wig off in the middle of the gig and shouted, 'It's ironic, you fucking idiot!'

I put the wig back on and everyone laughed.

★   ★   ★

Paul Calf was so popular that, after eight weeks, someone suggested bringing Paul's girlfriend Julie to life. Although he talked about her a lot, it somehow didn't feel right. I thought it would be funnier to do his sister, Pauline, and I knew what kind of woman she'd be like: the ballsy, assertive and predatory girls who had started at my school when it became a comprehensive.

I'd found the new intake of girls vaguely threatening because they came from the local council estates. They were definitely not victims; I'd have been intimidated by Pauline had I met her during my adolescent years.

I tried Pauline Calf out for the very first time on national television on *Saturday Zoo*. I didn't test her anywhere else beforehand, I simply walked out in front of the cameras dressed in a big peroxide wig, a short skirt and white stilettos.

Pauline was an instant hit, pretty much like Paul. The key to Paul, in particular, is the fact that he's old-fashioned and vaudeville. It's just gags. He's basically a thin Les Dawson with a feather-cut; the rhythms of his speech are certainly Dawson's.

At the same time, there is a crossover between Paul Calf and Alan Partridge. Paul has this lack of self-awareness and earnestness that's also evident in Alan, though Paul is more self-knowing.

Paul's relationship with the audience is very much, 'You know what I'm saying is wrong, but I know you secretly agree with me.'

It was cheeky, almost challenging you to remonstrate. Nobody did.

Sometimes I could swap material between Paul Calf and Alan Partridge. If a gag I was writing for Paul was too long, I'd tweak it and give it to Alan.

Alan is more nuanced, so I had to push him into more of a caricature if I took him on tour. But whenever I did Paul Calf live, I knew I could just go onstage and relax. He's so low energy that it was almost like taking a break.

There's a twinkle in his eye when he knows he's being bad. He's a bit daft, a bit naughty, and he knows he's saying things he shouldn't say. I would delight in the delivery of the lines.

It's traditional, old-fashioned shtick. Paul Calf is a proper comedy character. Unadulterated fun, guiltless joy. I miss him. Sometimes.

CHAPTER 41

Jan Murphy wanted me to move to London as soon as I finished college, but I was reluctant to leave Manchester. I bought a house with Martin Murray in 1989 and we rented a room out to Alan Francis, who went on to co-write *Jeffrey Dahmer is Unwell* at the 1995 Edinburgh Festival.

Martin and I played a trick on Alan once. Martin bought a couple of blank-firing pistols that were very realistic: a Browning 9 mm and a Walter PPK. We used to mess around with them; I could exactly mimic the sound of the gun being loaded and then fired. The blank bullets were deafening and quite dangerous because they gave off this charge.

Alan came back home one day to find me downstairs and Martin upstairs. Martin and I staged an argument and then suddenly I pulled a blank-firing pistol out of my jacket pocket and started shooting down the stairs. Martin was shooting back up at me. The house was full of smoke and the noise deafening.

We completely traumatised poor Alan, who was screaming at us to stop before someone was hurt.

I did eventually rent a flat in Balham, south London, with Miles Harvey, who had been at Manchester Poly with me. I was aware that I was working all the time and Miles was always waiting for the phone to ring. It was brutal enough for him, without me doing well.

Miles was the brother of Marcus Harvey, one of the Young British Artists who would later shock the tabloids with his portrait of Moors murderer Myra Hindley. Damien Hirst often came round to the flat; I always encouraged Miles to invite him because he was very funny.

Damien once showed us a photo of himself leaning on a dead man's head.

I thought, 'Well, that's not very nice.'

I didn't think it was art, I just thought it was a stupid photo he'd taken for a laugh. There was no indication at all that he was going to become one of the highest-paid artists in the world.

I didn't settle properly in London; I got my work done there and went back up to Manchester whenever I could. My personal life was complicated. I was seeing a woman called Lizzie when I bought the house with Martin. She had been Martin's girlfriend and, as one of my best friends, he wasn't delighted. But he got over it – he says now simply that it was 'awkward' – and Lizzie moved into our house.

Lizzie and I were together for three years. She was great. She was very organised, so it was like having a PA as well as a girl-friend and she helped me get the Edinburgh show ready for the summer of 1992.

While I was still with Lizzie, I met Anna Cole.

I caught Anna's eye in a pub in 1991. She was a student in Manchester and she didn't have a landline, so I used to sneak out of the house I shared with Martin and Lizzie and throw rocks at Anna's window. Eventually she'd let me in.

When Anna moved to London in 1992, I used to see her there and Lizzie up in Manchester. Neither of them knew about the other. I was such a fool. It wasn't even exciting after a while; it just became normal once I got into the rhythm of it.

In fact, it was often just exhausting.

There were a number of times I went to Euston and put Lizzie or Anna on the train, went to a cafe and waited for the next one to turn up. I just had to make sure the train times allowed a gap of around an hour.

Lizzie came up to Edinburgh for the festival in 1992 and then, after she'd gone back to Manchester, Anna came up from London.

I knew it would all catch up with me eventually.

In the end, one found out about the other and they had a long conversation on the phone. Remarkably, instead of dumping me, they both told me I had to make my mind up. I ran away and hid in London.

Eventually, I chose Anna; Lizzie went on to forge a successful life in the theatre. I think she dodged a bullet.

Anna and I moved into a flat in Belsize Park. But I had to work for her affection. She wasn't remotely interested in my work, which was good in a way. I liked the fact that she was conscientious about things. She was smart, provocative, very political, very left-wing.

I could assuage my occasional bouts of guilt about earning proper money by subsidising Anna as she studied to be a lawyer.

I was happy with Anna, but I had endless flings. For about a year, when things started to happen for me, I slept around. If women came my way, I wouldn't avoid them. And there were always girls hanging around. Slightly wild girls I met in the pubs and clubs of the comedy circuit.

I had been cloistered as a Catholic teenager, and now I was like a kid in a candy shop. Or a bull in a china shop. Take your pick.

There's a strange Victorian morality about being sexually active that I don't share, as long as it's consensual. Judging people's behaviour has become a national sport.

I don't regret sleeping with all those girls. Not really. I thought I was Byronic.

I had a long, delayed adolescence.

Having said that, I did hurt people and I'm not proud of it. But I felt slightly disconnected from it, and at the time I didn't really think about the consequences. Sex is just sex. It doesn't necessarily carry any emotional involvement. When you're young it doesn't really matter. If I was still shagging around now it would probably be a bit grim. Contrition has been shown and apologies made to those affected. I don't intend to elaborate here out of respect for those people. And I will say that

I can still count as friends all the women I ever had a relationship with.

In the late eighties and early nineties, however, it was a big adventure. It was a big wide world populated by women who seemed quite sophisticated and who wanted to have sex with me.

I thought, 'Gosh, I must be interesting.'

It wasn't, at the start at least, about being famous, because I wasn't *that* famous; I'd only been on TV a few times.

Famous is when you get in a taxi and the driver says, 'Here, you're that fella on the TV!' That didn't happen to me until 1994, when *Knowing Me Knowing You with Alan Partridge* moved from radio to television.

The girls I met in the early nineties were just responding to me as the funny guy who'd performed earlier in the club. They were attracted to the fact that I was funny. They also seemed to like the fact that I wasn't an alpha male. I was a bit square, a bit nerdish. Never cool. I slowly realised that some women liked the fact I wasn't urbane, nor was I trying to be.

With my daughter, Clare. The ever-present Alan Partridge is on the telly.

With the late, great Tony Wilson in Cannes for *24 Hour Party People*.

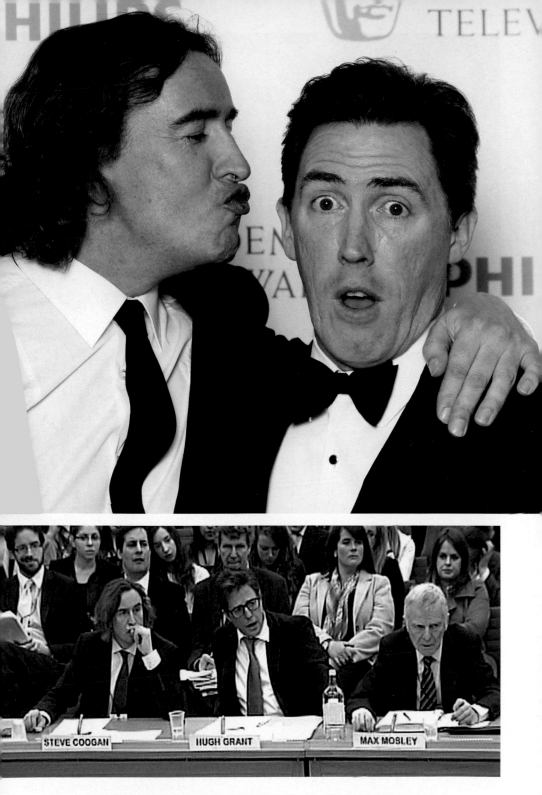

Top: Rob Brydon and me at the BAFTAs for *The Trip* in May 2011.

Above: With Hugh Grant and Max Mosley in front of the Select Committee during the phone-hacking scandal in November 2011.

Above: At the premiere of *Alpha Papa* in Leicester Square in July 2013.

Opposite, top left: Neil and Rob Gibbons, also a
the premiere of *Alpha Papa*

Opposite, top right: Dame Judi as Philomen
Lee and me as Martin Sixsmith in *Philomena*

Opposite, bottom: With Philomena Lee

Top left: With Martin Sixsmith.

Top right: With Dame Judi.

Above: With my *Philomena* co-writer Jeff Pope.

Top: A-ha! Arriving at the BAFTA party in February 2014 after winning a screenwriting BAFTA for *Philomena*.

Above: With John Cleese, my childhood hero, after chairing a Q&A with him in December 2014.

Mum and Dad, without whom . . .

CHAPTER 42

In 1991, as I was feeling sorry for myself in Rhodes, Patrick Marber had moved to Paris to try to write a novel. I was lost and lonely in Rhodes, and Patrick was lost and lonely in Paris.

In the meantime, Armando Iannucci, who had been working for the BBC since the late eighties, was working as a light entertainment radio producer. He was on a BBC training course learning how to make feature programmes. He didn't want to make a straight feature or news programme, however, and he was fed up of conventional radio comedy. Instead he came up with the idea of a spoof news comedy programme called *On The Hour*.

He put together an informal pilot that was too straight because it used real reporters. For the proper Radio 4 pilot, he assembled a group of performers including me and Patrick, Chris Morris (who also wrote for the show), David Schneider, Doon Mackichan and Rebecca Front, and writers including himself, Stewart Lee, Richard Herring, David Quantick and the late Steven Wells.

It was an extraordinary collection of people, all in their twenties. And, best of all, I was in their gang.

Armando had used Patrick on *Week Ending*, the satirical current affairs sketch show on Radio 4, which he had produced, and Patrick had recommended me. Armando had also seen me doing impersonations and thought I'd be useful in a repertory group because I was versatile and quite funny.

I don't think he adored my comedy, but he could see I wasn't just doing silly voices, that I was trying to do something a bit different. Perhaps he recognised, consciously or otherwise, my own burgeoning frustration with the comedy I was doing.

Back in the day when people still wrote letters, Armando wrote to me.

Apparently I didn't write back for six weeks.

Armando says that when we finally spoke on the phone, I was horribly quiet and monosyllabic.

When I turned up at the studio and we physically met for the first time, Armando was surprised by how low-key I was. He wasn't sure how to interact with me.

I was low-key because I was nervous. I thought it better, as Mark Twain said more eloquently, to keep my mouth shut and be thought an idiot than to open it and remove all doubt.

The *On The Hour* writers had come up with a script, and to loosen us up, Armando suggested we play with it a little. He remembers the transformation in me: I went from shy to fearless when I started doing impressions and improvising. I could deal with anything and everything that was thrown at me. He says I came alive.

I had turned up at *On The Hour* knowing it was a spoof current affairs show, but not quite realising how special it was. On that first day, Armando read something that Stewart Lee and Richard Herring had written. It didn't follow the normal rules. It was properly funny, Python funny. Avant-garde, different, fresh.

On The Hour felt experimental, for me at least. I learned that you don't have to be conventionally funny to get a laugh. You can laugh at things without quite knowing why they're funny.

Armando knew exactly what he wanted to do with *On The Hour* – and, when it transferred to BBC2 in 1994, *The Day Today*. He was brilliant at pushing me away from punchlines and the more traditional comedy formats that I was still hanging on to.

In turn, I brought some accessibility to the characters and made them approachable. Not that we sat for hours and hours discussing character motivation. Most of the time we just chucked ideas around: 'What about a guy who talks like this?' Or 'Who has this kind of voice?'

We recorded *On The Hour* in the Paris Studios in the bowels of the BBC on Lower Regent Street. Photos of the Goons and Tony Hancock adorned the walls, and I was exactly where I wanted to be – and, unusually, I knew it at the time rather than only with hindsight: following in the footsteps of the BBC comedy giants that I'd listened to on vinyl time and again as I was growing up.

We'd talk about things, improvise, go out for lunch, then try to spin things one way or another. Writing comedy isn't always funny, but we were always laughing. It occurred to me that the Pythons must have felt the same when they first met.

Some of the sketches were scripted, some had bullet points to be covered and others were improvised. I remember reading scripts and crying with laughter, but knowing I'd be hard-pushed to explain why.

Armando's comedy was funny partly because it was so silly. He didn't employ the normal cadences and rhythms of traditional comedy, where the audience is given a green light to laugh. There was a nervousness about it.

I was incredibly excited by the material, some of which was very abstract. I loved the fact that *On The Hour* wasn't derivative. It was its own thing. Fresh and confident, with this brilliantly acerbic quality, a kind of 'we don't care if you don't get it, we don't care if you don't like it, we're doing it because it amuses us' attitude. It was quite elitist, and very uncompromising. Radio 4 had faith in the talent and therefore let us get on with it; it was the BBC at its very best.

It quickly became clear that we were making the kind of cutting-edge comedy that would make *French and Saunders* and *The Comic Strip Presents . . .* look dated. In fact, I felt like I was in on a big secret that reduced much of the other comedy around at the time to hot air.

We all felt like we'd discovered treasure.

On The Hour felt like a TV show on the radio, and that's what made it funny. It was arrogant enough to believe it was more important than TV. Paris Studios was isolated from Oxford Street, so you felt like you were in a timeless bubble of radio comedy. We knew there wouldn't be anything like *On The Hour* for at least another five years.

There was no one in my line of work who I would have swapped places with. It was what I'd been working towards for years. I would read the material and be impatient to record it. Not just the sports commentator who became Alan, but all the characters.

On The Hour might have been innovative, but it was none-theless made in an old-fashioned way; we all sat around wearing Bakelite headphones with a woven cord. It was always pre-recorded, and it was very ad hoc. There's something special about radio: you feel you can do anything. You could have an idea at lunchtime and execute it that same afternoon. The expediency of it made for very fresh, spontaneous material.

I remember watching Armando, who was doing a radio course, edit with a razor blade. It seems prehistoric now. We were still in an analogue world, but *On The Hour* laughed at the past as well as presciently mocking a digital future dominated by surreal soundbites.

I occasionally listen to radio comedy now, and it seems the affable, jocular, avuncular, middle-class nature of Radio 4 remains unchanged and undimmed.

We played around with the formula, challenged it and ignored the rules. There was nothing friendly about *On The Hour*, and that's what was so delicious about it. It was incredibly acerbic and a total release.

★   ★   ★

I wasn't very sophisticated when I joined *On The Hour*. At drama college I was surrounded by people who would talk endlessly about the process, while I was just chomping at the bit to 'do it'.

When I did my impressions at college, people were often surprised at my detailed observations. But I can pick up mannerisms easily, and I like observing the oddness of people. I have always been able to dip into this big bucket of observations in my head, to change my voice and find voices for characters.

I knew I had a skill, but I felt self-conscious and slightly out of my depth in Armando's gang.

Everyone on the *On The Hour* team was clever and confident, and I wanted to be like them. I wanted some of their smartness. I'd been frustrated on my drama course, but I was learning from Armando et al. every day; they made me think, they raised my game.

I was more aware than I should have been about the fact that most were university-educated – Armando went to Glasgow and then on to Oxford to do an MA; Patrick, David and Rebecca had gone to Oxford; Chris had gone to Bristol and Doon to Manchester – while I had been to a polytechnic. I certainly felt like I was punching above my weight.

Neither Armando nor Patrick was remotely judgemental about my education; it wasn't important to them, or to anyone else for that matter. It was all in my head. In fact, Patrick later told me that he considered me the big cheese in the room after Armando because I'd been on TV and drove a sports car.

As much as I was in awe of them all, I knew I wouldn't be in their gang if I wasn't good enough. I made up for my lack of a university education by having a great ear and being able to come up with characters quickly. But sometimes Patrick, David or Rebecca would talk about Oxford and I'd have nothing to say.

I'm sure for some people this screams 'Alan Partridge subtext', and they are of course right, but it was a while before I learned to turn my shortcomings and flaws into strengths. I wasn't liberated creatively; I had a self-inflicted repression.

Still, while I might laugh and say something funny about

being at a polytechnic, I thought Oxford sounded great and secretly I wished I'd gone there instead. I was impressed, yet envious and irritated at the same time.

I didn't always help myself.

My mild inferiority complex didn't exactly propel me forward at the start. It didn't turn me into a swot. Despite my resolve to put in the hours, I was, as ever, prone to laziness. Patrick pushed me and encouraged me in equal measure. He didn't let me get away with anything.

Thank goodness for Patrick.

★   ★   ★

When Patrick came back from Paris to work on *On The Hour*, I rented out my London flat to him. I was also, later, a landlord to Simon Pegg and Nick Frost, but that's another story.

I naturally gravitated towards Patrick, and I grew dependent on him very quickly; there was a time when I wouldn't make a career move without asking his advice. He became my mentor, my sage. I had to know what he thought about everything. I sought his guidance and approval. Patrick's role in my development was crucial. It was exciting for me to be around him, though no doubt I drove him crazy at times.

Patrick was thoughtful and smart, exceptionally well read and knowledgeable. I used Patrick like Google for all things creative. He could answer most of my questions. He was my search engine for anything literary. He would just know.

He could discuss things without necessarily having an opinion about them, whereas I'd been brought up to discuss things with a view to arriving at a conclusion. He taught me to think independently, freely and confidently.

He even asked my point of view on things, which I found hugely flattering.

If I was impressed by his mind, Patrick was impressed by my talent.

I never doubted that I had more confidence than Patrick as a performer. But it was intuitive and instinctive with me, rather than intellectual. I didn't think too much about it: I'd run at something, whereas Patrick would endlessly mull things over.

He can be a curmudgeon, but I was drawn towards him because he was the opposite of light entertainment and I was desperate not to be a light entertainer. I wanted to be doing work that I felt mattered, that had substance.

We became very close, both professionally and personally. When I later fell out with Patrick, it was like getting a divorce.

My relationship with Armando was very different. He was the head teacher, a young fogey who had a kind of woolly, academic, BBC fustiness. And yet he was super-sharp, fiercely bright and forensic. He was, in some ways, like the man behind the curtain in *The Wizard of Oz*, controlling all the action but hidden from view.

Chris, meanwhile, very much fronted *On The Hour*. He was odd. Polite, but posher than Armando. And even sharper. A bit spiky, like John Cleese. His focus was absolute and he was quite militant about things being done in a certain way.

Rebecca, meanwhile, was the most respectable woman I knew. She was so grown up and well presented that you couldn't quite believe she had this wicked sense of humour.

Doon was a bit more down and dirty. She was mischievous and had more of a filthy laugh. She was naughty. She could really make me laugh.

But it was Arm's show. He was in charge, and if *On The Hour* carries a kitemark with anyone's name on it, it's his.

The show was cold and austere in a way that was really refreshing. It wasn't trying to be liked, it didn't try to charm you, and compromise wasn't on the agenda.

Right from the start, Armando's way of doing comedy was hugely inspirational for me. For all the run-ins I've had with him over the years, I talk about him like he's a relative. Part of me still can't figure him out, but he's been a huge part of my life.

I've never socialised with Armando, though; we have very little in common. Armando, for example, has zero interest in cars. He once told me how he picked up Colin McRae, the late rally driver, from the airport in an Austin Metro with an automatic gearbox. Armando really couldn't understand why it would be the antithesis of everything a driving enthusiast would want in a car.

There might have been some dignity if it had been a manual.

Knowing Armando as I do, the idea of him driving Colin McRae all the way back home from the airport in an Austin Metro is just hilarious.

When we were writing *I'm Alan Partridge* for television and Armando and I were a little more comfortable around each other, I would sit there leafing through a car magazine.

Someone asked him what I was like and he said, 'Steve's someone who reads car magazines.'

That's all he knew about me because that's all I did when I was in the office when we weren't writing.

My relationship with Patrick was more intimate. We were close friends and I trusted him implicitly. I would tell him my troubles; he would counsel me on my professional and personal life with great patience. It would never have occurred to me to go to Armando for advice about either.

And yet, when he sent me that letter, Armando changed my life in ways that I couldn't ever have anticipated. I still get goosebumps when I think about it.

CHAPTER 43

Once *On The Hour* had been commissioned as a series, Lee and Herring wrote a brilliant, incisive sketch about a sports reporter. It became increasingly surreal and there were no punchlines, but it was incredibly funny.

Armando turned to me. 'Steve, can you do a generic sports reporter's voice that's not an impression?'

The voice was very different from the way Alan now talks. It wasn't, in fact, that different from my own voice, except more nasal and monotone. A bit like Elton Welsby, John Motson or David Coleman.

So far as I remember, Armando, Patrick, Rebecca and Dave Schneider were in the room when I first did the voice.

I've never been particularly interested in sport, but I know that commentators tend to sound very confident and simultaneously slightly stupid. They never stop talking, even if they're stuck for something to say.

Lee and Herring wrote some original scripts that had a strange, surreal quality, but none of the comedy was character-driven. It is sometimes said that they invented Alan Partridge. Let me be clear. They did not.

I started to improvise about how I wanted to get into light entertainment to get away from the serious news guys who I feared looked down on me, and then I improvised as a racing car commentator, which was immediately funny because I know so little about the rules of sport.

The more mundane the sports reporter, the better.

'There they go, racing around that bend. Along the straight now. Down the dip. Through the chicane. Around the bend again. Down. Up a bit.'

Everyone started laughing. Armando says it's as though Alan emerged fully formed.

Although, at that early stage, he didn't yet have a name. He was simply 'sports reporter'.

At a certain point we decided that he should have a name. I thought it should be a name that sounded familiar, that you felt you'd heard before.

'Alan' seemed like an appropriately sporty, Middle England name. It didn't sound bookish; literary people aren't generally called Alan. Alan would have a nice car on the drive and wear golf sweaters.

I'm pretty sure I came up with 'Partridge'. We had to check in the phone book to see if an Alan Partridge – or a list of Alan Partridges – already existed. But there was only the news reporter Frank Partridge.

'Alan' and 'Partridge' fitted well together. It didn't sound overly comical.

One of the first good pieces of advice Patrick gave me was to change Duncan Disorderly's name to something more anonymous. Paul Calf doesn't sound like a nice, cosy name for a character. It's deliberately unpoetic.

Names of comedy characters usually have some history to them, and mine were no different. Duncan Disorderly was a stupid pun and Patrick was right to make me change it. Gavin Gannet then became Gareth Cheeseman. Someone called Gareth Cheeseman wrote me a very angry letter saying that everyone laughs at him now, which is unfortunate.

Ernest Moss was previously Ernest Ickler. Being a health and safety officer he was a stickler for things . . . not great, I know. Terrible, in fact. Patrick only let me keep Duncan Thickett because I pointed out that it was a real person's name; someone at drama school knew of a social worker with that name.

After we'd named Alan, we talked about where he was from. Milton Keynes was too obvious. We pored over a map of Britain. I was tired of hearing Liverpool and Midlands accents in comedy, and Norwich was interesting because it isn't en route to anywhere and as such is probably the most isolated city in England. Patrick liked Norwich because he'd recently been there to watch Arsenal play at Carrow Road, and I was keen because I immediately thought of 'Naughty Norwich' and fondues and BBQs. Norwich isn't the north or the south; there's a kind of otherness to it. It doesn't have an overwhelming sense of itself, like, say, Yorkshire or Cornwall does.

I didn't know what the Norfolk accent was like, so I didn't attempt it. If anything, Alan speaks received pronunciation, but I occasionally use flat, northern vowels for comic effect. He's ostensibly well spoken, but a bit nasal, which is a northern idiosyncrasy.

It was obvious to me that Alan would drive a Ford Granada. He felt like a type: a bloke with a collection of golfing sweaters who religiously washed his car at the weekend, who was slightly right-wing and very judgemental. Very clean. Catalogue man.

Alan is a Thatcherite more than a Tory. There's a small appreciation of high culture in one-nation Conservatism that you don't get with Thatcherism. Alan is a typical Little Englander, one of those Napoleonic shopkeeper people. For him it's about status and being respected in a very superficial way. He measures himself against success. For him, knowledge is something one could acquire by ordering the wipe-clean vinyl edition of *Encyclopaedia Britannica* and a subscription to *Reader's Digest*.

If you look at the pantheon of loved British comedy characters, they have a common denominator, a thread running through them. *Dad's Army*'s Captain Mainwaring, *Fawlty Towers'* Basil Fawlty: they are all frustrated. Frustrated at not being properly recognised for who they are. They are essentially disappointed with their lives – more Dunkirk than D-Day.

And the humour comes from that frustration.

We love them because we recognise that fallibility, that vulnerability. It's cathartic for an audience.

Alan was the perfect character for me to immerse myself in

and, because he was on the radio, he evolved organically. I was given scripts to work from when I sat at the sports desk, but when I was doing interviews with sportsmen or -women, the writers would suggest funny things Alan could say and use in his own way.

In the second episode, for example, Armando suggested that I become obsessed with groin injuries in a matter-of-fact way. It was even picked up by the press: the sports presenter who can't stop asking athletes about their groin injuries.

It certainly set a pattern: on *The Day Today*, Alan interviews a topless female jockey in the changing room. He's like a little boy lost and doesn't know what to say. I just played it for real, like a boy who can't quite believe that a woman has unself-consciously taken her top off in front of him.

By the time we were doing *The Day Today*, we were officially a new generation of comic talent. The BFI website reliably informs me that *The Day Today* was 'the most radical satire seen on British screens since the 1960s', but *On The Hour* was more of a cult radio show with an audience built on word of mouth.

Although we knew we were on to something, without the benefit of a live studio audience we had no way of knowing what people thought of *On The Hour*. Occasionally a member of the public would come up and say a particular sketch was really funny, but the audience was just getting to know certain characters in the series.

By the time we came to recording the pilot of *Knowing Me Knowing You with Alan Partridge* in front of a live audience, in the spring of 1992, Alan's fanbase had really gained momentum: the queue outside the BBC stretched around the block.

★　　★　　★

I had no idea, of course, that Alan Partridge would come to define my work in Britain for the next two decades. In the beginning I didn't even regard him as a stand-up character, never mind a character who might be loved as much as Captain Mainwaring or Basil Fawlty. He did, however, feel special and different.

If you were to draw a Venn diagram of Alan and me, there would clearly be an overlap. I would explain to people who asked that I used Alan Partridge to channel all the things about myself that I was embarrassed about. And then they would want to know more.

Am I as incompetent, narcissistic and socially inept as Alan? Sometimes. But aren't we all? Isn't that why we respond to him?

Alan's foibles aren't unique; there is an unfiltered honesty coupled with ignorance. Some critics have been very reductive about my relationship with Alan Partridge; they seem to think I might be wounded by the observation that I'm a bit like him. As if it's something I'm not completely cognitive of.

People still say, in a surprised manner, 'Ah, Steve Coogan actually *is* like Alan Partridge'.

To which I say, 'Well, yes, of course I am. Alan is a conduit for all my demons. Clearly he's a bit like me. I have inadequacies and that's OK. What makes it work is my being comfortable with that and giving vent to them through Alan.'

What irritates me is when I do other characters and they still say, 'Oh, that's a bit like Alan Partridge.'

Well, no, that's actually me you're seeing in those other characters. And Alan is a bit like me.

To be reductive myself, I knew that if I wanted to make the shift from *Sunday Night at the Palladium* to *The Day Today*, I had to offload my flaws on to Alan Partridge.

Alan allowed me to make a virtue of my innate ignorance about certain things. I very quickly learned in improvisation sessions that the key to Alan was using my immediate reactions to anything anyone said. Those reactions, unedited as they were, had a childlike quality to them.

Actually, it was rather like seeing the world through a child's eyes, because Alan was giving his first, visceral response to virtually everything. I almost didn't want to foster anything too eloquent. I had to pretty much say the first thing that came into my head. It was a technique that made us all laugh simply because it was so reductive while being profoundly honest.

I could use Alan as a dumping ground for my insecurities and at the same time say, 'This is not me. It's someone else.'

Later on, I would be writing Alan with Patrick and Armando and I'd say something as myself.

In unison they would respond: 'Just say that as Alan! It's perfect!'

As I felt self-conscious about having been to poly, so I was still aware of my lack of sophistication. I would play to it, but I really was green about certain things. When I first started working with Armando and Patrick, there were terms and references I just didn't get.

They would casually refer to architectural styles or writers I'd never heard of. A few times I would scribble down a reference and look it up later at the library. The Internet had yet to be invented.

Patrick remembers me being as assertive and confident as him and Armando in those writing sessions. He says I mocked their Oxbridge intellectualism and vetoed gags that I considered too highfalutin. He says he and Arm regularly deferred to me because I was Alan. However, I remember clearly feeling like the world of clever comedy was almost out of my reach, but not that far away. I felt like I could just about jump off the riverbank and grab hold of the branch without falling into the river.

★   ★   ★

Once or twice when we were making *On The Hour* and *The Day Today*, I did a sketch that reduced the cast and crew to tears of laughter – usually the improvised chats with Chris where Alan was mercilessly bullied.

Patrick and I wrote a sketch for *The Day Today* about a night attendant at a public swimming pool called Keith Mandement. The morning of the recording, I was studying the script and said I had two voices for Keith, both painfully monotone, but one much sadder and more pathetic than the other. We chose the latter. That was the extent of the discussion.

Talking to a documentary maker (played by Armando), Keith spoke in a voice that sounded at times as if he was almost flatlining:

KEITH: 'I'm the night-time supervisor. I basically watch the monitors at night to see if anything occurs. There was one incident, I remember it quite clearly. I was filling in a puzzle and I heard a noise, a commotion, up in the rafters and somehow, we will never know even to this day, a pigeon had got in and was flapping about in the rafters. We called the bird specialists and they removed it in the morning. I'm never tempted to use the pool myself at night, although some time ago I used to go down and take showers. And on one occasion I went down and found a woman's swimming costume which I put on and paraded around, singing a Joan Baez protest song. This pool has been open nearly forty years and in all that time I only slipped up once in my mind. I was engaged in a particularly tricky word puzzle and forty people had broken into the pool and were playing around, ducking, bombing and doing all manner of prohibited activities and eventually someone was killed.'

DOCUMENTARY MAKER: 'But given that your sole responsibility is to maintain the security of the pool, isn't that an indictment against yourself?'

KEITH: 'Well, I would say this. I've been working here for eighteen years. In 1975, no one died. In 1976, no one died. In 1977, no one died. In 1978, no one died. In 1979, no one died. In 1980, someone died. In 1981, no one died. In

1982, there was an incident with the pigeon. In 1983, no one died. In 1984, no one died. In 1985, no one died. In 1986 . . . I mean, I could go on.'

DOCUMENTARY MAKER: 'No.'

I knew it was funny because I could see the cameraman's shoulders shaking with laughter while he was trying to keep the camera steady. He had tears streaming down his face.

Chris Morris said I should stop doing comedy because I'd never do anything as funny as the night attendant ever again. I think he's right. It may be the funniest thing I've ever done.

CHAPTER 44

Armando knew Alan Partridge was funny, but he didn't give much thought to Alan's future because he was buried beneath *On The Hour*. And if you listen back to *On The Hour*, Alan doesn't really stand out among the clever silliness.

So when Patrick proposed an Alan Partridge chat show, both Armando and I laughed. We were dismissive. I thought the character could stretch itself to, at best, ten minutes. Given half an hour, he would surely run out of steam.

We made Patrick write a proposal for the chat show. It had already been established that Alan liked Abba, so even in its primitive form Patrick knew it should be called *Knowing Me Knowing You*. I think Armando added '*with Alan Partridge*'.

Patrick's pitch said that the show would be six thirty-minute episodes for Radio 4, with the *On The Hour* cast playing guests. He sold it as a spin-off of *On The Hour*, and pointed out it would be cheap and funny – why not do a pilot?

Armando initially thought it would be like Radio 4's weekly discussion programme *Start the Week*, but then we all agreed it should be a chat show to appeal to Alan's more mainstream side.

Alan Partridge really came to life when Patrick started pushing me to think about Alan in terms of his family life, whether he had kids or not, if he was divorced, what sort of music he liked and hated. Things I hadn't bothered to think about. Patrick teased the information out of me.

He was a little obsessed with Alan, and I wasn't.

Patrick says now that people love Alan because there's a little bit of Alan in us all; a confident, perennial fool, he speaks to a universal small-mindedness that we would prefer to conceal.

He points out too that Alan was a fan of the Thatcher regime, which we detested as young, studenty lefties; to play the enemy was great fun.

Patrick saw an opportunity to make Alan greater and he wanted to be the person to do it. He thought Alan just too good to be a small part of a cult radio show.

And so I went round to Patrick's house in Islington to write with him.

He would give me five minutes' grace and then fine me a pound for every minute I was late. He refused to give it to charity because he knew I wouldn't mind paying up. I was pretty much never on time, and the most he charged me was a fiver. Despite being preposterously late year after year, Patrick always found it in himself to forgive me.

Patrick carried on pushing me, asking me endless questions about Alan.

Knowing Me Knowing You with Alan Partridge was written almost entirely by me and Patrick, with Armando producing, editing and guiding the show. When it came to the television show in 1994, Armando became fully involved as a writer as well.

When we finally recorded the radio pilot of *Knowing Me Knowing You with Alan Partridge* at the Paris Studios, I nipped out to Lillywhites in Piccadilly Circus during a break in rehearsal.

I bought some slacks, slip-on shoes, a shirt, a tie and a nice pink-and-green Pringle golf jumper. I still have the sweater in as-new condition, hardly worn. My affection for it grows with the years.

Back in the studio, I parted my long hair down the side and combed it across my head as if I was covering up a bald patch.

Photos of myself as Alan in the early nineties show that I look way too young. It doesn't really work. But I wanted to walk out in front of the radio audience as Alan. People wanted to believe he was real, and I was happy to oblige. We kept the conceit going when it became a TV show; I would welcome the studio audience and tell them that we'd be starting shortly and ask them to be patient. In other words, do the normal warm-up that would be expected if Alan were real. It was easy that way. If there were any technical issues, I'd go out and talk to the audience as Alan.

For the Radio 4 show, the guests, most of whom had been in *On The Hour*, didn't come onstage and huddle around a mic. Radio 4 has this stilted and very idiosyncratic way of delivering drama and comedy drama that generally involves three people leaning into a mic and the characters being very earnest, endlessly sighing and talking in received pronunciation.

We wanted to be more naturalistic and so we set it up as a real TV chat show, with guests sitting on chairs perpendicular to me.

When the show was first on the radio, one of my greatest pleasures was people telling me they had to pull over because they couldn't listen properly if they were driving. When you tune into most Radio 4 plays, you know within two seconds that it's a radio drama rather than someone talking for real. With *Knowing Me Knowing You with Alan Partridge*, listeners were totally thrown.

They couldn't quite believe what they were hearing and didn't know if it was for real or not. It was the perfect response.

I had letters of complaint from listeners who thought it was real.

I have one such letter framed in my downstairs toilet:

December 9, 1992

Dear Mr Iannucci,

I was appalled by yesterday's 6.30pm Alan Partridge broadcast. If this is the level to which Radio 4 has sunk, the BBC is in need of real help.

The Simon Fisher 'interview' was tasteless and cruel. Partridge's only means of countering the intellect of a quite exceptional 9-year-old child was to ridicule him and apparently after striking him, to reduce him to tears. It ended with Partridge calling Simon a 'little shit'.

The pseudo-hypnotic segment gave Partridge a five minute opportunity to tell listeners on countless occasions that at school (and having heard him, I was surprised to learn he ever went to school) he was nick-named 'Smelly Fartridge'. How very entertaining.

At this stage, I switched off.

Of all the communication media, radio is my first love and usually I have a high regard for the standards set by the BBC, but this example of witless drivel presented by an individual who gives me the impression of being verbally uncontrollable has greatly concerned me.

I hope Sir Michael Checkland and Michael Green both caught the programme and share my concern. Please let me have your comments and by copies of this letter, I would make the same request of them.

It's a compliment, I suppose, that anyone thought Alan was real.

I was chuffed to be mentioned in Sir Roger Moore's autobiography. His father was still alive when I did *Knowing Me Knowing You with Alan Partridge* on TV. One of the jokes in the first episode was that special guest Roger Moore had failed to turn up because he was stuck in a car at Heston services on his way from Heathrow.

His father later said to him, 'It was very rude of you not to turn up to that talk show.'

Roger replied, in that smooth, baritone drawl, 'Father, it's a satire.'

I'm also still staggered by how many public figures have a crass, Partridgesque world view. More than anything, Partridge represents those economically libertarian, socially progressive Tories who like to think of themselves as fun and not fusty. Touchy-feely. You know, suits with open-neck shirts, PR-ed to within an inch of their lives. At least those old-money bastards in their top hats were easy to spot.

★ ★ ★

The script for *Knowing Me Knowing You with Alan Partridge* was only delivered the night before and we rehearsed on the day in the Paris Studios. The show was then recorded in ninety minutes and edited down to half an hour. It was loose and scary, but it gave the show a certain freshness and at least we all knew each other very well from *On The Hour*.

I didn't learn the scripts: I could crib off a clipboard because I was a chat-show host. When the show moved to television, I cribbed in two ways: the script was on the autocue, so occasionally I'd look up and ask a question and the audience would laugh. I used to look at the autocue and the clipboard and combine an awkward look of self-consciousness with an opportunity to look at my lines.

I also had an earpiece. Armando would occasionally throw in the odd phrase from the control room or give me a prompt, tell me to ask a certain question. There's a famous moment where a horse did a shit as we were filming and I couldn't see it because it was behind me. Armando alerted me to it and told me to make a reference to it, so I did so without having seen it.

Just before the radio pilot went out, I did a corporate job and a woman asked me what else I did.

'Oh,' I said, 'I do bits and bobs, *On The Hour*. I do a sports presenter called Alan Partridge.'

Her eyes widened: 'Oh my God! That character is genius!'

She started eulogising about Alan. Her response both shocked and pleased me.

But I still didn't expect people to be queuing around the block for the pilot. I couldn't quite believe it. When an audience turns up, you're not quite so cocky. If they don't laugh, it's not funny.

The brutal nature of comedy is in fact what's enjoyable about it. I've always loved its lack of ambiguity. People can say what they like, they can have an opinion. But if lots of people laugh at it, they can't say it's not funny.

Michael McIntyre is not my cup of tea, but I can't deny that people find him funny. He was reported to be the highest-grossing comedian in the world in 2012, and you can't argue with that. You can say someone has bad taste if they're laughing at something you don't find funny, but you can't say it's not funny.

Our *Knowing Me Knowing You with Alan Partridge* audience was flesh and blood. They were real. There was nowhere to hide.

I need not have worried about the pilot. The audience was mostly, so far as I could tell, made up of *On The Hour* fans who had heard about Alan Partridge going solo.

The recording was dynamite.

It was the first time I thought, 'Oh, people like Alan. They *really* like him.'

Afterwards I went to a pub round the corner with the *On The Hour* gang.

I don't know why Patrick wasn't there, but I remember calling him from a phone box.

He said, 'This character is going to change your life. I hope you're ready for it. People are going to be shouting "A-ha" at you across the street.'

I was floating on air after that recording. Everything was lining up perfectly.

CHAPTER 45

When I first started seeing Anna Cole properly in early 1992, I apparently told her I was going to be incredibly successful and famous within a few years.

She thought I was slightly deluded. Charming, but deluded.

It sounds arrogant to say so, but sometimes you just know you're on to something. We knew collectively with *On The Hour*; it's different saying it about your own comedy creation.

Yet my toughest critics were gushing about the radio pilot, including my dad.

When I played it to him, he laughed all the way through and then asked how many episodes I was going to record.

When I said five, he laughed again. 'You'll have a job keeping that up.'

And yet Alan was advancing on three fronts.

As well as the radio show, Patrick and I were filling in his backstory for *Knowing Me Knowing You with Alan Partridge*, and *On The Hour* was transferring to television as *The Day Today*. There was a discussion about which should be shown first, *The Day Today* or the Partridge chat show. Introducing Alan to television as part of an ensemble was perfect, so *The Day Today* started on the BBC in early 1994 and his chat show went out later on that year.

I was also pulling material together for a show I could take to Edinburgh in the summer of 1992.

Patrick asked if I had a director. I didn't so I asked if he'd like to do it, for a fee of £1,000. It sounded pretty reasonable. It was a bargain in retrospect, of course.

I did two shows in Edinburgh: the one with John Thomson that Patrick directed, and a much less successful one during the day at Pleasance Two called *The Dum Show* with Patrick, Stewart Lee, Richard Herring and Simon Munnery. It wasn't anyone's fault; the chemistry that existed in *On The Hour* wasn't there and it just didn't work.

We fooled around on the last night and Stewart told us off for not taking it seriously. I felt guilty, but it was hardly cataclysmic.

There has been speculation about internal tensions in the group when we were making *On The Hour* as Lee and Herring weren't, in the end, involved in *The Day Today*. I can't account for anyone else, but I didn't fall out with Stewart and Richard. We were just different. I wanted to be successful, but on my own terms. I was intuitively more commercial and gravitated towards broad characters like Partridge and Paul and Pauline Calf.

I was wrapped up in what I was doing, but it's easy to see how my ambition might have irritated them. Maybe they even thought, 'Fucking hell, he could do with a bit of self-doubt.'

I was driving around in my racing-green Mazda MX-5 with BBR turbo conversion. I think I used to vault into the car without opening the door.

What a tit! But I was having the time of my life.

Meanwhile, Lee and Herring were quite purist, and confident with it. They were esoteric and elitist, but not in a bad way. They didn't want to pander to populism. It's amazing to see what Stewart Lee has become. He has his own idiosyncratic style – his is a unique comedy voice. I think he is the best stand-up comedian in Britain.

I did, however, briefly fall out with Patrick when we were working on *Knowing Me Knowing You with Alan Partridge* for the BBC.

The fight is now long forgotten and it is, in retrospect, ludicrous that tension about my inability to ever be on time came to a head over a pair of shorts.

It was a hot, humid day in the summer of 1994 and I had

spent my lunch hour searching for a pair of shorts. All the shops seemed to have sold out and I ended up getting back to work half an hour late.

Patrick was immediately angry. 'Where have you been? You know we're up against it.'

'I was hot. I couldn't find any shorts.'

He said, 'What goes on in that little mind of yours when you know you're late?'

'I'm not answering that.'

He was furious. 'I really want to know. I'm genuinely fascinated.'

I looked at him. 'Button it.'

He went for the door, but I stood in his way. I raised my fist.

He said, 'Don't you dare raise your fist at me,' then stepped round me and walked out.

Armando was left there saying, 'Should we . . . er . . . have a break?'

That evening I bumped into Patrick and immediately apologised.

My memory of the row is different from Patrick's. I was convinced that he suggested we take a break because our professional relationship had become quite intense. He insists that we put our differences aside, came into work and carried on writing. We did, in fact, carry on working together on various projects after 'Shortsgate'. We did a Pauline Calf Christmas special that year, and then, in early 1995, I went to the opening night of his play, *Dealer's Choice*. Perhaps the truth is that we drifted apart when the second series of *I'm Alan Partridge* was commissioned and for various reasons Patrick wasn't involved.

I went off and edited *Live 'n' Lewd*, a video of a national tour I'd done earlier in the year that was directed by Dominic Brigstocke. I was supposed to be editing it with Patrick, but I did it on my own and it went really well.

About six months later, Patrick said he'd have a look at it for me.

He watched it and said, 'This is really funny.'

Ironically, it was his unqualified praise for something I'd done without him which set me free.

I had wanted and needed his approval since *On The Hour*, but suddenly I'd developed my own voice.

He has asked me a few times to take Alan back to the radio, but there just hasn't been time. The beauty of radio is that it's a short step from conception to execution; on television there's always the danger a project will have its vitality sucked out of it at every turn.

I will always love Patrick. He held my hand and led me past the pitfalls and potholes on the rocky road to success. Yes, I know, Partridge could have written that sentence, but unfortunately I did. It doesn't matter.

We worked together for five really important, formative years and, in a strange way, as the years go by, that time I spent with him becomes more, rather than less, important.

CHAPTER 46

K nowing Me Knowing You with Alan Partridge was first broadcast on Radio 4 in December 1992. We recorded the pilot three months before going to Edinburgh and the five episodes that made up the first series straight afterwards.

As Alan's chat show was going out on Radio 4, I did a Prince's Trust gig. The next day, Charles and Diana announced their separation. People asked what I'd said to Diana. It's not as though I even got the chance to stir it up; we had a banal conversation in which she asked if I practised my voices in front of the mirror.

At the start of 1992, however, my focus wasn't on royal gossip but on planning my Edinburgh show.

John Thomson and I decided to do an extensive warm-up tour of adult education centres in the north-west in a Volkswagen Golf. We were endlessly refining the show, but keeping it away from London.

We even drove all the way to Aberdeen and about fifteen people turned up.

They said, 'Steeleye Span was here last week and they got 200.'

John and I just looked at each other.

In the boot of the Golf we had a projector and a lectern, and a ghetto blaster and a bunch of cassettes that I would give to the sound man at each venue for cues.

It was complicated: I had to talk each sound man through the cues because I'd designed the show so fastidiously.

John and I, obsessed with amassing as many strange photos as possible for the show, had driven around in the Golf to take them and then had them developed into slides. John would compère as Bernard Righton, his hilarious, politically correct Bernard Manning creation, while I was changing characters.

At one point, John and I asked my dad if we could take some photos in his cellar.

He said, 'What do you want to do that for?'

I tried to explain. 'There's so much technical equipment down there, it would be great texture as the background of the photos for this handyman character I'm doing. I think it's got the right kind of feel because it's full of . . .'

He finished off my sentence. '. . . junk? You mean junk.'

In the awkward silence that followed, John stared at the floor and kicked his heels.

My dad finally broke the silence. 'You should just go and take photos outside a substation somewhere. That will look technical.'

I tried to argue: 'But it doesn't really have the requisite detail.'

Firmly, finally, he said, 'I'd rather you didn't. Some of the wiring I've got down there is quite unorthodox. If you show a slide at a public event and someone from the council happens to be in the audience and they see behind you on one of the slides how the circuit-breakers in my cellar are arranged, they will realise it's technically against health and safety regulations.' He took a breath. 'They could come round and insist we change it all.'

We both said, 'OK then.'

And that was the end of that.

But I was allowed to look through the old science magazines that my dad kept piled up in the cellar, and found random black-and-white photos of men with Brylcreemed hair, operating blades in the 1960s. When the images were transferred onto slides and projected onto a white screen, they had a pleasing retro look about them.

I took a photo of my Fiat Uno being towed by my dad's Volvo. And then I switched the cars around, so the Fiat was towing the Volvo.

Operating the projector myself, I would later ask the audience, 'What is wrong with the photo?'

The audience would look baffled; the joke couldn't possibly be that simple, could it?

It could.

The simplicity was part of the joke. It was a very stupid but funny joke.

I'd point impatiently at the screen with a stick. 'The car in front is broken down. That's what's wrong with the second photo. The Fiat has to be behind the Volvo, not in front of it.'

I'd switch the slides around again, so the Volvo was once more in front. 'That's better. The car that is broken down is at the back, where it should be.'

John and I dressed up as the health and safety officer Ernest Moss and his son Robin and drove around Manchester with a photographer from Hulme. We would find an image and then write around it. It was really silly and brilliant fun.

We stood next to a burned-down sandwich bar called the Butty Bar Plus on an unfinished section of the Mancunian Way. We also posed in front of the Stockport Viaduct, and the Stockport Pyramid, which was being built at the time. Later, in the show, I would point at them and describe Stockport Viaduct as the 'longest brick-built structure in Europe' and talk about the quite ridiculous Stockport Pyramid. 'You won't find Nefertiti in there, but you will find the finest sprinkler system this side of Chadderton.'

John gave me that line. It still makes me laugh now.

And we particularly liked Rochdale multistorey car park. We took photos of John standing in the car park and then on a ledge, looking down. I rehearsed the narrative.

'There's Robin on level three, which is his favourite.' Beat. 'He later returned to that level when he threw himself to his death some years later. It's only now, when I look at his eyes, that I can see he was lost.'

It was dark and the car park was deserted, but John and I were helpless with laughter.

★　★　★

As the same time as preparing for Edinburgh, John and I met up with Caroline Aherne at her flat in Didsbury to write a sketch-show pilot for Granada called *The Dead Good Show*. Andie Harries, then a producer at Granada, thought we might work well together, but it didn't go to series in the end as we all had other things in the mix.

While we were sitting around writing the pilot, however, I played a brilliant trick on John.

He had taken a break from writing to do an interview with Mark Radcliffe on Radio Manchester. Caroline and I listened in as John did an impression of Tony Wilson. Caroline has always been able to make me laugh, mostly by relentlessly taking the piss out of me, but this time our focus was on John.

He kept sniffing, insinuating that Tony was taking cocaine.

Caroline immediately said, 'Why don't you ring up Radio Manchester as Tony Wilson and complain?'

I rang Liz, the producer, straight away.

'It's Tony Wilson here. I just heard John Thomson doing impersonations of me on the radio and insinuating that I was taking cocaine. I'm a big fan of John's, but this time he's gone too far. Unless I hear a retraction on the radio in the next half an hour, you'll be hearing from my lawyers on Monday morning.'

Liz stuttered a profuse apology. We tuned back into the radio and Mark Radcliffe was at great pains to point out that it was John Thomson doing an impression of Tony Wilson and not Tony himself.

Liz had obviously been spooked.

Mark kept on saying, 'Just to reiterate one more time, it was just John Thomson doing an impression. We love Tony. We'd love to have him on the show.'

Caroline and I couldn't stop laughing.

I phoned Liz and told her it was me who'd made the earlier call, not Tony. She said I should've been on instead because my impersonation was much better than John's.

When John came back to the house, Caroline and I asked him how it had gone.

He sighed and hung his head. 'Tony Wilson might be suing me.'

Caroline and I were both mock incredulous.

He continued. 'He said he was a big admirer of my work, that a lot of my work was brilliant . . .'

He started exaggerating, bigging himself up. And then talking slightly hysterically about lawyers.

I asked if he was absolutely sure it was Tony Wilson, and he didn't even pause to consider it. He was sure.

I said, 'Just think about it, John. It could've been a prank.'

John: 'No way.'

'Who knew you were doing the show?'

John: 'No one. Just you and me. Maybe Rob Newman could do an accurate Tony Wilson, but he had no idea I was doing the show.'

'Let's ring up the producer and check to see if it really was Tony or not.'

I rang Liz. 'Hi, it's Steve Coogan here. I've got John here, who's very concerned . . .'

She was laughing at the other end of the phone.

John took the phone, all beleaguered. Then he looked massively relieved.

He put his hand over the phone and mouthed, 'It was a prank.'

I told him to ask Liz who the prank caller was. She told him the caller was sitting in front of him.

His face changed.

He yelled, 'You fucking bastard!'

But, in time, he got his revenge.

★　★　★

In 1993, I was staying in a provincial hotel after a gig. I was something of a philanderer in those days, and I secreted a girl I'd met in Edinburgh into my hotel room.

Just as we were settling in, I had a phone call from reception.

'Good evening, Mr Coogan. Are you aware of the fact that we don't allow additional guests in the room unless you're willing to pay a supplement?'

I said, rather tartly, 'Why are you making the assumption that because I have a guest in my room she is staying over? She is a friend of mine.'

The female receptionist refused to listen. She insisted a further charge would be added to my bill.

I went ballistic. 'How dare you talk to me like this! This is shoddy behaviour from a reputable hotel. I want to talk to the manager. Right now.'

The manager came on the line. He was apologetic and asked if he could send some champagne up.

I said, 'I don't want champagne. I will be checking out of the hotel as soon as I've packed, and I don't expect to be presented with a bill.'

The manager kept on apologising, but I wouldn't change my mind.

The girl and I went downstairs to reception.

I said, 'We're checking out.'

The receptionist looked mystified. 'May I ask why, sir?'

I was livid. 'Because of the appalling behaviour of the staff at this hotel. It's atrocious.'

The girl I was with was sitting out of earshot on a sofa in the lobby.

The receptionist politely asked if I knew the names of the staff members I'd spoken to. I didn't.

I was becoming increasingly impatient.

The receptionist was trying to calm me down, but I was apoplectic.

One of her colleagues appeared with a fax. 'This might explain the situation, sir.'

The fax was for my attention. It had one word on it, in giant block capitals.

'SUCKER'.

I suddenly remembered that I'd been on the phone to Patrick Marber before the receptionist had called my room.

Just before I'd hung up, he'd said, 'Have you got a girl in the room with you?'

I said, 'Yeah, I have.'

I was standing at reception, looking at the fax and thinking to myself, 'Oh fuck.'

The receptionist said, 'Would you still like to check out, sir?'

I said, 'No. No, I don't. I'm very sorry for being so rude.'

She laughed. 'It's OK. You'll just have to think of a way to get them back.'

I went over to the girl and told her that everything had been sorted out.

I later found out that Patrick had rung John Thomson with an idea of how to get me back for the Tony Wilson trick. He had given John the hotel phone number and John had got Zoë Ball to ring and pretend to be the receptionist.

I had been so cross that I hadn't noticed her giggling as soon as I asked to speak to the manager.

Nor had I recognised either of their voices. Without even leaving Patrick's flat they had made me look like a total dick. They were over the moon that I'd made everything worse by having a stand-up row at reception.

It was an elaborate prank, but it worked perfectly.

We were finally quits.

★   ★   ★

As Edinburgh approached, Patrick came up to Manchester and stayed with me, and we rehearsed at Bury Metro Arts.

I was sometimes late, but I did at least try to get there on time. Patrick was bossy and strict from the outset, but he says I was easy to believe in and just needed someone to crack the whip.

I was more disciplined than John, who could be sloppy at times, but Patrick was more ruthless than either me or John. He'd insist on routines being cut down or binned altogether.

Patrick always seemed to be shouting, 'Cut that! That joke doesn't work!'

I'd try to argue back, saying I liked the joke.

He would simply respond with: 'It never gets a laugh. You've got to make sure the show is funny. No one will miss that joke if it's not there.'

I always had the final say, but Patrick knew that he not only had to organise us and give us notes. He knew we needed to treat it like a theatre show. He'd never directed before, but he knew how to do the light and sound and he has an organised mind.

When I was road-testing the show with John, we'd got it down to seventy-five minutes. Ruthless, brilliant Patrick shaved a further fifteen minutes off the show, which was called *Steve Coogan in Character with John Thomson*.

He says now that he was never as confident as he pretended to be. But I believed in him, and he thought I was a genius – his word, not mine – and so it worked.

His genius was this: he told me to drop Gavin Gannet and replace him with Alan Partridge.

I initially argued against it. I didn't think Alan was a good enough character to put onstage. He was, at that point, just a voice on the radio. Patrick insisted and I relented.

As I've already mentioned, John's compère character was Bernard Righton, his politically correct Bernard Manning, very of its time.

A typical Righton joke was: 'A black man, a Pakistani and a Jew are in a pub having a drink. What a wonderful example of an integrated community.'

John was incredibly funny. Just fantastic.

Pauline Calf didn't yet exist, but I did Paul Calf, Duncan Thickett, Ernest Moss and Alan Partridge. I was twenty-six and too young to be playing any of them really. Alan and Paul Calf were both in their mid to late thirties, while Ernest Moss was probably in his mid-forties.

But I couldn't wait till I was slightly older and looked more suited to playing these characters. I knew I would have a future because nothing I was doing was dependent on my youth. I didn't have the problem of being a pretty boy who would inevitably age.

John and I, Henry Normal, Caroline Aherne, Dave Gorman, Lemn Sissay and 'Guitar' George Borowski, who is name-checked in the Dire Straits song 'Sultans of Swing' – 'Check out Guitar George, he knows all the chords' – were all performing at the Greenroom in Manchester, at the same time. John and I did three warm-up shows together there, and the progression between each show suggested it was going to be really good.

It was quite a simple show – some silly slides and some well-crafted characters – but it was quite original at the time because straight stand-up was still very much in vogue.

By the time we got to Edinburgh in the summer of 1992, the show was as tight as a drum. It was unrecognisable from the show I'd done with Frank as support two years earlier.

I wanted to show those bastards who'd given me bad reviews how good I really was.

We were in a small venue called Gallery 369, which was adjacent to the Gilded Balloon before it sadly burned down twenty years ago.

Although I had dressed up as Alan in front of a small audience for the pilot of *Knowing Me Knowing You with Alan Partridge*, this was the first time I had properly introduced him to the public.

A review in the *Independent* from 18 August only slightly hedges its bets:

Sandwiched between a gallery of grotesques from Steve Coogan (a voice from *Spitting Image*), Thomson's growling, beer-bellied banterer brilliantly subverts audience expectations with crass racist, sexist or superannuated jokes for which the punchlines never come. Coogan, meanwhile, specialises in repellent oiks, from a lecherous drunk to the supremely patronising sportscaster Alan Partridge ('Of course, women are allowed to compete in the Olympics, which gives the whole thing a bit of glamour'). The material is variable, but the timing is flawless.

The first one or two shows only drew an audience of six or seven, but by the end of the week the venue was full and it was almost impossible to get a ticket.

And yet, when we were nominated for the Perrier, we didn't think we'd win.

CHAPTER 47

I didn't have much experience of drugs in my late teens and early twenties. Apart from a terrible acid trip once when I was working on *Spitting Image*. I went to a party, took two tabs and went bonkers.

At first I thought it was great because I was dancing with everyone else. As soon as I got in a taxi home, though, I felt like I was on a roller coaster. I was convinced the driver was laughing at me as he took me on a ride to hell. He was definitely looking over his shoulder at me and sniggering.

Once I was home, the paranoia grew.

I started talking into the Dictaphone I kept handy for recording ideas. 'I've just taken some acid and I think I'm dying. I want to leave this last message in case anyone finds it.'

There was a car magazine lying around, and the driver on the front appeared to be waving at me.

I looked in the mirror and my face started to melt.

I asked Miles, my flatmate, for help. I was utterly convinced I was dying and that he hated me.

He nonchalantly said, 'You're just having a bad trip. And I don't hate you.'

He thought he was helping by giving me a bottle of water, but it turned into a slithering snake in my hands.

Eventually it wore off and I realised I was neither disliked nor dying, but I never took acid again.

I didn't start taking cocaine until I was living in Edinburgh in the summer of 1992. And even then I didn't buy it; people just kept giving it to me and I kept accepting it.

And then, the week before the Perrier winner was announced, I had a truly terrifying cocaine-induced panic.

I'd been up all night doing drugs, and when I sat down to have breakfast I started to feel dizzy. My blood-sugar level had dropped really low and I was on the verge of blacking out.

I could feel pins and needles in my left arm and my heart was thundering.

I was surely having a heart attack.

Patrick and Simon Munnery put me in the car and drove through red lights to get me to hospital. I cried all the way.

Patrick later told me he really thought I might die.

When we arrived, the nurse put me on a gurney and then left me lying there. The panic intensified. I was having a heart attack and no one seemed to be paying any attention.

I couldn't stop thinking, 'I'm going to die. This is it. My headstone will say: "Stephen Coogan, born in Middleton in 1965, died in Edinburgh in 1992, aged 26 years."

What a waste!

Finally, a doctor appeared. He examined me and very quickly said, 'You're fine.'

'No!' I shouted. 'You've missed something. I had this thing . . . my heart was going bang, bang, bang.'

He said, 'You're fine, honestly. It was just a panic attack.'

They gave me an ECG and told me they were going to keep me in overnight for observation.

Jon Thoday came to the hospital to see me because he was producing *The Dum Show*. I told him I wasn't in any shape to make the show that afternoon.

Jon said, 'You have to get out of your hospital bed and do the show.' He made me feel as though I had no choice.

He told me I had an hour and then he left.

★   ★   ★

I was scared of what might be written about me in the papers. I pulled the electrodes off my chest, got dressed, walked out of hospital and did the show that afternoon.

And the next day I had another panic attack. And another. They wouldn't go away.

I started to think I was going mad. I didn't know what was wrong with me.

I'd be having dinner in a restaurant, surrounded by people I did and didn't know – or anywhere I felt I couldn't easily escape – and I couldn't breathe. I had to get out or I would start to hyperventilate. It was hell.

I really thought I was losing my mind. I very quickly became depressed.

I went back to hospital. They said there was nothing wrong with me. But it didn't feel like this illness was a fiction. It felt horrendously real.

When I came back from Edinburgh, I saw a therapist. He asked if I had a feeling of impending catastrophe. That was the perfect word: catastrophe.

He then described a panic attack and I was immediately calmer.

I wasn't going mad. This was a condition. As soon as I could label it, I felt better.

The therapist taught me breathing exercises. And then he taught me how to play a trick on my mind: as soon as I felt an attack coming on, I had to start a drill.

He told me to breathe slowly and to think of a place where I was happy as a child. I had to imagine sitting somewhere calm and looking out at the landscape. I always think of Ireland, of the farmhouse where I used to sit as a child and gaze out of the window at the rain.

Initially I thought I wouldn't be able to make the drill work. Then I felt a panic attack coming on and I started to breathe slowly and think of Ireland. To my amazement, the attack subsided.

Eventually he told me to try to induce a panic attack and then stop it, so that I would feel I had ultimate control. I induced an attack just once and managed to stop it, which was a great feeling.

Anyway, as the panic attacks became less and less frequent, so I started doing cocaine again. It was always around, always on offer. I didn't actually start to buy it until years later. In those early days it was all recreational and relatively controlled. I'd have a line or two and stop.

Like everyone who took it, I liked cocaine because it gave me confidence when I lacked it. I always thought, 'I'm not really one of those people who does cocaine, so I'll be OK.'

As soon as I could control the panic attacks, I quit therapy. It can be quite useful to talk to someone who won't just tell you what you want to hear, but I don't embrace the blame culture that is sometimes associated, however indirectly, with therapy – the notion that I'm like this because of my parents.

I did a spell in rehab much later and I hated the idea that I was there because of my childhood or some incident of bullying at school. I was there because of my own selfishness. I had to accept personal responsibility.

When I was in rehab I wanted to say, 'I don't take cocaine because I feel terrible about myself, I take it because I feel fucking great about myself and I deserve a reward for working so hard.'

At the same time, I wanted to stop. Wanting and then needing some sort of constant stimulus becomes debilitating. I thought that maybe I needed a hobby as a distraction.

I don't take drugs or drink any more, but I am in no denial about my past: I will always be a recovering addict.

The problem with all my excesses is that, unlike those people who reach rock bottom when they're hooked on drugs, I could still function. Being a functioning addict is a curse; my life didn't ever quite fall apart.

My personal life had gone to shit, but I had maintained a certain quality in my work that almost gave me a licence to misbehave.

It wasn't healthy.

I put a number of people through rehab at my own expense while I was still abusing drugs.

I spent tens of thousands of pounds on everyone else's addiction, but it took me a long time to face up to my own.

CHAPTER 48

When I wasn't in hospital or having a panic attack, I had a routine going in Edinburgh. I would do my two shows, get totally wrecked, get up at midday, get some lunch, do the next two shows, get totally wrecked.

God knows how much I was drinking. But I was also taking notes from Patrick and making sure our show was good. I was, as I say, good at functioning while abusing drugs and alcohol.

One morning I was lying in bed ill in the Edinburgh flat I shared with Patrick and John. No doubt I'd overdone it the night before.

I heard Patrick in the hallway, talking on the phone. 'I think the best place to give it to him would be onstage.'

He thought John and I were both asleep because we were still in our respective bedrooms.

He says he had this feeling of immense pride and power because he'd been given this wonderful piece of news which we were as yet oblivious to.

After a minute, unable to contain himself, he knocked on our doors.

He looked at us both. 'You've done it! You've won the Perrier Award!'

We all grouped together in a big manly hug and danced around the room, laughing, unable initially to absorb the news.

We kept saying, in unison, 'I can't believe this.'

We'd really come from behind.

We were completely confident about the show, but we genuinely never thought we'd win. We'd come from nowhere in a really strong year.

Everyone thought Jo Brand was a dead cert – Jeremy Hardy came up to me at one point and said, 'I hear you have a very good show, but of course you do know it's Jo's year' – and Graham Fellows had also been nominated for his brilliant show *Guide to Stardom*. John Thomson and I were huge fans of his comedy creation, John Shuttleworth. Graham was a kindred spirit, a big influence.

Precisely because we didn't think we had a chance, winning the Perrier was a truly magical moment. I felt as though I'd conquered the comedy scene and planted my flag on the summit.

Only a year earlier I'd been sitting on my own in a box room in Rhodes overlooking an air-conditioning duct, reading about Frank Skinner winning the Perrier and feeling utterly irrelevant.

But I had used my frustration to motivate myself and I'd let Patrick crack the whip. My plan had worked perfectly.

I'd only done one impersonation, in the encore of the Edinburgh show, of Robert De Niro messing around. And I'd still won the Perrier.

I was no longer just this lad from Manchester who was good at voices. I could create comedy characters worthy of a Perrier Award. I knew I was finally starting to get it right: I was finally being taken seriously not only by *On The Hour* fans, but by the comedy world.

I thought, 'They can say what the hell they like now. I don't care. I'm a Perrier winner.'

It remains the most exciting award I've ever won in my life. More than any of the BAFTAs, although the Oscar nominations come close. You can go from zero to hero in four weeks in Edinburgh; it's like having a career in microcosm. If comedy was a game of snakes and ladders, winning the Perrier was the biggest leap up the longest ladder.

Lucy Porter, who was not yet a comedian herself but who served as a lay member of the jury in 1992, later told me that it was a tie between Graham Fellows and me. She had the casting vote and she voted for me.

I owe Lucy for what was without a doubt a life-changing moment.

Thank you, Lucy.

★   ★   ★

We weren't allowed to tell anyone we'd won, because the Perrier was to be awarded to John and me onstage that night. It was so exciting doing the show and knowing that the audience would find out we'd won at the end.

Nica Burns and Johan Magnusson came onstage and handed me the award, and the Gallery 369 filled with tumultuous applause.

I think it was a popular win.

Apart, perhaps, from the fact that I drove to the 369 in my British racing-green Mazda MX-5 with its tan seats and £4,000 of souped-up engine. You don't really need a car in Edinburgh, but the flat had a private garage and so I kept the Mazda there.

I know people sneered at me for turning up in a sports car. It just served to re-emphasise the fact that I wasn't exactly the model of the struggling artist finally picking up the big prize.

I could almost hear them whispering behind my back, 'There's that wanker Coogan in his stupid fucking car!'

★   ★   ★

That summer I was exactly where I wanted to be again. I had won the Perrier unexpectedly, and I had the *Knowing Me Knowing You with Alan Partridge* pilot in the can.

When I was asked if John and I were going to take the Perrier show on a national tour, I politely declined. I kept saying I had this other thing to do, and people looked puzzled; surely I wanted to capitalise on my success?

Sometimes they would ask what the 'other thing' was, and I'd tell them I was recording a series on the radio called *Knowing Me Knowing You with Alan Partridge*.

Nobody knew what I was talking about. It made no sense to them. They clearly thought I was mad.

As often as not, they would say, 'You don't want to waste your time with that. You want to get your live show on the road.'

But I knew I had something much better. Something that was going to be much bigger than anything else I'd ever done.

Delighted as I was to win the Perrier, I knew that being accepted into the comedy club wasn't enough.

★   ★   ★

I had only left college in 1988, and by 1992 I had risen and fallen and risen again.

Rob Brydon bumped into David Walliams around the time *Philomena* came out and David apparently said, 'Steve hasn't put a foot wrong in his entire career.'

It's not true, of course, and I'm only in a sweet spot now because I learned to do the work.

Whatever might be going wrong, do the work.

And surround yourself with people who are bloody clever. Without Patrick pushing me to take Alan further, Partridge might only have existed on *On The Hour* and *The Day Today*.

I suppose that, in some ways, by giving Alan my neuroses, I was also giving him my shiny Burton suit. It was rather bizarre that Alan's distinct *lack of* cool made me cool.

As a child I watched *Fawlty Towers* and said to myself, 'If I can create a character that has the impact of Basil Fawlty, my life will be complete.'

I fully realised my childhood ambition and of course my life *wasn't* complete.

In the years following Alan's success, my personal life descended into turmoil. And I had no idea where to go with my career.

I was lost.

The two BAFTAs I'd won in 1998 sat on my parents' mantelpiece, growing more and more tarnished. They seemed to mock me, reminding me of when I'd been good.

It was to be more than a decade before I started to win another slew of BAFTAs for *The Trip* and *Philomena*, thanks to both Michael Winterbottom and an 80-year-old Irish lady from St Alban's.

And, of course, the character who had become something of an albatross had a renaissance against the odds.

Thanks, Alan.

Alan: 'You're welcome. Sorry, you don't mind me interrupting at this late juncture?'

Of course not.

Alan: 'Great. I enjoyed the book by the way. Not perfect, but pretty solid.'

Thanks.

Alan: 'You're welcome.'

OK, well I'd like to have the last word. I suppose there is a corner of my mind that will be forever Alan Partridge.

Alan: 'Lovely.'

INDEX

SC indicates Steve Coogan.

Abba 213, 311
Abbott, Paul 279
Academy Awards (Oscars) 28, 33–5,
    43, 65, 85, 164, 337
Adoption Rights Alliance 40–1
Agutter, Jenny 179
A-ha 8, 85, 316
Aherne, Caroline 324, 325, 329
Allen, David 240, 284
Allen, Jim 177, 178, 240, 284
Allen, Woody 26, 174
Allsop, Paul 171
Alpha Papa 70
    Armando Iannucci and 53, 54
    Ben Stiller advice on 49, 54–5
    casting 51–2, 55, 248, 253
    cinematic influences upon 50
    director 51, 52, 55
    evolution of Alan Partridge char-
        acter and 54
    financial backing for 47–9
    Neil and Rob Gibbons and 52–4
    origins of 46–50
    Philomena effects preparation of
        51
    plot 47–50
    research for 56–7
    SC's fame in England and 34
    SC's necessary ruthlessness whilst
        working on 54–5
    SC's pride in and regrets over
        57–8
    SC's workload on 52–3, 68
    script 51–5
    shoot 51–3, 54, 55–7
    success of 85
    title 50
Anderton, James 117–18
Apatow, Judd 52
Archer, Jeffrey 272
Arkwright, Ziggy 216
Arndale Shopping Centre,
        Manchester 97, 194, 205
Ashdown, Paddy 272
Astoria Ballroom, Plymouth Grove,
        Manchester 98, 99, 100, 101
Auslander, Shalom 66
Avalon 280
Ayckbourn, Alan: *Just Between
        Ourselves* 247

Baby Cow Productions 18, 280
BAFTA 4, 65, 337, 340
Bagpuss 171
Ball, Zoë 274, 327
Barclays Bank 250
Barraclough, Roy 97
Barrie, Chris 271–2, 273
Barry, John 133
Baynham, Peter 46, 47, 48, 49, 252
BBC:
    Alpha Papa plot ideas and 47, 48,
        57
    Armando Iannucci and 295, 297,
        301
    BBC Films and *Philomena* 20
    BBC Manchester, SC sketches for
        251, 252
    BBC Scotland, SC sketches for
        251

BBC2 4, 180, 189, 296
comedy heritage of 58, 186, 189
I'm Alan Partridge filming in BBC
    TV Centre 57–8
influence upon SC's comedy
    175–6, 186, 189, 190
influence upon SC's youth 99,
    172, 175–8, 179, 180, 186
*Knowing Me Knowing You with
    Alan Partridge* and 306, 313,
    314, 318
On the Hour and 295, 297, 301
Paris Studios 58, 297, 298, 312,
    315
SC's straight acting roles for 15
The Day Today and 317
Wednesday Play series 177
Bearcat Club, Birmingham 284–5
Beasley, Miss 181
Beatles, the 33, 189, 213, 218
Bee Gees, The 90, 213
Bennett, Alan 259
Beyond the Fringe 236
BFI 306
Big Flame 177
Blackadder 261, 272
Blackshaw, Rosie 256
Blake, Juliet 260, 262
Blake, William 163, 230–1; 'The
    Garden of Love' 36
Blondie 90, 213
Bloody Sunday, 1972 130
Blue Peter 151, 172
Blur 71
Boggart Hole Clough, Blackley 144
Bolt, Robert: *A Man for All Seasons* 127
Bond films 109, 133, 171, 175, 185,
    195, 201, 202, 209, 225
    *see also under individual actor and
    film name*
Bono 45
Borat 49
Borowski, 'Guitar' George 329
Bouquet of Barbed Wire 179–80

Bowie, David 125, 210, 213
Boyle, Danny 174
Bradley, Simon 160
Brambell, Wilfrid 192
Branagh, Ken 27
Brand, Jo 11, 337
Brighton 6, 56, 75, 158
Brigstocke, Dominic 319
Brooks, Rebekah 76, 79
Brydon, Rob 61–3, 64, 65–7, 68, 69,
    70–1, 253, 339
Bryson, Bill: *Notes from a Small
    Island* 174
Budd, Trisha 256
Burns, Nica 338
Bury Metro Arts 327–8
Bush, George 229
Bush, Kate 213
Buzz, The 251
Buzzcocks 90, 216
Byron, Lord 29, 36, 69, 238, 293

Caldwell, Phil 251, 252
Calf, Paul (SC comedy character) 3,
    131, 175, 253–5, 287–8, 289,
    290, 304, 318, 319, 329
Calf, Pauline (SC comedy character)
    3, 118, 149, 209, 283, 289,
    318
Callaghan, James 203
Cameron, David 76, 77, 82, 130, 265
Cant, Brian 171
Cardinal Langley Roman Catholic
    High School, Middleton 114,
    163–4, 194–206, 207–12,
    220–1, 230–1, 235, 236, 239,
    240
Carry On films 142
Cash, Craig 15
Castle, Roy 99
Catenian Association, The 122
Catholic Children's Rescue Society,
    The 141
Cathy Come Home 177

Central School of Speech and
    Drama, London 236, 238
Channel 4 260–1, 287
Charismatics 210–11
Charles, Prince 321
*Chaucer's Knight: The Portrait of
    a Medieval Mercenary* (Jones)
    163
Cheeseman, Gareth (SC comedy
    character) 286, 304
Chow, China 17, 18, 20
Christian Brothers 98
Clangers 171
Clark, Alan 229
Clash, The 90, 213, 214
Cleese, John 84, 173, 175, 188, 189,
    190, 301
Clement, Alex 243
Clement, Dick 192
CND (Campaign for Nuclear
    Disarmament) 228, 258
Cock and Bull Story, A ix, 59, 60, 61
Coffee and Cigarettes ix
Cohen, Sacha Baron 70–1
Cole, Anna 292, 293, 317
Cole, Clare (daughter) v, 6, 35, 73,
    75, 95, 148, 152, 221
Coleman, David 259, 277, 303
Coleridge, Samuel Taylor 62
Comedy Awards 4, 336–8
Comedy Store 266, 281, 282
Comic Strip Presents…, The 297
Connery, Sean 176, 253
Conservative Party 76, 128, 144,
    226, 227, 229, 236, 265, 274,
    278, 305, 314
Coogan, Brendan (brother) 110,
    112, 115, 121, 123, 141, 209,
    210, 221–2, 223
Coogan, Clare (sister) v, 3, 26, 89,
    90, 91, 101, 103, 105, 107,
    108, 110, 121–2, 123, 141,
    162, 179, 213, 217, 220, 223,
    269

Coogan, David (brother) 110, 121,
    123, 131, 157, 189, 205, 213
Coogan, Kathleen (mother):
  birth 97
  Catholicism 122–3, 124, 143, 211
  character 117–18, 145, 154–5
  childhood 97, 129
  class and 93, 95–6, 129
  eightieth birthday 36
  family background 96. 97–8
  fiftieth wedding anniversary 94
  football, love of 118
  fostering of children 102, 136,
      139–44
  holidays in Ireland 111
  humour 118
  Irish Troubles and 226
  James Anderton and 117–18
  maiden name 97
  marriage 101, 118, 119, 151, 166
  meets husband 100–1
  Morris Minor 155
  musical taste 217–18
  politics 226–7
  running of Coogan household
      during SC's childhood 102,
      103, 104, 105, 111, 112,
      154–5, 170
  SC's meningitis and 157, 158,
      159–60
  SC's teenage sexuality and 181,
      182, 183, 184, 185
  SC's success and 5, 33, 169,
      278–9
Coogan, Kevin (brother) 108, 109,
    112–13, 121, 122, 123, 160,
    186, 195, 210, 237
Coogan, Martin (brother) 102, 110,
    112, 114, 116, 121, 123, 125,
    136, 144, 179, 191, 203, 213,
    214–15, 216, 217, 218, 223,
    225, 259
Coogan, Nana (paternal grand-
    mother) 97–8, 158

Coogan, Patricia (aunt) 225, 236–7

Coogan, Peter (uncle) 98, 99, 221–2, 228

Coogan, Pierce 'Pop' (paternal grandfather) 97, 98, 99, 100

Coogan, Steve:
  acting career ix, 8, 15–16, 17, 18, 22–5, 34, 49, 51, 52, 59, 60, 61–3, 64–72, 161–2, 228, 284 *see also* Manchester Polytechnic *and under individual film or TV show name*
  agents v, 12, 13, 28, 261, 263, 275, 279, 286, 291
  audiences and 4, 8, 10, 16, 148–50, 249, 266, 267, 276, 278, 279, 281, 284, 290, 312–13, 315, 316
  awards 4, 32–5, 43, 65, 117, 250, 255, 330, 331, 336–7, 338–9, 340
  birth 121
  birthdays, childhood 130–2
  Brighton, life in 6, 56, 75, 158
  cars, love of 105, 124, 127, 155, 204–5, 211–12, 213, 268–9, 318, 338
  Catholicism and ix, 17–18, 30, 31, 36–9, 40, 41, 42–3, 44, 89–91, 93, 96, 98, 107, 108, 122–5, 126, 143, 164, 170, 181, 188, 196, 201–3, 210–11, 222, 226, 269, 293
  characters, comedy *see under individual character name*
  childhood ix, x, 5, 17–18, 43, 89–92, 93–110, 111–19, 120–9, 130–232
  cinema and 109, 132, 133, 171, 175, 180–1, 185, 195, 201, 202, 209, 225
  class and x, 5, 17, 19, 20, 26, 83, 84, 93, 94, 95, 96, 98, 128, 137, 170, 174–5, 177, 210,

  214, 227, 240, 265, 288, 298
  collaboration, preference for 26, 251–2
Coogan name 97
corporal punishment, experience of in childhood 195, 196–7, 198, 201, 207, 221
corporate gigs 269, 276, 315
creative angst 11–12
Daily Mail and 22, 75, 80, 85, 95
decision to be true to self 14–15
drama schools, applies to 236–45, 246 *see also* Manchester Polytechnic, studies drama at
drug taking x, 7, 46, 331–5
Edinburgh Festival and *see* Edinburgh Festival
education/intelligence/academic record and 18, 114, 160–1, 163–5, 196, 199, 208, 230–1, 235, 239, 240
Englishness and 173–5
equality of opportunity, on British problem with 264–5
fame and ix, 34, 73, 294, 317
film work *see under individual film name*
finances 3, 4, 11, 73, 81, 82, 89, 90, 99, 102–3, 104, 105, 113, 222, 235, 236, 250, 251, 252, 258, 263, 267–9, 271, 279, 281, 317, 335, 338
fraud, feeling like a 11–12, 14
funniest performance 309–10
Greater Manchester Theatre Company 240–2
guilt, feelings of 83, 108, 181, 269, 271, 288, 290, 293, 318
holidays, childhood 90–2, 105–7, 109–10, 111–12, 333
impressions/voices ix, 11, 12, 64, 148, 166, 185–6, 191, 203, 204, 239, 253, 258–9, 260,

261, 262, 263, 265, 267, 270, 271–4, 275, 278, 280, 285, 286–7, 296, 299, 303, 324, 325, 330, 331
inferiority complex 299–300
jobs 99, 254–5, 256–7, 258
kiss-and-tell stories and 74–6
lateness 220, 312, 319, 328
Leveson Inquiry and 82, 83
loss of memory during childhood after bicycle accident 113–14
Lourdes, childhood trip to 89–91
love/sex life and 6–7, 12, 36, 70, 75–6, 80, 85, 91, 94, 102, 111–12, 115, 117, 130, 131, 141, 172, 180–5, 202, 207, 208–10, 212, 255–6, 281, 292–4, 317, 326
managers and 275–6, 280
Manchester Polytechnic, studies drama at 8, 242–4, 246–8, 250–7, 258, 261, 262, 263–5, 268, 291, 299, 300, 308
media and 6–7, 46, 73–85
meningitis, childhood 114, 157–8
middle age, effect of approach upon 95
music and 90, 125–6, 211, 213, 214–18
name 231–2
News International, sues 76–8, 79–83, 85
nostalgia for childhood 105–6
Owen Wilson alleged suicide attempt and 75
parents and see Coogan, Kathleen (mother) and Coogan, Tony (father)
patriotism and 174
Philomena and 36–9, 123
philanthropy/duty and 108
phone hacking and 76, 77–8, 79–85
poetry and 36, 62, 163, 230

politics and 76, 93, 128, 131, 144, 176–8, 190–1, 226–7, 228–9, 235–6, 240, 241, 254, 264, 265, 272, 273, 274, 277, 278, 302, 305, 312, 314–15
postmodernism and 54, 61, 285, 288–9
practicality 112, 113
press regulation and 83–4
radio appearances see under individual radio show name
Rhodes residency, 1991 13–14, 295
schooldays 18, 89–92, 113, 114, 161–2, 163–5, 190, 220–1, 226
screenwriting see Alpha Papa and Philomena
self-doubt 18–19, 193, 237, 318
silliness/fooling around in childhood 166–9
snobbery and 19, 90, 170, 173, 199, 213, 216–17
stagehand, Royal Exchange Theatre 256–7, 258
stand-up ix, 3–7, 8–16, 117, 169, 251, 252, 258, 259–61, 262, 264, 266–7, 278, 279–82, 287, 292, 306–7, 317–18, 321–4, 327–8, 327–30 see also under individual gig or venue name
style 135–6, 137–8, 194–5, 281–2, 339
success and failure, reaction to 8, 30–1, 65–7, 339–40
therapy 73, 333, 334
TV, first appears on 259–61
TV, influence upon as a child 170–8, 179–80
TV shows see under individual TV show name
voiceover artist 11, 171, 258, 259, 261–2, 263, 267, 271–2, 283
Coogan, Tommy (uncle) 98, 99

Coogan, Tony (father):
  appearance 100, 118–19
  as authority figure during SC's
    childhood 116, 117, 167, 168,
    218, 219, 222
  birth 97
  Catholicism 98, 122–3, 124, 132,
    210, 211, 222
  'charmer' 118–19
  childhood 97, 98, 99, 100, 102–3
  cinema and 132
  conservative style 111, 134–6,
    137–8, 155, 156, 217–18
  contradictions within nature of
    223
  egalitarian character 123
  Encyclopedia Britannica and 93,
    170
  family background 96, 97–8
  family holidays and 109, 110,
    209
  fiftieth wedding anniversary 94
  fostering of children 102, 139–44
  grammar, emphasis on impor-
    tance of 93, 94, 163
  house fire and 223–4
  humour 191
  IBM job 20, 101–2, 110, 112,
    114, 123, 134, 135, 151, 153–4
  Knowing Me Knowing You, reac-
    tion to 317
  lateness 225
  marriage 101, 102, 118, 119
  media stories about SC, reaction
    to 117
  meets wife 100
  morality and 122, 135, 139,
    228–9
  Morris Oxford 103, 132, 135,
    155, 156
  musical taste 217–18
  Philomena and 36–9, 123
  politics 226–7, 228–9
  practical nature 20, 101–2, 110,
    112, 113, 118, 120–1, 152–4,
    155, 168, 171, 286
  questioning of received wisdom
    222–3
  Round Table and 224–5
  sax playing 99, 101
  SC's comedy characters and 286
  SC's meningitis and 157, 158,
    159
  SC's prurience/silliness and
    166–9, 181, 219
  SC's success and 117, 169, 278–9,
    317
  SC's teenage sexuality and 183
  science and technology, belief in
    132, 134–5, 145–6, 222
  Second World War and 98
  talkative character 120–1
  telephone manner 219
  temper 116
  TV comedy and 191–2
  Volvo car 109, 122, 154, 155–6,
    246
Coogan and Hayley's Seaside Special
  280–1
Coogan's Run 256, 260
Coonan, Bernard (uncle) 111, 134
Coonan, Nana (maternal grand-
  mother) 75, 97, 185
Coonan, Pop (maternal grandfather)
  97
Corbett, Harry H. 192
Corbett, Ronnie 259, 273, 280
Cornfeld, Stuart 34
Cottrell Boyce, Frank 174
Coulson, Andy 75–6, 77, 80, 84
Courtenay, Tom 237
Coward, Noël: The Vortex 263–4, 265
Crosby, Stills and Nash 217
Cruise, Tom 71
Curtis, Tony 172

Dacre, Paul 80, 85
Dad's Army 58, 173, 305

Daily Mail 22, 75, 80, 85, 95
Daily Mirror 73–4, 78
Daily Telegraph 84
David, Larry 174
Davies, Nick 80, 83
Davies, Windsor 181
Davis, Julia 3, 4, 6, 55
Davy, John 13
Dawkins, Richard 42
Dawson, Les 97, 99, 175–6, 191, 289
Day Today, The 270, 296, 306, 307,
    308, 309–10, 317, 318, 339
Day, Simon 287
de La Fontaine, Jean 188
De La Salle Brothers/De La Salle
    Foundation 97, 195
De Niro, Robert 259, 337
Dead Good Show, The 324
Dench, Judi 20, 22, 24, 30, 44, 118
Des O'Connor Show 275–6
Desplat, Alexandre 33
Diana, Princess 321
Disorderly, Duncan (SC comedy
    character) 287, 304
Dixon, Anthony 185
Doctor Who 176
Dodd, Ken 276
Dog Day Afternoon 50
Doonican, Val 214
Dowler, Gemma 84, 85
Dowler, Milly 76, 79, 80, 82–3, 84
Downton Abbey 174–5
Dr No 185, 253
Duff, Graham 56
Dum Show, The 318, 332
Durst, Will 280

Earle, Kenneth 275–6
Easy Riders, Raging Bulls (Biskind) 172
Eddisford, Maurice 143, 184
Eddisford, Michelle 184
Edge, The 45
Edinburgh Festival 9
    1988 269–70

1989 280–1
1990 9–12
1991 12–13
1992 12, 13, 14, 117, 250, 255,
    287, 292, 317–18, 321–4,
    327–8, 331–5, 336–9
1995 291
Edmondson, Ade 191
Elephant Man, The 34
Elizabeth II, Queen 226, 272
Elton, Ben 190, 261, 272, 275, 276,
    277
Emmy Awards 33
Enfield, Harry 272, 281, 286–7
Equity card 8, 252, 259

Fast Show, The 255
Fawcett-Majors, Farrah 213
Fawlty Towers 4, 58, 173, 186,
    189–90, 305, 339
Fellowes, Julian 174–5
Fellows, Graham: *Guide to Stardom*
    337, 338
Ferrell, Will 17
Ferrino, Tony (SC comedy character)
    3, 276
Festen 29
Financial Times 80
First Exposure 259–60, 262, 266, 280
Firth, Tim 266
Fix, The 48, 265
Fleetwood Mac 213
Fluck, Peter 258
Foot, Michael 235, 236–7
Fox Searchlight 48
Foxx, John 216
Francis, Alan 246, 291
Francis, Pope 38–9, 40–1, 42, 44
Frears, Stephen 20, 30, 36, 38, 84
Free Trade Hall, Manchester 126
French and Saunders 297
Friday Night Live 275
Front, Rebecca 295, 299, 301, 303
Frost, Nick 300

Fry, Stephen 84, 261, 272, 275
Fun Boy Three 211

Gallagher, Liam 27
Gallery 369, Edinburgh 329, 338
Gallery, Neil 253
Galton, Ray 192, 193
Gannet, Gavin (SC comedy
    character) 286, 304, 328
general election:
    1979 209, 227
    1983 235–6
    1992 274
Generation Game, The 173
Generation X 214
Genesis 213
Gervais, Ricky 70–1
Gibbons, Neil 26, 52–4, 55, 83, 148
Gibbons, Rob 26, 52–4, 55, 83, 148
Gide, André 69
Gilbert, Colin 251
Gilded Balloon, Edinburgh 11, 329
Gleeson, Brendan 51
Glover, Jon 286
Good Life, The 173, 190
Goon Show, The 168, 191, 236, 297
Gorman, Dave 329
Gort, Sandy 10, 261, 263, 275
Granada TV 12–13, 162, 239, 262,
    263, 287, 324
Granada Up Front 12–13
Grant, Hugh 84, 85
Grease 90, 217
Greater Manchester Theatre
    Company 240–4
Green, Theresa 182
Greenroom, Manchester 259, 280,
    329
Greenall, Simon 250, 251, 252–3,
    255
Greengrass, Paul 20, 48, 265
Guardian 14, 17, 22, 72, 79, 80, 83,
    150, 254
Guildford pub bombings, 1974 98

Hacked Off 84–5
Hague, William 227
Haircut 100 211
Hammer Horror 180
Hancock, Nick 288
Hancock, Tony 58, 191, 192, 297
Hancock's Half Hour 191, 192
Happy Mondays 60
Hardee, Malcolm 266, 267
Harding, Keith 201
Hardy, Thomas 188
Hardwicke, Edward 239
Hardy, Jeremy 337
Hare, David 84
Harries, Andie 324
Harris, Rolf 273
Harry, Debbie 213
Hartley, L. P.: The Go-Between 95,
    112, 184
Harvey, Marcus 291
Harvey, Miles 291
Hayley, Mike 280, 281
Hazlegrove, Jane 237
Healey, Denis 34
Heath, Edward ix, 203
Heaven 17 211
Hennessey, Brother David 202, 203,
    206, 210, 227
Henry VIII, King 126, 127
Herring, Richard 280, 295, 296, 303,
    318
Heseltine, Michael 259, 272
Hesketh-Harvey, Kit 281
Hess, Michael 28
Hill, Benny 142, 181
Hill, Bernard 250
Hirst, Damien 291–2
Hollywood 17, 28, 47–9, 59, 70–1,
    287
Hooper, Tom 32
Howarth, Mrs 143, 144
Howe, Geoffrey 272
Hughes, Sean: A One Night Stand 12
Human League, The 90, 211, 216

Hunt, Gareth 172
Hurd, Douglas 272
Hurt, John 176
Hutton, Will 84
Hytner, Nic 256

I, Partridge 147–8
Iannucci, Armando:
    Alpha Papa and 46, 49, 53, 54
    education 18, 299, 308
    I'm Alan Partridge and 252
    Knowing Me Knowing You with
        Alan Partridge and 311, 312,
        315, 319
    On the Hour and 18, 295, 296,
        297, 298, 299, 301–2, 303,
        304, 306, 308
    SC writing process with 26
    SC's relationship with 301–2
IBM 101–2, 110, 112, 123, 134, 135,
    151, 153–4
I'm Alan Partridge 3, 4, 7, 15, 57–8,
    250, 252, 302, 319
Ickler, Ernest (SC comedy character)
    304
Independent 80, 329–30
Independent Talent v, 28
Industrial Revolution 94, 115, 227
IRA 98–9, 226–7, 228
Ireland 52
    Philomena and 19, 21, 26, 37, 38,
        39, 40–1, 44, 45
    SC's ancestry and 37, 93, 96–100
    SC's childhood holidays in
        17–18, 26, 40, 105–7, 108–10,
        111, 147, 221–2, 228, 333
    Troubles and 98–9, 130, 226–7,
        228
ITV 20, 172, 173, 176, 237, 258, 271
Izzard, Eddie 282

Jam, The 90
Jarre, Jean Michael 216
Jefferies, Christopher 84

Jeffrey Dahmer is Unwell 291
Jerry Springer: The Opera 280
Jobs, Steve 135
Jóhannsson, Jóhann: IBM 1401, A
    User's Manual 101–2
John Paul II, Pope 40
Jones, Bernadette 40, 210, 211, 212,
    281
Jones, Maggie 281
Jones, Mar 201–2
Jones, Terry 163, 176, 186
Jongleurs 13, 266, 281
Joy Division 213
Joyce, James 106

Karcher, Monsignor Guillermo 43, 44
Keane, Roy 118
Keats, John 69
Keelan, Claire 69
Kempinska, Maria 13
Kennedy, John F. 120
Kes 177, 197
Key, Tim 54, 55
Kick up The Eighties, A 191, 251
Kidd, Jerry 125
King Jr, Martin Luther 159
Kinnock, Neil 261, 271, 272, 273,
    274
'kiss-and-tell' stories 74–5
Kit & the Widow 281
Knibb, Mike 112
Knibb, Mrs 112, 113
Knibb, Timmy 112
Knowing Me, Knowing You with Alan
        Partridge:
    birth of idea 311–12
    complaints from listeners to
        radio series 313–14
    radios series 58, 193, 294, 306,
        312–16, 317, 318–19, 321,
        329–30, 338, 339
    title 311
    title music 3–4
    TV series of 54, 294

Kraftwerk 90, 216
Krypton Factor, The 279

L'Arche community, France 107–8
La Frenais, Ian 192
Labour Party 17, 93, 177, 226, 227,
     228, 235, 236, 274
Lam Dien 142
Langan, Christine 20
Langley, Greater Manchester 129,
     196, 210
Lao-Tzu 285
Laurel, Stan 272
Law, Roger 258
Lazenby, George 133
Leach, Rosemary 244
Lederer, Helen 251
Lee, Philomena 17–18, 19, 20, 22,
     23, 24, 26, 27, 28–9, 31–2, 37,
     38, 40–1, 42, 43, 44, 45, 123
Lee, Stewart 14, 280, 295, 296, 303,
     318
Les Dawson Show, The 175
Leveson Inquiry 82, 83, 84, 85
Leveson Royal Charter 84
Libberton, Jane 22, 41, 42, 44
Liddiment, David 262–3
Likely Lads, The 192
Little Englanders x, 94, 173, 175,
     235, 241, 305
Live and Let Die 133, 185, 225
Live 'n' Lewd 319–20
Lloyd, John 261–2
Loach, Ken 177
Loaded 285, 288
Locke, Josef 99
Lohan, Susan 40, 41, 44
London Weekend Television (LWT)
     259, 269, 270
Look of Love, The 51, 70, 228
Lowney, Declan 51, 52, 55
Lucas, George 133
Lumet, Sidney 50
Lumley, Joanna 172

Luther, Martin 126
Lyceum Theatre 3–6, 169
Lyric Hammersmith 281

Macabre, James 11
MacKenzie, Kelvin 84
Mackichan, Doon 270, 295, 299, 301
Macnee, Patrick 172
Madden, John 142
Magdalene Sisters, The 38
Magnusson, Johan 338
Magpie 172
Major, John 272, 274
Majors, Lee 213
Man for All Seasons, A 127
Manchester ix, 5, 8, 18, 40, 60, 94,
     97, 98, 99, 102, 108, 115, 118,
     122, 126, 128–9, 131, 146,
     177, 181, 191, 200, 215, 218,
     237, 240, 245, 251, 252, 259,
     260, 261, 266, 267, 268, 269,
     274, 275, 291, 292, 299, 323,
     327, 329, 337
Manchester City 131
Manchester Polytechnic 8, 242, 243,
     244, 245, 246–9, 250–7, 258,
     261, 262, 263–4, 268, 291,
     298–9
Manchester United 118, 131
Mandement, Keith (swimming pool
     attendant character) and 309–10
Mani 208
Manning, Bernard 99, 181
Mantel, Hilary 175
Marber, Patrick:
     Alan Partridge and 270, 303, 304,
        305, 308, 309, 311, 312, 316,
        317, 318, 339
     Alpha Papa and 49
     Armando Iannucci and 295
     Dealer's Choice and 319
     Edinburgh Festival, directs SC's
        1992 show in 317, 318, 327–8,
        336, 337

Edinburgh Festival, 1990 and 11
education 18, 240, 244, 299
Knowing Me Knowing You with Alan Partridge and 311, 312, 316, 317, 318, 339
On the Hour and 18, 295, 299, 300–1, 302, 303, 304, 305, 308, 311
Paris, moves to 295
Paul Calf and 287, 304
SC relationship with 11, 18, 26, 270, 280, 295, 299, 300–1, 302, 318–20, 327, 332
The Day Today and 309
The Parole Officer, reaction to 18
Week Ending and 295
writing process with SC 26
Marple Hall School 201
Mayall, Rik 191, 251, 261
Maycock, Lucy 244
McBreen, Gerard 125, 171, 201, 214
McDiarmid, Ian 256
McFadden, Cynthia 43
McIntyre, Michael 316
McIntrye, Phil 6
McQueen, Steve 35
McRae, Colin 302
McWhirter, Ross 98–9, 186
Meacock, Lucy 12
Meaney, Colm 52
Melody Maker 213
Merton, Paul 11
Metropolitan Police 77
Mid Morning Matters 54
Middle England 174–5, 304
Middleton, Greater Manchester 94–5, 99, 106, 107, 111, 120, 127, 129, 132, 133, 159–60, 164, 176–7, 190, 194, 219, 260, 271, 332
Mike Yarwood in Persons 272
Mission Impossible 71
Mitchell, Joni 146, 217
Mock Turtles, The 215, 248, 259

Molly, Aunt 139–40
Monkees: 'Pleasant Valley Sunday' 128
Monkhouse, Bob 46, 276
Monty Python 126, 168, 176, 187, 188–9, 191, 230, 236, 296, 297
Monty Python's Flying Circus 176
Moore, Roger 133, 172, 176, 185, 213, 225, 314
Moran, Caitlin 15
Moran, Johnny 253
More Roper, Margaret 127
More, Thomas 127
Morecambe & Wise ix, 128, 168, 173, 217
Morgan, Piers 74, 84
Morris, Chris 18, 295, 299, 301, 308, 310
Morrissey 126
Moss, Ernest (SC comedy character) 286, 304, 323, 329
Moss, Robin (SC comedy character) 323
Moss Side, Manchester 208
Motson, John 303
Mounfield, Gregory 208
Mulcaire, Glenn 79
Mullan, Peter 38
Mulligan, Andrew 240, 241, 242, 243, 244
Munich Olympics, 1972, killings at 130
Munnery, Simon 280, 318, 332
Murdoch, Rupert 76, 81, 82–3
Murphy, Jan 12, 13, 275, 286, 291
Murphy, P. B. 204, 206
Murphy, P. K. 206
Murray, Martin 246, 248, 249, 291, 292

Naked Civil Servant, The 176
Naked Video 251
Nallon, Steve 273
National Lottery Live, The 276

Nestor, Martin 246–7, 263
Network 50
New Avengers, The 172
Newman, Rob 267, 273, 288, 325
News International 76–8, 79–83, 85
News of the World 73, 76, 79, 80, 82–3
NHS 114, 174
NME 213
Noah 43
Noakes, John 172
Normal, Henry 18, 55, 56, 280–1, 287, 329
Normal, The: 'Warm Leatherette' 216
Norman, Barry 172
Not the Nine O'Clock News 189, 190, 236, 260

Oakey, Phil 216
Oasis 71
Oliver, Denis 228
Olympic Games:
   1972 130
   2012 174
On Her Majesty's Secret Service 133
On the Buses 173
On the Hour 320, 337
   Alan Partridge and 303–6, 308, 311, 313, 315, 316, 317, 339
   Armando Iannucci and 18, 295, 296, 297, 298, 299, 301–2, 303, 304, 306, 308
   cast and 270
   educational background of people involved with intimidates SC 18, 298–300
   Keith Mandement (public swimming pool attendant) character 309–10
   Knowing Me Knowing You with Alan Partridge and 311, 313, 315, 316, 317
   Lee and Herring and 295, 296, 303, 318
   origins of 295

Patrick Marber and 18, 295, 299, 300–1, 302, 303, 304, 305, 308, 311
   recording of 297–8
   SC becomes involved with 295–6
   SC's realisation of quality of 297–8, 317
   transfers to TV as *The Day Today* see *Day Today, The*
Onion 217
Opus Dei 122–3
Ordinary People 34
Orwell, George 163
Other Guys, The 17
Owen, Wilfrid 163
Oxford University 131, 177, 191, 202, 240, 244, 299, 300, 308

Palin, Michael 186, 188, 189
Paramount City 11
Paris Studios 58, 297, 298, 312, 315
Parole Officer, The 18
Partridge, Alan (SC comedy character) x
   'A-ha' catchphrase 8, 85, 316
   Armando Iannucci and 46, 53, 54, 302, 303, 311
   BBC and 57–8, 175, 190
   birth of 298, 302, 303–8
   car 305
   change/evolution in character over time 3, 54
   Cleese/Basil Fawlty and 175, 190, 305, 307
   clothes/style of 54, 312–13
   comedy of embarrassment and 243
   comments on this book 340
   complaint letters misread as real person 275, 313–14
   corner of SC's mind that will be forever 340
   definition of SC's career as a performer and 19, 306–7

Downton Abbey and 175
evolution of character in first
    radio series 305–6
fanbase 306, 315, 316
frustration as a thread running
    through pantheon of loved
    British comedy characters and
    305
I'm Alan Partridge 3, 4, 7, 15,
    57–8, 250, 252, 302, 319
killing off of 46
*Knowing Me, Knowing You with
    Alan Partridge* 3–4, 54, 58, 193,
    294, 306–16
Leveson and 83
Little Englander 173, 305
live audience and 150
makes SC laugh 47
Michael the Geordie 250, 252–3
Mid Morning Matters 54
movie *see* Alpha Papa
name 304
Neil and Rob Gibbons and
    rebirth of 53–4 *see also*
    Gibbons, Neil *and* Gibbons,
    Rob
Norwich and 304–5
offers to take back on radio
    320
On the Hour and *see* On The Hour
Patrick Marber and *see* Marber,
    Patrick
Paul Calf and 290
'peak Partridge' 3
Peter Baynham and 46, 47, 252
politics 305, 312, 314–15
Rigsby and 173
SC on funniest incarnation of
    54
SC prefers *Saxondale* over 15
SC's affection for 53
SC's father and 119
SC's success with *Philomena* and
    34
similarities to SC's character ix,
    47, 66, 92, 168, 299, 307–8,
    339, 340
as stand-up character 306–7
*Steve Coogan in Character with
    John Thomson* (Edinburgh
    show, 1992) and 328, 329
*Steve Coogan: The Man Who
    Thinks He's It* and 3, 6
The Day Today and 306, 308,
    309–10
writing of 26, 47, 302, 303–6
Partridge, Frank 304
Paul Calf's Video Diary 255
Pegg, Simon 3, 4, 6, 71, 148, 300
Penhaligan, Susan 179–80
Perkins, Geoff 261, 262, 283
Perrier Award:
    1990 12
    1991 14, 337
    1992 117, 250, 255, 330, 331,
        336–7, 338–9
Persuaders!, The 172
Pertwee, Jon 176
Philomena 46, 53, 68, 70, 192, 248,
    339
    Alpha Papa and 51, 52
    as an open letter to SC's parents
        about faith 36–9, 123
    BAFTA and 340
    BBC Films and 20–1
    China Chow and 18, 20
    Jeff Pope, SC's collaboration with
        20–1, 23, 27, 28, 29, 34, 35,
        192
    Judi Dench and 20, 22, 24, 30,
        44, 118
    Martin Sixsmith, SC meetings
        with 22, 23
    origins of 17–18, 19–22
    Oscars and 28, 33–5, 43, 65, 85,
        337
    personal resonance of story for
        SC 17–18, 19

response from women to 31
SC buys film rights to *The Lost Child of Philomena Lee* 19
SC finds artistic nourishment in 19
SC first meets Philomena Lee and Jane Libberton 22, 23
SC first reads Sixsmith piece in *Guardian* 17–18, 21
SC's background and 18–19
SC's role as Sixsmith 19, 22
screenplay, SC writes 18–25, 26–9, 31–2, 36–9, 40–5
Sean Ross Abbey, Roscrea, SC visits 23–5
Stephen Frears as director of 20, 30, 36, 38, 84
Vatican, papal audience at 38–9, 40–5
Weinstein and 27–8
world premiere, Venice Film Festival, 2013 30–1
Philomena Project 41, 45
Piccadilly Radio 258
Pilger, John 84
Pips, Manchester 215–16
Planer, Nigel 191
Playhouse, Edinburgh 280
Pleasance Theatre, Edinburgh 10
Pleasance Two, Edinburgh 318
Poet's Corner, Salford 266
Pope, Jeff 20–1, 23, 27, 28, 29, 34, 35, 192
Porridge 58, 172, 192
Porter, Lucy 337–8
Posner, Geoff 260, 261
Postgate, Oliver 171
postmodernism 54, 61, 285, 288–9
Potter, Dennis *177*
Powell, Enoch 159
Poyzer, Darren 279
Presley, Elvis 133, 217
Primal Scream 208
Prince's Trust 321

Protestantism 126, 127, 141, 226, 280
Proust, Marcel 109, 188
Pulp: 'Disco 2000' 146

Quantick, David 295
Quigley, Pierce 251

RADA 238–9, 244–5
Radcliffe, Mark 324
Radio 4 18, 58, 193, 275, 295, 297, 298, 311, 313, 321
Radio Manchester 251, 252, 324
Raging Bull 34
Raymond, Paul 70, 182, 228
Record Breakers 98–9, 186
Red Guitars 125–6
Redford, Robert 34
Resurrected 265
Rhodes, Greece 13–14, 295
Richmond, John 125
Ripping Yarns 186, 189
Rising Damp 173
Robbins, Kate 272
Rocky 254
Roeg, Nic 179
Ross, Jonathan 287
Rossiter, Leonard 173
Rowling, J. K. 84
Roxy Music 213, 218
Royal Exchange, Manchester 191, 237, 256–7, 258
Royal Irish Constabulary 227
Rushdie, Salman 84
Ryan, Christopher 191
Ryan, Fran 262

Sanchez, Bishop 41, 43, 44
Saturday Live 260–1, 275
Saturday Zoo 287, 289
Saxondale 15
Sayle, Alexei 191
Scarborough, Adrian 256
Schneider, David 295, 303
Scorsese, Martin 34

SDP 227

Sean Ross Abbey, Roscrea 23–5

Second World War, 1939–45 97, 98, 131

Sellers, Peter 285

Sessions, John 279

Sex Pistols 90, 213, 214, 215, 216, 217

Shakespeare, William 36, 230, 243

Shameless 279

Shapps, Grant 57

Sheen, Michael 65–6

Shelley, Percy Bysshe 69

Shepperton Studios 180

Shuttleworth, John (comedy character) 337

Simpson, Alan 192, 193

Singh, Rav 75–6

Siouxsie and the Banshees 90, 215

Sissay, Lemn 329

Sisson, Richard 281

Sixsmith, Martin 17, 19, 22, 23, 24, 28–9, 31–2, 44, 77–8; *The Lost Child of Philomena Lee* 19

Skinner, Frank 10–11, 12, 14, 282, 284–5, 329, 337

Smith & Jones 251, 272

Smith, Joan 84–5

Smithills, near Bolton 104

Smiths, The 125–6

Sneddon, Gary 246, 248, 249

So It Goes 213

Soho House, London 6

Some Mothers Do 'Ave 'Em 165

Sony Radio Awards 193

Sounds 213

South Africa 250

Spearpoint, Andy 253

Spencer, Frank 54, 165, 238

Spinal Tap 250

Spitting Image 148, 258–9, 261, 262, 265, 267, 270, 271–4, 275, 280, 286–7, 330, 331

Spongers, The 177–8, 240

St Cassian's Centre, Kintbury 210–11

St Thomas More RC Primary School, Middleton 127, 163

Stallone, Sylvester 210, 254, 259

Stand and Deliver 279

Stand Up, Nigel Barton 177

Stanislavski, Konstantin 239, 247, 258

Star Trek 71

Star Wars 217

Start the Week 311

Steptoe and Son 192–3

Steve Brown Band 3–4

Steve Coogan in Character with John Thomson (Edinburgh show, 1992) 12, 13, 14, 117, 287, 292, 317–18, 321–4, 327–8

Steve Coogan: The Man Who Thinks He's It 3–6, 169

Stiller, Ben 34, 49, 54, 55

Stone Roses, The 208

Stoppard, Tom 84

Sun 75–6

Sunday Night at the Palladium 6, 270, 278, 307

Sunday Times 75, 78, 80–1

Sunshine 15

Superstars 201

Sweeney, The 138, 185, 219, 259

T. Rex 213, 218

Tanner, Gaby 20

Tarbuck, Jimmy 6, 270, 278, 279

Tarbuck, Liza 263

Tati, Jacques 132

Taylor, Alex 248

Taylor, C. P.: *The Magic Island* 240

Taylor, Julie 251

Taylor, Mike 199–201, 283, 284

Tebbit, Norman 258, 259

Ten Glorious Years 279

Thatcher, Denis 272

Thatcher, Margaret 143, 174, 191, 203, 209, 227, 228, 241, 258, 259, 261, 273, 277, 279, 286, 305, 312, 336

Thaw, John 237
Thickett, Duncan (SC comedy character) 3, 10–11, 243, 244, 264, 278, 280, 286, 304, 329
Thoday, Jon 280, 332
Thomas, Richard 280
Thomson, John 250, 253, 255, 268, 274, 287, 317–18, 321–5, 327, 328–9, 330, 336, 337, 338–9
Threlfall, David 250, 256
Tierney, Brendan 121, 125, 131, 140–1, 144, 161, 171, 181, 199, 215
Time Out 13
Times, The 15, 80–1, 84
To Russia with Love 201
Tonioli, Bruno 283–4
Top of the Pops 142, 172, 215
Tower of London 127
Trip, The ix, 34, 61–3, 64–7, 68–72, 253, 340
Trip to Italy, The 41, 68–9, 70–1
Tropic Thunder 71
Trumpton 171, 251
Tunnel Club, London 266–7
Twain, Mark 296
12 Years a Slave 35
24 Hour Party People 34, 59, 60, 70, 284
Two Ronnies, The 168, 173
2001: A Space Odyssey 132

U2 45
Ultravox 216
Undertones, The: 'My Perfect Cousin' 90, 213–14
Universal Studios 49
Up the Junction 177

Vanier, Jean 107–8
Vatican 38–9, 40–5, 127, 203
Veep 53
Venice Film Festival 30, 38
Vic and Bob 9
Vinterberg, Thomas 29

Wahlberg, Mark 17
Walkabout 179
Walliams, David 339
Walter, Harriet 256
Walters, Julie 250
Watching 263
Watergate scandal 130
Wayne, John 209–10
Webster, Miss 181–2
Week Ending 295
Weinstein, Harvey 27–8, 40, 41, 43
Wells, Steven 295
Welsby, Elton 303
Whitehouse, Mary 184
Wilde, Martin 203
Williams, John 33
Williams, Shirley 226
Willis, Bruce 253
Wilson, Harold 179, 226, 227
Wilson, Owen 75
Wilson, Tony 12, 124, 213, 284, 325, 327
Winterbottom, Michael 59–60, 61–3, 64, 66, 68, 69, 70, 340
Wogan, Terry 259, 273
Wood, Victoria 250
Wordsworth, William 62

X-Ray Spex: 'Germfree Adolescents' 216

Yarwood, Mike ix, 272, 281
Young Ones, The 190–1, 236, 260, 272

③ I think I'll do PHYSICS, CHEMI. I'm
not sure of the ~~ao~~ ARTS or CRAFT.
I find FRENCH very hard but I feel i
is a waste after 2 yrs of French. Also
I feel I would really like to communic
with the french well. I want ~~the~~ to take
SPANISH because it is easy and I
find it interesting and different. I lov
HISTORY and the whole 1st and 2nd y
have heard the tape of Gred McBreer
and I made with Pop Groogran abo
unemployment in the 1930s. I find GEE
very hard but interesting. I love ma
with Mr Wilde because you can ha
good conversations with him and beat
him up and throw snow-balls at him
He's just GREAT! English is not ba
we have Mrs Elton (Previously Miss Lewi
But she's a bit too corny and serious. Ou
French Teacher is INSANE he is in hi
early 20s and has a moustache and
shoulder length hair. He is just one
big corny cliché. He is into Bee gee
~~Greese~~ and other commercial rubish.
I'm into the really heavy punk. Clash,
Sex Pistols, Siouxsie + the Banshees bu